How to Teach a Play

Online resources to accompany this book are available at: https://www.bloomsbury.com/how-to-teach-a-play-9781350017528/. Please type the URL into your web browser and follow the instructions to access the Companion Website. If you experience any problems, please contact Bloomsbury at: contact@bloomsbury.com

RELATED TITLES

The Arden Introduction to Reading Shakespeare: Close Reading and Analysis
9781472581020
Jeremy Lopez

Creative Shakespeare: The Globe Education Guide to Practical Shakespeare
9781408156841
Fiona Banks

Essential Shakespeare: The Arden Guide to Text and Interpretation
9781408158739
Pamela Bickley and Jenny Stevens

*ShakesFear and How to Cure It: The Complete Handbook for
Teaching Shakespeare*
9781474228718
Ralph Alan Cohen

Teaching Shakespeare with Purpose
9781472599612
Ayanna Thompson and Laura Turchi

*Script Analysis for Theatre: Tools for Interpretation, Collaboration
and Production*
9781408184301
Robert Knopf

How to Teach a Play

Essential Exercises for Popular Plays

EDITED BY MIRIAM M. CHIRICO AND KELLY YOUNGER

methuen | drama
LONDON • NEW YORK • OXFORD • NEW DELHI • SYDNEY

METHUEN DRAMA
Bloomsbury Publishing Plc
50 Bedford Square, London, WC1B 3DP, UK
1385 Broadway, New York, NY 10018, USA

BLOOMSBURY, METHUEN DRAMA and the Methuen Drama logo
are trademarks of Bloomsbury Publishing Plc

First published in Great Britain 2020

Cover design: Louise Dugdale
Cover image © Remus Kotsel / Getty images

A catalogue record for this book is available from the British Library.

A catalog record for this book is available from the Library of Congress.

ISBN: HB: 978-1-350-01752-8
          PB: 978-1-350-01753-5
          ePDF: 978-1-350-01755-9
          eBook: 978-1-350-01754-2

Typeset by Integra Software Services Pvt. Ltd.
Printed and bound in Great Britain

To find out more about our authors and books visit www.bloomsbury.com
and sign up for our newsletters.

CONTENTS

ACKNOWLEDGMENTS

The editors wish to thank the following for their generous support:

At Loyola Marymount University, Dean Robbin Crabtree, Bellarmine College of Liberal Arts; Prof. Barbara Rico, Chair, Department of English; Dean Bryant Keith Alexander, College of Communication and Fine Arts; Prof. Kevin Wetmore, Chair, Department of Theater; Nathan Faust, Taran Drummond, and Jordan Rehbock, Research Assistants; Oscar King IV, Editorial Assistant.

At Eastern Connecticut State University, President Elsa Nuñez; Former Provosts Rhona C. Free and Dimitrios Pachis; Dean Carmen R. Cid, School of Arts and Sciences; my colleagues on the Research Reassigned Time Committee and the Sabbatical Leave Committee for granting valuable release time; Miranda Lau, Administrator of the English Department, and the assistance of our student workers.

The Comparative Drama Conference Board Members as well as the participants on and attendees at our many panels. This book truly found its origin in your company, and we appreciate your encouragement over the years.

Our friendly readers, Suzanne Maynard Miller, Verna Foster, William Boles, and Kerri Ann Considine.

Finally, our students who participated in early versions of many of these exercises and offered their smart and thoughtful feedback.

Introduction

If you teach plays, you most likely also go to see plays. But how often do you go to see others teach?

The answer is probably only when mentoring new faculty or when observing a colleague applying for promotion. Rarely do faculty willingly invite colleagues into their classroom of their own volition to observe or critique their teaching. That is not to say that we resist feedback, as most of us do strive to improve our teaching methods. Why else would you have picked up this book? And yet, there are a dozen reasons why we wouldn't willingly put ourselves into this professionally and even personally vulnerable position.

But who wouldn't love to be a fly on the wall in somebody else's classroom?

Recognizing this predicament, we saw the need for this book and started a conversation with colleagues from around the country and the world. As a result, the generous and talented contributors in *How to Teach a Play* are inviting us into their classrooms. They come from many different departments, including Classical Studies, Modern Languages, Literature, and Theater, as well as all levels of experience, from the graduate teaching fellow to the newly minted PhD to the venerable professor emeritus. We also have exercises from professional playwrights, theater directors, dramaturgs, and artistic directors. What unites all of our contributors, however, is their shared spirit of collaboration, inspiration, and dedication to the dramatic arts.

These exercises are meant for all instructors—literature and theater; college and high school; dramaturgs and directors. Whether you specialize in drama and only teach plays, or your speciality is another genre but you include the odd play every now and again in your curriculum, these exercises will inspire you to reflect upon your own teaching practices. Ultimately, they are a testament to the strength and vitality of our shared discipline, dramatic literature.

English Departments and Theater Departments

English and theater departments have an intertwined history based on their commitment to dramatic literature. Theater departments, over one hundred years ago, began separating from English departments in order to teach drama as inherently distinct from literature. Carnegie Mellon University began its Department of Drama in 1914, and Yale followed suit in 1924. One central reason for creating drama departments was the belief that a play could only be fully understood through its performance: that the script was a skeletal outline of the playwright's vision that could only be realized through its production. This division of purpose still persists to this day; dramatic literature is taught in literature or foreign language departments as one of several kinds of literary genres, next to poetry, fiction, essays, memoir, etc., while theater departments teach plays with an eye toward performance. The repercussions of such disciplinary differences are clear: by categorizing drama as akin to poetry and fiction, literature instructors tend to draw attention to its literary nature: that is, they point out the aesthetic qualities valued in literature. Thus, even while professors of literature might remind the class out loud, "Of course we should not be treating a play as a poem or a short story," the instructor inevitably defaults to teaching the literary aspects of dramatic texts, such as the richness of poetic dialogue or the differences between the flat and the round characters.

Furthermore, literary history courses in drama focus on how the politics and social conventions of the particular period shape the literature: i.e., the cultural influences affecting the play's construction are taught, but the emphasis is still elsewhere, and not on performance. For example, a unit on Roman comedy might focus on character types (the irate father, the hen-pecking wife, the parasite); in an encounter with poetic drama such as Shakespeare's, the conversation might turn to prosody and imagery; and a lesson on Restoration comedies might attend to rhetorical devices, like ripostes or chiasmus. When courses teach the history of *theater*, the emphasis tends to reduce plays to cultural by-products of history's shaping force, indistinguishable from other artistic developments. These lectures will center on elements such as how the large space of an amphitheater required masks and broad acting, while the advent of realism demanded a more nuanced, intimate form of acting. While this knowledge is certainly valuable, a basic factor still eludes these history of theater classes: the play's intrinsic difference from other literary forms based on the interactive relationship with an audience.

In theater departments, often the reverse is true. The play script is assumed to be a blueprint, an architectural rendering of a three-dimensional building that is second-place to the actual building, or in the case of dramatic literature, to the performance. The text is often demoted or jettisoned even in favor of getting students to inhabit the space and envision the complementary sound, costume, and scenic designs. The instructor, while teaching a play, may remark, "Well, we are only reading a blueprint here; we have to imagine how this would appear in performance," and consequently imply that the script is only a pretext to a larger, more substantial piece. This premise, while it has some truth to it, comes with its own pitfalls: the belief that the play itself only comes to life in performance and that the text is only an *ersatz* version.

Demoting the play to a mere blueprint does not accurately depict the relationship between text and stage. It disregards too much, chiefly the initial creative vision of the playwright. Furthermore, although there is one complete and finished building for every blueprint, the same cannot be said for plays. If Arthur Miller's play *Death of a Salesman* were only a blueprint, we would be hard-pressed to determine which particular production over the years would be the actual constructed building, the "true" rendering of the play. If anything, each individual performance with its particular creative vision adds to the meaning of the original play script, an important point to share with students. Our goal for all of these exercises is to illustrate this productive tension between the literary text and the dramatic performance.

How *Not* to Teach a Play

Alarmed by theater's "march toward extinction" and the observation that "there is no longer any such thing as habitual theatergoing," the much revered (and feared) *New York Times* theater critic Walter Kerr penned a treatise called *How Not to Write a Play* (1955). In it, he places the blame for the decline in audiences solely on playwrights. Their hackneyed attempts at imitating "Ibsenism" (which even Ibsen abandoned) as well as writing for the elite intelligentsia have corrupted theatrical culture and contributed to its inevitable demise. Kerr pleads for the next generation of playwrights to accept that plays can be both entertaining and artistically sophisticated. He says, "We are willing to acknowledge that the theater is unpopular in the sense that people don't go to it. We are not willing to admit that it is unpopular in the sense that people don't like it."

Despite the emergence of many groundbreaking, dynamic, and diverse plays and playwrights since 1955, Kerr's words may have an uncomfortable resonance with today's academics, especially in the arts and humanities. There are too many national sources to cite, but we are aware of the declining numbers of students pursuing literary and performance studies. We can all point to reasons why—blaming cultural factors like economics or the media, or even university decisions on core curricula or budgetary support—but what role might we as the instructors of drama play in this conversation? It is important, here, to examine our own pedagogical situation and our own performance in the classroom. Is there such a thing as how *not* to teach a play? Are we teaching plays in the same ways we teach other genres such as poetry, fiction, nonfiction? Are we imitating the teachers who taught us, who were imitating the teachers who taught them? Are we teaching to smaller and smaller classes of the elite who choose to major in our departments or to larger and larger classes of nonmajors who are only reading plays because they have to fulfill a requirement (if we're lucky enough to teach at an institution that requires students to read plays)?

We are not suggesting that teachers must be popular entertainers. Far from it. We are, however, interested in thinking about the ways we often teach plays and how we might show new ways to highlight the most distinguishing and exciting element of our genre: performance.

Yet the goal of this book is not to increase the number of students pursuing literary and performance studies (although, that too would be nice). The goal is to help students and instructors connect with their dramatic imaginations and enter into the world of a play through a more immediate, meaningful way. We wish to help them see dramatic connections in their studies, appreciate the artistic spirit of the works, and open a creative portal in their own lives that they did not think was possible.

Through conversations with many colleagues, some of the most common phrases we hear when discussing the teaching of drama are "how to bring a play to life" or "how to get this play on its feet." While these sentiments intrinsically convey to those in the theater world the sense of rendering a two-dimensional script into its three-dimensional expression, how, exactly, to accomplish this is less obvious.

How to Teach a Play

Or, "How do *you* teach a play?" This was the question we asked each other years ago at the annual Comparative Drama Conference. Both of us value the written word and how those words create/imagine fictional worlds that take on the weight of reality in performance, yet we come from different backgrounds and approach teaching drama in different ways. Kelly, with an MA in Classics and a PhD in Drama Studies, is also a professional playwright and screenwriter. He is a tenured professor in an English department but also an affiliate faculty member of the theater department, and he teaches both surveys of dramatic literature and playwriting courses from workshop to production and performance. Miriam, having earned her MA degree in Text and Performance and her PhD in Literature, is also tenured in an English department where she teaches drama survey and criticism courses. Her scholarship focuses on staged productions, playwrights, and theater directors. Meeting as we did at the Comparative Drama Conference, we discovered we were both invested in finding new ways of teaching dramatic literature that could capitalize on the power of performance without losing the prescience of text.

We were concerned about the all-too-apparent gap between teaching dramatic literature as text *only* and teaching drama *only* as performance. We recognized that the campus path between the theater department and the literature department was not a well-worn path at all, but oftentimes one filled with sizable obstacles and misdirections. Faculty in literature departments held strongly to the sanctity of the text, refusing to consider theater productions that challenged traditional understandings ("Set *A Midsummer Night's Dream* on a golf course? Impossible!"), while theater departments often prioritized the materiality of performance over the value of the script's themes and insights. We understood that teaching dramatic literature involved techniques such as close reading and textual analysis while simultaneously requiring a vision of how this text might look beyond the printed page. Yet, we recognized that the training of scholars of dramatic literature often does not include training in what makes this form of literature *dramatic*. For example, even if an instructor knew enough to signal to her students to incorporate the pauses in a Beckettian piece, she might not possess the performance knowledge necessary to elicit meaning from that silence. We both agreed that the ideal teaching method would illustrate how the performance complements and supplements the meaning inherent in the text, which is gained through close reading and analysis.

And so we decided to take a risk.

The following year, we submitted a panel idea to the Comparative Drama Conference asking participants to bring copies of their "Intro to Drama" syllabus so that we could distribute, share, and discuss with fellow faculty members. The questions were simple: *What plays do you teach? In what order? What assignments do you give? How many essays do you assign? How large are your classes? Who are your students?* We had willing participants from across the country who generously shared not only their syllabi but also their teaching anecdotes, including successes, failures, insights, fears, questions, and possible solutions. The most meaningful discovery was the admission that teaching can be a lonely venture. It takes real vulnerability to ask for help, guidance, mentorship, or even for someone else's materials: that there is an insecurity to teaching sometimes, especially when teaching a text that is not within one's immediate area of expertise. The biggest surprise, however, was the follow-up to the panel: so many conference goers were interested in what took place. We were stopped constantly and asked questions about what was said, what we learned, and above all, "Are there copies of all those syllabi?" It was clear that many instructors wanted the materials on how *others* teach plays but were afraid to pay the price of admission: that is, they were apprehensive about admitting how *they* teach plays. So, the following year, we proposed another panel, this time called *How to Teach a Play*. We asked several of the prior year's participants to pick one play from their syllabus and share one of their class exercises that not only focuses on text but also highlights performance.

The panel was standing room only, not because of the organizers but because of the remarkable panelists who led the way in modeling generous, collaborative, and honest exchange of teaching practices. Moreover, the attendees expressed an earnest desire to improve and expand their own teaching repertoire.

Thus, the idea for this book was born. For the next several years, we created panels centered around teaching strategies for plays. The enthusiastic response revealed how eager instructors were—when given encouragement and a platform—to share a clever strategy to introduce a play or how hungry they were for more inspiration on teaching dramatic literature. Our panels were filled with scholars from around the country and the world who had traveled to the Comparative Drama Conference to present their scholarship, but who also wanted to leave with practical strategies to improve how they taught plays. Ultimately, we discovered to our delight that faculty from Classics, Modern Languages, English, and Theater departments—as well as playwrights, dramaturgs, directors, and artistic leaders—are indeed eager to collaborate and support one another as we all strive to be the best teachers we can be.

We cannot thank our colleagues of the Comparative Drama Conference enough for their enthusiastic support over the years by encouraging our pedagogical panels. Founded in 1977 at the University of Florida by Dr. Karelisa Hartigan, the Comparative Drama Conference is an international, interdisciplinary conference that brings together scholars in the fields of Classics, Theater, English, and Modern Languages and Literatures from a variety of international universities. Over the past ten years, the Conference has expanded to include workshops for playwrights, recognizing the unique opportunity to bring together practitioners with theater scholars and examine the hybrid nature of dramatic text. Many board members encouraged our plans for the book from the beginning book, attended our workshops, presented at the panels, and were early contributors to the book. Special thanks to Bill Boles, Jose Badenes, Andrew Ian McDonald, Michael Schwartz, Bill Hutchings, Verna Foster, Baron Kelly, Graley Herren, and Janna Segal.

Furthermore, participants of a Pre-Conference Session at the Association for Theatre in Higher Education (ATHE) Conference in Boston (Summer 2018) provided us with enthusiastic feedback for the book, illustrating that there is both wider appeal and need for it. A travel grant provided by ATHE allowed sample exercises to be shared during a workshop organized by the Theatre as a Liberal Art committee. The comments offered by the participants made it clear that the book could serve as a resource for dramaturgs and directors, as well as classroom instructors, and that the exercises worked equally well in an acting classroom as a literature one. These workshop participants, in noting how the exercises could offer an alternative to the script analysis during early stages of play rehearsal, provided the balanced expertise we needed on the project.

New Ways to Teach Plays

What could a new strategy for teaching drama look like? The answer to that question became this book. Nearly two hundred scholars and theater professionals responded to our request for teaching ideas based on their experiences either in the classroom or directing. Many shared excellent ideas at the Comparative Drama Conference, such as using a metronome to create a soundscape (*Machinal*), taping off the parameters of a room corresponding to a tenement (*Juno and the Paycock*), or vocally punching the second-person pronouns in a Pinter play (*The Homecoming*). Even as we collected ideas and lesson plans from contributors, we refined and sharpened our mission. We wanted to emphasize that performance is the way that a play speaks its message, so we sought out exercises that connected textual themes to performance elements.

We pursued our goal to ensure that each exercise pertained to a specific play, asking contributors to connect the performative exercise to a pattern or motif inherent in the text. Yet, to our delight, several contributors provided exercises that justifiably worked for several different plays, which made for intriguing pairings: the use of optical illusions to teach a mistrust of reality brought together *Life Is a Dream* and *Six Characters in Search of an Author*; enacting asides to understand social context linked *The Country Wife* and *The Importance of Being Earnest*; substituting emotionally charged phrases for the actual dialogue in order to emphasize subtext made *A Raisin in the Sun* and *Oleanna* echo one another, while playing musical clips for students became a way for students to understand *Flower Drum Song* and *The Glass Menagerie*.

Although some exercises require technology, most, like theater itself, rely on basic tools and the imagination. The exercise for *The Dutchman* incorporates the flashlights from students' cell phones, while the one for *The Eumenides* asks students to use a Twitter account. So many instructors seem to incorporate games in the classroom as active learning techniques that easily transferred to the performative: for example, the game of Witches and Werewolves (*The Crucible*), social status games of one-upmanship (*The House of Blue Leaves*), invented detective stories (*Oedipus Rex*), and three-card monte (*Top Dog/Underdog*). Other instructors draw on public rituals with which students are already familiar: such as an auction ("*Art*"), a trial (*The Merchant of Venice*), or a collectively made quilt (*Angels in America*). We also have a few non-play specific exercises that focus on key dramatic terms (*hubris* and *hamartia*) or dramatic eras (Restoration audiences). These are just a handful of the many excellent, diverse, and inspiring contributions.

Instructors were more than eager to revise exercises several times in order that their ideas could be clearly understood, speak to as wide a teaching audience as possible, and conform with the overall goals of the book; we have overwhelming gratitude for the enthusiastic refrain we heard regarding our requests to revise: "Sure, when do you need it by?" Even when we had to turn down teaching ideas from contributors, most did not balk when asked to pitch us another idea for an entirely different play, again reminding us of the flexibility and creativity so many teachers in the field possess. Still others were generous enough with their efforts to willingly adapt their exercises for one play to a different play if we had a duplicate, such as a ball-bouncing exercise applied to the dialogue in *Rosencrantz and Guildenstern Are Dead*, or using ropes to physically dramatize a conflicted mind in *Hamlet*, or illustrating the tension between political context and personal subtext in *Sweat*. Scholars from all over the country have shared their ideas, as well as those far-flung scholars who sent us teaching strategies from Turkey (*Death and the King's Horseman*), Greece (*Antigone*), England (*The School for Scandal*), Spain (*Trifles*), and South Africa (*"Master Harold" ... and the Boys*). Finally, many contributors tested their revised exercises in the classroom, reshaping them based on feedback from their students—perhaps the most important editors of all.

The Plays

Often, in creating any kind of anthology or literary compilation, one considers the opportunity to redefine the canon or to reconsider what *should* be taught in the drama classroom. While we have resisted this temptation in order that this book might be accessible by the greatest number of instructors, ultimately, we had to make some decisions about what would or what would not be included here. In order to identify the most frequently taught plays—or "most popular" in the sense of how often they populate the reading list on syllabi—we referred to the most frequently used anthologies in the classroom in determining our request for exercises, drawing from *The Wadsworth Anthology of Drama,* edited by W. B. Worthen; *The Bedford Introduction to Drama*, edited by Lee A. Jacobus; *Stages of Drama*, edited by Carl H. Klaus, Miriam Gilver, and Bradford S. Field, Jr.; *Types of Drama: Plays and Contexts*, edited by Sylvan Barnet and William E. Burto; *The Norton Anthology of Drama*, edited by J. Ellen Gainor, Stanton B. Garner, Jr., and Martin Puchner, as well as the *Longman Anthology of Drama and Theater*, edited by Michael L. Greenwald, Roger Schultz, and Roberto Dario Pomo.

Moreover, we shaped our chosen list of exercises based on the research of Janet Gardner. In her essay "What We Teach When We Teach Drama: Current Drama Pedagogy in American Colleges and Universities,"[1] she investigated the instructional practices by which faculty introduce college students to

---

[1]Janet E. Gardner, "What We Teach When We Teach Drama: Current Drama Pedagogy in American Colleges and Universities," in *The Theater of Teaching and the Lessons of Theater*, edited by Domnica Radulescu and Maria Stadter Fox (Lexington Books, 2005).

drama and theater studies by collecting syllabi from eighty-three classes offered between 1997 and 2001 in American colleges and universities. Sixty percent of these classes used one of the aforementioned anthologies; 31 percent require students to perform a scene in the classroom; and 45 percent require students to attend some form of live performance. Of greater value for our purpose, however, was her compilation of plays that are actually taught in English and theater departments as documented by the syllabi she received. She discovered that the "plays included on the syllabi represent a quite conservative notion of what constitutes the theatrical experience and tradition" when compared to the research projects of most current faculty. Through constructing an "imaginary class syllabus modeled on the national average," Gardner identified the top ten most frequently taught plays:

Oedipus Rex by Sophocles
A Doll's House by Ibsen
Hamlet by Shakespeare
Lysistrata by Aristophanes
The Cherry Orchard by Chekhov
Endgame by Beckett
Everyman by Anonymous
Fences by Wilson
Trifles by Glaspell
Death of a Salesman by Miller

Clearly, this list is as familiar as it is under-representative. In selecting exercises for our collection, we made a concerted effort to include exercises for non-Western dramatic texts commonly taught in the classroom. In sum, the contents of the teaching exercises in the book range from classical to contemporary plays from France, Spain, Japan, England, Germany, Norway, South Africa, Mexico, and more. Admittedly, it is still incomplete, which is why we include a blank exercise template on the Companion Website for you to download and complete, thus adding to the list and joining the conversation.

The Exercises

The goal of this book is to provide practical, performance-specific exercises that teachers can use in the classroom to identify key performative moments in the plays. Grounded in research of the playwright's work, each exercise aims to point out the performance elements of the specific play while indicating how that performance element illuminates the play's larger themes or significance. By focusing attention on such performative elements, teachers can animate the dialogue or challenge the script's interpretation for the students. All of the exercises connect close textual analysis with performance and provide play-specific performance techniques in order to reveal to our students how performance and text work together to create meaning. In other words, the aim of this book is to inspire and cultivate the dramatic imagination in our readers, so that they in turn can nurture the dramatic imaginations of their students.

Like a recipe, we purposefully emulated a "cookbook" style where contributors provide simple, concise, bullet-point steps that guide the instructor through the exercise. Our aim is to make them as accessible and as jargon-free as possible so the teacher can immediately apply the activity to practice in the classroom. We have tried to avoid exercises that would require specialized knowledge or outside research, and we have purposefully not included exercises that are already used in classrooms, such as reading aloud or watching a clip from a movie version. We have limited the exercises that require students to have acting skills to ensure that they could be practiced in literature classrooms, although many are useful early in the rehearsal process. Over and over, we have worked with contributors to emphasize turning the classroom into a performance space, with students performing while others listen or watch a message being enacted or created live.

The defining feature of this book is that each of the teaching exercises foregrounds performance attributes. While each exercise is tailored to teaching a particular play, each exercise emphasizes at least one (if not several) performance element, such as sound, tempo, tension, movement. The performance attribute is specifically identified in the "In Brief" section so instructors can immediately see what will be taught. The contributions that follow also state the "Purpose" of the exercise, detail any advanced "Preparation" required, list any "Materials" needed, outline the "Nuts and Bolts" to facilitate, and finally offer a "Reflection" on the exercise as a whole. Often, the reader will be directed to the Resources and Appendix on the Companion Website for bibliographic citations specific to the play and/or exercises that can provide further support, discussion questions, downloadable handouts for students, etc. It is important to note that all bibliographic sources referenced by in-text citations for either plays or scholarship can be found under Resources on the Companion Website.

As an instructor incorporates different exercises in the classroom that emphasize various performance categories, the cumulative effect is that they gradually underscore to the students that *drama is a qualitatively different genre than fiction or poetry* and deserves to be treated as such. To give an example: one exercise instructs teachers to incorporate a metronome for the opening scene of *Machinal* to underscore the performative attribute of "time/tempo," even while this use of a metronome connects to the play's larger theme: mechanization in society. Another exercise, for example, on Pinter's play *The Homecoming* asks that instructors emphasize the second-person pronoun in speech so that students might hear the aggressive nature of Pinter's dialogue, thus drawing attention to "voice/emphasis" in that play. Consequently, by the end of a semester filled with exercises drawing attention to performative attributes, students will begin to see for themselves how timing or spatial arrangements change a scene, or how voice or costuming can supplement meaning.

We wish to make clear what these exercises are *not*: they are not lesson plans in the traditional sense of a structured trajectory through historical background, discussion questions, and in-class activities. They are not intended to be exhaustive summaries of themes and motifs or studies in symbolism and figurative language. Nor are they script analyses, which correspond more closely to the work actors do preparing characters for performance. Rather, these exercises are meant to introduce a performative attribute that offers insight into the play's meaning, not to provide the definitive understanding of the play. Most of the exercises in the book focus on a single scene or a moment, meant to spark students' imagination regarding performance possibilities; oftentimes, the exercises take as little as 15 minutes to implement and get the students excited and talking. Each exercise provides instructors with a tool for focusing on a performative aspect that will deepen the background knowledge instructors already bring to the play.

A Few Rules before You Begin

Trust yourself: You are the instructor. You are the authority. And even if you are teaching a play for the first time, you have a deep understanding and appreciation of the theatrical. So be theatrical.

Trust your students: Whether they are in your classroom by choice or by requirement, remember they all played as children. Remind them of that. Talk about play and games and roles and rules. Encourage them to be a little foolish, a little histrionic, a little goofy.

Be transparent: Let your students know you are trying an exercise for the first time. It will be new for all of you. Give them ownership in the process. Collaborate with them. Follow the instructions, step by step. Don't pretend you're not using a recipe. Don't act like you're inventing this exercise on the go. Share the steps with your students. Talk about "how to teach a play" and why you are focusing on the performative elements of this particular play. You may be teaching a future teacher how to teach a play.

Embrace the process: Even with all the step-by-step instructions, these exercises are not set in stone. There will always be variables and events and personalities that will shape the direction a certain exercise takes on a certain day. If one of the steps doesn't work, stop and try it again. Ask the students for help. What changes need to be made in order to make it work? How might this exercise be made more specific to your particular class? Start over and make changes to the rules. Figure it out together.

Make it your own: Good cooks can't resist making a recipe their own. That's why they're good cooks. The same with teachers. Feel free to improvise, add elements, skip others, adapt into larger exercises that take several class periods or pick and choose only a few components for a shorter class. Whatever works for you and your students.

Make your own: You may have several plays you love to teach that are not in this book. You may have exercises for them as well. Again, we have provided a blank exercise template on the Companion Website. Join the conversation. Add your experience and expertise. Share with others how *you* teach a play!

Enjoy it: You became a teacher for a reason. You became a teacher of plays for a reason. Remember what those reasons are. You're reading this book because you want to be better at both. And now, it's showtime.

Break a leg,

Miriam and Kelly

The Exercises

HUBRIS AND HAMARTIA BASED ON ARISTOTLE'S POETICS

Betsy S. Goldman, Boston Shakespeare Project

IN BRIEF

Students test their luck at "hitting the mark" in a game of darts.

PURPOSE

The themes and philosophical questions raised in Greek tragedies can feel both overwhelming and irrelevant to our current lives. Greek plays are so old, and the stories are often so fantastical that students can find it difficult to connect to them in any personal way. This exercise introduces students to the concepts of hubris and hamartia; helps them understand the dramatic role these terms play within Greek tragedy; encourages them to explore themes and questions of knowledge and fate in both embodied and intellectual ways; and asks them to draw connections between characters affected by hubris and hamartia and their own lives.

PREPARATION

Students may read chapters 12–14 of Aristotle's *Poetics*. The instructor should introduce the terms *hubris* and *hamartia* as well as their definitions (see the Appendix on Companion Website).

MATERIALS

A dart board, darts, and index cards. Some options may include a homemade dart board made of velcro or cork board and homemade darts that either stick to or pierce the cardboard; a floor dart board, resembling hopscotch where students can throw an object that will land and stay in place; a purchased multicolor dart board and darts; a purchased children's dart board (velcro or with knobs) and darts. A very basic option is to draw a large dart board on the classroom chalkboard/whiteboard and have students crinkle up pieces of paper to throw at it. The instructor can then mark the general location where the "dart" strikes.

Nuts and Bolts

1 Introduce or review the definitions of hubris and hamartia.

2 Take a quick poll of how each student is feeling that day. They may write down these answers or answer in the moment.

  a On a scale from 1 to 7, rate how confident are you feeling about being in class today? (1 = not confident at all—not feeling self-assured, optimistic, or positive about class; 4 = neutral; 7 = extremely confident! You are feeling self-assured, optimistic, and positive about class.)

  i Before you take the poll, you may want to have the class agree on what "feeling confident" means—for example, self-assured, optimistic, and positive about class.

  b From 1 to 7, rate how good you feel about today in general? (1 = not good at all—perhaps you're in a bad mood or you're feeling unwell, not self-assured or self-confident; 4 = neutral; 7 = you feel great! You're feeling positive, self-assured, and/or in a good mood.)

3 Distribute the index cards to the class. Each card will communicate one of three sets of instructions:

  a Set (A) "Go for it."

  b Set (B) "Each color on the dart board is connected to in a different outcome. You will learn that outcome after the game is played."

  i Note: If your dart board does not have colors, substitute accordingly. For example, if your dart board has numbers indicating the spaces, write on the index card: Each numbered space on the dart board will result in a different outcome.

  c Set (C) "Each color indicates a different outcome: blue = you get to decide what happens in the next class, yellow = your instructor will bring you the candy of your choice to the next meeting, black = you must bring the instructor the candy of their choice for the next two meetings, white = we will finish the game and then proceed with class as scheduled, red = you must balance a book on your head for the remainder of class."

  i Note: These are mere suggestions and may be modified; each outcome should have some direct effect on the student's experience within the class or rehearsal while remaining fun and appropriate.

4 Play darts.

  a Each student gets three throws. The color on which the third throw lands indicates the outcome for the student.

5 Share the outcomes.

6 Celebrate or reward the ones whose outcomes were positive.

7 "Punish" those whose outcomes were negative.

8 Share that each student received an index card with varying levels of information.

    a Take the poll again (see Step 2).

9 Play again, if time allows.

Reflection

This exercise encourages students to draw connections between the concepts of hamartia and hubris and their performance during the game of darts. Encourage your students to think about the role(s) that circumstance, attitude/intention, information about the game, and sheer chance played in their successes or failures in this activity. Begin by debriefing their experiences with the game they just played.

    Suggested reflection questions:

1 What strategies did you use?

2 How did you prepare?

3 What were the stakes for you?

4 How did the information you had on your index card affect how you played?

5 How do you think students with different information on their index cards approached the game?

6 Would you have preferred to know more/less information than you did?

7 Did the outcome of this game affect your attitude or mood?

These questions will challenge students to think about factors that influenced their performance in the game. Some of these factors were (more or less) within the students' control, while many were not. Discuss the circumstances of the game and students' reactions to how these circumstances may have affected their performance. Connect these reflections back to the concepts of hubris and hamartia.

    For example:

1 Did anyone feel "overconfident" when stepping up to play?

2 Did anyone believe that their level of confidence changed the course of the game?

3 Did anyone try to bend the rules?

    a Discuss how these are examples of the Greek concept of hubris and how hubris may have played a role in students' attitudes or behaviors during the game.

4 Did anyone aim for a particular color and miss?

5 Did anyone close their eyes and throw or throw in a silly way?

6 How do students feel their level of confidence affected the outcome of the game?

   a Discuss these and other examples of how hamartia may have been evident in the game.

7 Challenge students to find other examples of hubris and/or hamartia in their experience of playing darts.

Competitive games (such as darts) are performative in nature. The students throwing the darts may feel others' eyes on them as they attempt to hit the target. Perhaps the students who are watching will cheer, boo, or even attempt to sabotage the thrower. The performative nature of the darts game will help to illustrate the interconnections between external circumstances and internal attitudes/intentions of the players.

The common usage of "tragic flaw" when referring to heroes of Greek tragedy—and many other plays and media since then—is misleading and simplifies the philosophical landscape of the Greek tragedy. Clarifying and expanding students' understanding of the terms *hubris* and *hamartia* and their roles within Greek tragedy by performing a simple game that embodies some of the aspects of the question of "fate versus free will" provide opportunities for personal connections to Greek tragedy and its tragic heroes.

Toward the conclusion of your reflection, ask a few more questions that will deepen students' understanding of hubris and hamartia:

1 What is your understanding of hubris and hamartia now that we have played this game and discussed the definitions in relation to the game?

2 How are the terms *hubris* and *hamartia* connected to circumstances, attitude/intention, information, and chance?

3 How do you think that hubris and hamartia connect to the exploration of fate versus free will in ancient Greek tragedy?

AGAMEMNON BY AESCHYLUS

C. W. Marshall, University of British Columbia

IN BRIEF

Brainstorming contemporary adaptations to deepen students' understanding of *nostos*, or homecoming.

PURPOSE

We have all seen productions of classical plays that were "authentic" (with period costumes, for example) but that were utterly disconnected from the contemporary audience's experience. And we have seen productions whose recontextualizations (to new places or periods) seem incomprehensible or unmotivated. The goal of this exercise is to help students recontextualize the *Agamemnon* with both purpose and meaning. The key to doing so is in understanding the nostos of Agamemnon, that is, the return home of a hero following great challenges or trials. Reframing the nostos in terms of another soldier's homecoming from war will help develop theatrical imagination and encourage understanding of what is gained and lost in directorial choices for dramatic adaptation.

Students are encouraged to find varying contexts (period, nation, war) for a modern production of *Agamemnon* and to consider the opportunities for performance driven by that choice. No one historical period is better than any other; students are simply encouraged to consider various choices of postwar periods and compare how each time frame changes the representation of Agamemnon and his circumstances.

PREPARATION

None. A short writing assignment to develop the idea of nostos can be used in advance to ensure students are familiar with the concept.

MATERIALS

None.

Nuts and Bolts

1 Lecture (10–15 minutes): At the start of class, summarize Agamemnon's nostos as Aeschylus presents it: after the setup, Agamemnon arrives with a chariot and retinue with spoils, with Cassandra standing beside him (lines 782–809). The victorious general with the riches of Troy, and Cassandra silent but present throughout the initial greetings (810–930) and temptation by Clytemnestra inviting Agamemnon to tread on the tapestries (931–57), Clytemnestra's allusive speech as he does so (958–74), the subsequent choral song (975–1034), and the scene that follows (1035–71), before she begins to speak, not properly understood by the chorus throughout her song as she approaches and eventually enters the palace (1072–330).

2 Group work (20 minutes): In small groups of 4–5, students are invited to consider what Aeschylus values in this homecoming and which modern wars or historical events might illuminate these values. Students can be invited to discuss and prepare answers for the following questions:

   a What aspects of Agamemnon's nostos are relevant to you?

   b Is there a modern event that can help illuminate those aspects in an imagined production of the play?

   c How could a production emphasize these associations without changing the words of the script? Consider costume, set, music, props, etc. Think particularly about the choices made with the appearance of Agamemnon, the appearance of Cassandra, and the victory trophies or war booty that might be brought back.

   d What are the repercussions of these choices? Would that help make an interesting/relevant production of Agamemnon? How would the choice affect other moments of the play? Does giving the play a period setting help communicate Aeschylus' message about war and homecoming to a modern audience?

   e Finally, what would be jarring or disconcerting about this decision?

3 Presentations (10–20 minutes): Once the questions have been discussed, groups can make short presentations that focus on answering the above questions. A time limit can be set, to encourage students to make short, enthusiastic, 90-second sales pitches. Ask the students to find analogies for Agamemnon's return, his war prizes, Clytemnestra's response, Cassandra's role, and the choral presence. Students could consider cultural context, technology, gender roles, and/or media in their pitch. A homecoming from a war depends upon certain inventions (automobiles, airplanes, or cell phones), social responses (protest or parades), and understanding of the conditions of war (peace treaty, prisoners of war, reparations).

4 Essay topic: This group work can then lay the foundation for a short (500-word) written assignment, with students developing an idea put forward by their own or another group. It can also lead to a reflection on the nature of directorial choices generally.

Reflection

Nostos is a key theme in Greek literature, beginning with the *Odyssey*. In an American classroom, the Second World War, Vietnam, and the war in Iraq are possible examples that students could offer. Knowing specific historical details isn't required: one can think about these wars as they are understood generally, known from movies, etc. The group environment can allow a collaborative picture to develop. Other plays with *nostoi* include Aeschylus' *Libation Bearers* and *Persians*, Euripides' *Heracles* and *Electra*, and Sophocles' *Women of Trachis* and *Electra*. The exercise could be reconfigured for any of these plays. Euripides' *Medea* (with its plot of a foreign woman who has been brought "home" and then rejected) also offers rich possibilities for thinking about appropriate modern settings.

In discussion, different groups might emphasize the booty (drawing comparisons with the looting of Iraq's museums), or the complete destruction of Troy (drawing comparisons with ethnic cleansing and the Rwandan genocide), or soldiers fighting in protracted wars far away and bringing home a foreign bride (compare, for example, the musical *Miss Saigon*). All of these are legitimate ideas for exploration. As long as the students can provide details from the context, they should be able to trace the implications for using that setting consistently in reimagining the play. "Modern" too can be understood freely: for examples of soldiers returning home at the end of the American Civil War or after V-E Day students might encourage other associations, such as the emphasis on weather and disease and filth in the camp (trenches) at Troy (cf. lines 555–67).

Ultimately, this is an exercise in theatrical imagination and perceiving how a single directorial choice can have ramifications for an entire play: what might be a cool idea for one scene may cause another scene to fall apart if the logic is pursued rigorously. For Greek tragedy, it is particularly important that a place be found for the chorus. How do we make sense of a collective character of old men? Are they the Senate? The media? Different choices will lead to different conclusions.

THE EUMENIDES BY AESCHYLUS

Ellen Moll, Michigan State University

IN BRIEF

Students perform a traditional and a nontraditional interpretation of a passage.

PURPOSE

This exercise will help students to articulate how *The Eumenides* performs the triumph of reason, democracy, civic justice, and "modernity" over irrationality, superstition, revenge, and tradition. This triumph depended on the artistic representation of ancient Athenian views of gender, including its connections to concepts of order, reason, the *polis* (city-state), and animality.

PREPARATION

This exercise is based on Froma Zeitlin's influential essay "The Dynamics of Misogyny: Myth and Mythmaking in the Oresteia." See Resources and Appendix on Companion Website for a discussion guide on historical and cultural contexts.

MATERIALS

Index cards (two different colors and two for each student).

Nuts and Bolts

1 Begin by having the students list as many binary oppositions as they can identify within the play.

    a For example: male vs. female, human vs. animalistic, positive vs. negative, reason vs. passion, light vs. darkness, mind vs. body, life vs. death, moderation vs. excess, city vs. home/house, polis vs. kinship, justice vs. revenge, order vs. chaos, past/old vs. future/young, above/

below (sky gods vs. earth gods who end up living under the polis), and culture vs. nature.

2 Distribute two index cards to each student: one that says "Orestes/ Apollo" and the other that says "the Eumenides." It helps if the index cards are two different colors, as the group can get a quick visual of where the majority of the class stands on a particular opinion.

3 Read through the list of binaries and ask the students to hold up the card that they think is more closely connected with a particular side.

  a In this way, it is easy to pause and discuss any binaries where the connection is not clear.

4 Discuss with the students how, in depicting these binaries, various concepts are gendered and otherwise given associations (i.e., masculine or feminine).

  a For instance, the side of Orestes includes Athene (who, as she states, is always on the side of men) and Apollo, who is portrayed as the side of men, the father (who argues for Agamemnon's primacy), reason, the sky gods, moral uprightness, the new, democracy, etc. The Eumenides are earth goddesses portrayed as animalistic, ruled by vengeance and emotion, associated with the old ways (they are older than the Olympian gods) and with the importance of motherhood (in their defense of Clytemnestra). The Othering of the Furies, and the play's vindication of Orestes, reason, democracy, law, the sky gods, and the new ways, depends on associating the side of the Eumenides with negative audience emotions such as fear, disgust, and revulsion—and notably also with the side of women. By constructing the two opposing sides in this way, democracy, the polis, reason, and the modern are gendered as masculine and positive, while revenge, kinship, unreason, and the old ways are gendered as feminine and negative; the misogyny is thus a vital rhetorical tactic for promoting democracy, reason, etc.

  b Discuss how the Athenian way, as exemplified by Aeschylus, of understanding progress and civilization has been used in later time periods (particularly in European colonialism from the early modern onward) to define some cultures as less "civilized" or "modern" and the ethical implications of these definitions.

  c Ask students to find examples of how modern society associates the feminine with nature, chaos, mystery, emotion, animality, and the body; next ask them for modern examples that associate the masculine or men with civilization, order, reason, democracy/politics/the public sphere, and the mind. These examples might be advertisements, movies/music videos/ TV shows, or articles related to women in politics or women in STEM or men in traditionally "feminine" fields, etc. Then, discuss the ways that the associations in the Eumenides still hold sway today. Explain that modern scholars problematize the way that the play uses misogyny to present the triumph of reason, progress, modernity, and democracy.

5 Place the students into groups and have them decide upon one passage (15–30 lines) that explores these binaries in interesting ways (or assign each group a passage).

6 Each group should provide two distinct staged readings of this play (including gestures and movements would be appropriate if there is room in the classroom). The students will need several minutes to plan and rehearse.

  a First, a reading that supports the traditional interpretation of the side of the feminine being the side of chaos, vengeance, excess, and emotion, and the masculine being the side of democracy, moderation, and reason.

  b Second, a performance that reflects modern critiques, particularly the portrayal of the gendered binaries. Some possible ideas:

  i Students change the way they read lines and body language to subvert the traditional interpretation

  ii Students are permitted to change one line of dialogue in the passage to challenge the message put forth in the passage

7 Once ready, each group will present their two different performances of the same scene before the class. Note: Depending on the size of the class, not all groups need to present. Volunteers may be called for instead.

8 Once both performances are completed, have the group ask the class in which order they were performed. It should be obvious, as most of these performances are a bit exaggerated, but it will help students identify the performance choices they made to emphasize a particular interpretation.

9 Lead the students in a discussion of these choices and how they influenced the performance of their particular scene. Misunderstandings can be addressed, and creative choices can be discussed in terms of how they reflect what these associations mean in ancient and modern contexts.

Reflection

This exercise can help students understand the traditional interpretation of *The Eumenides* as a narrative of the triumph of reason and democracy over tradition and superstition and revenge. It can help them see how more recent scholarly perspectives on this play, particularly feminist ones, shed light on both the play itself and its lasting impact on culture.

The interpretation of *The Eumenides* that has traditionally predominated is a valuable one for students to explore, both to understand the themes and historical contexts of the play and to understand the play's place in cultural history. We readily see how Western cultures defined their own values identical to the play's early conceptualizations of reason, democracy, and progress. According to this traditional interpretation, the acquittal of Orestes signifies the triumph of reason, jury trials, and democracy over older value systems based on kinship, superstition, tradition, and never-ending cycles of revenge. In the play, the gods acknowledge that a human jury, full of citizens participating in reason-based debates, can arrive at collective wisdom that no individual, including the goddess of wisdom Athene, could alone. The Eumenides are portrayed as driven by bloodlust and vengeance, and as clinging to the legitimacy of their age-old traditions, while Apollo and Athene demonstrate their reason through articulate arguments; the Eumenides are aligned with the old ways, and Apollo, Athene, and the jury trial are aligned with democracy and a new social order.

Through the dialogue, as well as the physical appearance of Clytemnestra's terrifying ghost and the monstrously bird-like Eumenides, the side of Clytemnestra is "Othered" in ways that emphasizes the superiority of Athene, Apollo, and Orestes and their values. At the end, of course, Orestes is acquitted but only through Athene's tie-breaking vote, and the Eumenides agree to take a lesser but still important role by residing underneath Athens. In this way, the play suggests a passing of the guard, in which Athens respects the old ways but ultimately (and by a narrow margin) embraces a new social order and value system, one that fits with the burgeoning democracy of the Athenian polis. Again, this narrative associates the new way with democracy, the polis, reason, and order, and associates all of these concepts with one another; similarly, the play enacts an association among tradition, emotion/animality, kinship, superstition, and chaos.

Furthermore, this exercise helps students to use a creative activity to "pick a side" and perform their understanding of traditional and modern feminist interpretations of this play. In particular, this exercise is good for them to understand the complex set of associations put forward in the play in a concrete way. Furthermore, the exercise helps students to examine how the cultural context of Aeschylus' time shaped the plot, characterization, and themes of the play, and to understand some ways that the play had a lasting impact on later cultures.

The exercise is also designed to help students understand why we study the portrayal of gender in other time periods; it is valuable to be explicit about how the study of gender in other time periods can reveal much about the nature of power and gender in our own time, and also to emphasize the complexity of cultural knowledge that goes into understanding gender roles (for example, associating reason with men and emotion with women is a culturally specific form of sexism, and understanding how misogyny functions in a society is far more complex than simply whether the average person believes women are bad; such conversations might come out of these activities if the similarities and differences between ancient and modern cultures are frequently explored). Most significantly, the activity offers a tangible way for students to pick a side and perform the abstract concepts at play in *The Eumenides*.

ANTIGONE BY SOPHOCLES

Avra Sidiropoulou, Open University of Cyprus

IN BRIEF

Create a space that limits or liberates the characters in order to reveal the principal conflicts.

PURPOSE

Antigone is a play of shifting perspectives. In order to identify with the title protagonist's resistance to autocratic rule, we should try to understand not only Creon's point of view but also the social and cultural milieu (or the world) in which the action takes place. To do so, we need to contextualize the play's central conflicts through a spatial configuration.

George Steiner, in his work *Antigones* (1996), identifies five principal constants of conflict within the play, namely, "the polarities of masculinity and of femininity, of aging and of youth, of private autonomy and of social collectivity, of existence and mortality, of the human and the divine."[1] As he points out, "the boundary-conditions of the human person are those set by gender, by age, by community, by the cut between life and death, and by the potentials of accepted or denied encounter between the existential and the transcendent."[2]

This exercise will lead students through an exploration of these boundary-conditions by creating physical spaces that limit, liberate, and reveal these five principal conflicts.

PREPARATION

Students should read the play in its entirety before class.

MATERIALS

None.

---

[1]George Steiner, *Antigones* (Yale University Press, 1996), 232.
[2]Steiner, *Antigones*, 232.

Nuts and Bolts

1 Create an open space for the exercise. The larger the better, but admittedly it may be limited to the size of the classroom. If possible, have the students push all the desks to the walls as a way to open up the center of the room.

2 Break the class into groups of 3–4. Ask them to imagine a potential staging of the play, for which they will be directors, designers, and actors, alternately.

3 Ask each group to decide upon a prevailing conflict they wish to explore.

    a masculinity and femininity

    b aging and youth

    c private autonomy and social collectivity

    d existence and mortality

    e the human and the divine

4 Once the students decide on one of the five conflicts, have them identify a specific passage in the play where they believe that conflict plays out on stage. They may, for instance, choose the emblematic Antigone–Creon scene (lines 441–525) to work on the conflict between private autonomy and social collectivity or the scene between Tiresias and Creon (lines 1000–1090) to focus on that between the human and the divine.

5 Now, ask the students to imagine they are directors and designers.

    a Have the groups create a mental or actual image—a sketch, a drawing—of a setting that captures this particular conflict.

    b Ask the students to throw in different design ideas, without censoring themselves. Would a cluttered space or a minimalist setting be more appropriate for portraying the themes of the human and the divine, respectively? Would opting for a bare stage reinforce the play's overriding mood of mortality and capture the coldness of a world where feelings of compassion have been replaced by a merciless adherence to the law?

6 After they have shaped their concept of scenography, you can also discuss sound and music.

    a What soundscape might clearly resonate a specific line of interpretation as well as a stylistic frame for the scene? What kind of instruments would best convey the aural world of their production? Would music, sound, or silence work better to communicate Antigone's private autonomy in the face of King Creon's adamant attitude to maintain order? If there were one single natural sound (water, wind, etc.) that could be used in performance, what would it be?

    b If possible, have the students create this soundscape by searching for those songs or sound effects on their smart phones.

7 Depending upon the size of the class, and how many groups, have the students take turns performing their scene.

> **a** They may only use the desks or any classroom furniture for their set. For example, if they want a cluttered, disorganized stage, they can fill the center with desks. If they want a bare stage, they should keep the center clear. If they wish Antigone and Creon to be separated, make a row of desks and have the actors on either side. In other words, have the students make the most of the classroom desks to create spaces that reflect their design ideas. Use whatever is available in the room to transform the space in order to accommodate the world they are building. Students may describe to the class their choices (these desks are the palace steps, this desk is the tomb, etc.) before they perform their scene.
>
> **b** As they perform, have the students play their soundscape on the phone as well.

8 Initially, have the students present the material/scene in front of the other classmates. Then, raise the level of excitement by introducing 1–2 new parameters, which you may have already determined (bringing in another silent character, adding a different song, adding a frozen tableau right before the scene opens, etc.).

9 When each scene is completed, have the group share the conflict they attempted to convey.

10 Finally, ask the audience to comment on how the scenography and the stage composition influenced the performance and how it heightened that particular conflict.

> **a** To illustrate: If the boundary-condition to explore was masculinity and femininity, and they had the actor playing Creon sit comfortably on a throne Center Stage, surrounded by the Chorus, while the actor playing Antigone stood in the Stage Left corner of the stage, how did that choice represent the gender politics in the play, by possibly reinforcing stereotypes of the masculine and the feminine?

11 Once all the scenes have been performed, ask the students what insights into the world of the play they now gained? Did anything change in the way the main event of the scene unfolded? In which way did the different spaces and stage compositions highlight the specific conflicts in the play? How did the scenography and spatial limitations/liberations affect the performance?

Reflection

This exercise is a resourceful introduction to the world of the play and a way of calibrating its fundamental story. It can help students explore which aspects of the text are central in their interpretation, particularly in reference to the multiple conflicts set out by Steiner, which define the world of the play. By considering directorial choices and perspectives, students can perceive the significance of Antigone in the here and now. While ideas and feedback are exchanged, a potentially strong vision can be shaped, clarified, as well as enriched through and beyond the presence of the text. In addition to bringing students together, as they become an audience for each other, this exercise also suggests different ways in which spatial perspective is manipulated and exposes the students to the mechanisms of building stage semiosis in order to emphasize dramatic situation. At the same time, the exercise can be useful for building rapport and developing a common vocabulary with one's team: working in groups, students can discuss fundamental performative insights, such as directorial vision and design concept in a condensed period of time.

OEDIPUS THE KING BY SOPHOCLES

Viviane Sophie Klein, Boston College

IN BRIEF

Demonstrate how different points of view and degrees of knowledge about a situation shape dramatic irony.

PURPOSE

This is an exercise in dramatic irony—when an audience understands something that the characters do not—which is the driving force behind *Oedipus Rex*. The tragic thrust of the play is not its infamous backstory about an ill-fated king who kills his father and marries his mother. Rather it is the protagonist's dawning awareness of his situation. The audience, therefore, derives suspense and satisfaction from watching the characters perform and put together the pieces of a puzzle that they have already solved.

PREPARATION

Download the role cards (see the Appendix on Companion Website).

MATERIALS

Printed copies of the role cards (see above).

Nuts and Bolts

This exercise consists of four activities, each taking approximately 10–12 minutes: an improv game, a post-game discussion, a performance of a scene from *Oedipus the King*, and a post-performance discussion.

Improv Game

The exercise begins with an improv guessing game, in which three supporting cast members provide bits of background information and a lead actor tries to deduce the full story. Adding new players and perspectives to the game, the exercise includes a chorus and two audiences (unknowing and all-knowing).

1 Ask for volunteers to play the Leader (1), the Supporting Cast (3), and the Chorus (1).

2 Divide the rest of the class into Audience A and Audience B.

3 Distribute the role cards (see Appendix).

    a Give the students a few minutes to read and think about—but not to share!—what's written on them.

    b Read the "How to Play" section aloud to the class.

How to Play

1 Premise of the game: A tragedy has just occurred. The Leader has gathered everyone together to try and figure out what happened as quickly as possible before an inspector arrives and shuts down their operation.

2 The Supporting Cast improvises conversation to guide the Leader along. They may read directly from either their role cards or ad lib based on the information provided there.

    a Important: Everyone wants to prove that he or she is innocent!

3 The Chorus is the only one who can interact with both the audience and the characters onstage.

4 Audience A and Audience B observe silently.

5 The game begins with the Leader, Supporting Cast, and Chorus, sitting in a semicircle at the front of the classroom.

6 The Chorus reads a passage aloud from his or her role card and sets the scene.

7 The Leader then begins to question the Supporting Cast.

    a The Supporting Cast members should feel free to interrupt one another and add to the conversation at any time.

8 The game ends when the Leader has figured out the time line of events and the cause of the tragedy, the instructor verifies that the Leader is correct, and the Chorus delivers its scripted line from *Oedipus Rex*.

Helpful Hint

1 If the students get stuck or begin to veer offtrack, instructors can steer the conversation back on course with the following prompts:

a Working backwards from the hours noted on your role cards, can you piece together the time line of events?

b Who was supposed to feed the lion and why? What was each character's motivation?

Discussion Questions

1 Discussion Questions for Audience A (unknowing audience)

a At what point did you figure out what had happened? What were the main clues that tipped you off?

b What were your impressions of the Leader? Did you feel any kinship or empathy toward him or her as you both attempted to solve the puzzle?

2 Discussion Questions for Audience B (all-knowing audience)

a What was it like for you to watch the episode unfold, knowing the full story?

b What were your impressions of the Leader? In what ways was it suspenseful to watch him or her solve the puzzle? In what ways was it frustrating? Tragic? Comic? Was it satisfying when (s)he finally solved it?

3 Discussion Questions for Leader, Supporting Cast, and Chorus

a At what point did you figure out what had happened? What were the main clues that tipped you off?

b What was the process of solving the puzzle like? Was there a sense of urgency to solve it more quickly as time went on?

4 General Discussion Questions for Class

a How did the Chorus affect your reception of the story?

b What did the Chorus' scripted line mean to you?

Oedipus Rex Performance

With this framework in mind, students next perform a short scene from *Oedipus Rex* (lines 950–1075):

1 Ask four volunteers to play Jokasta, Oedipus, Messenger, and Chorus.

2 Set the scene: "A messenger has just arrived to announce that Polybius, the man who raised Oedipus, has died of natural causes. The news brings relief to the king and queen, who lived in fear of a prophecy predicting that Oedipus would kill his father and marry his mother."

Post-performance Discussion

Following the performance, instructors should moderate a class discussion, underlining the role dramatic irony played in both the improv game and the ancient tragedy. Sample prompts include the following:

1 What was it like watching the episode unfold, knowing the full story?

2 What were your impressions of Oedipus? In what ways was it suspenseful to watch him solve the puzzle? In what ways was it frustrating? Tragic? Comic?

3 How did Jokasta and the Chorus affect your reception of the story?

Reflection

Dramatic irony is a powerful tool for modulating emotion, tension, and suspense in any play, but it is especially relevant to *Oedipus Rex*, a saga about vision and blindness that hinges upon its protagonist's awakening to his backstory. The tragic impact of the play lies not in the fact that he must commit his notorious crimes but rather in his realization that he has already committed them. The audience watches Oedipus undergo this process from a privileged point of view, either because they were familiar with the story beforehand—perhaps through mythology, psychology, or popular culture—or because they are able to piece together the narrative faster than the characters, especially when the characters resist the truth. The audience may assume that Oedipus will figure it all out in the end, but they remain suspended in a kind of uncomfortable limbo until he does. The more apparent the truth becomes and the more unwilling Oedipus is to see it, the greater the tension the audience feels. This dissonance between knowledge and uncertainty is what drives the plot forward and electrifies the pulse of the play.

The exercise highlights the key function of dramatic irony in *Oedipus Rex*. It calls attention to the variety of perspectives at play, both on and off the stage, and it examines the ways in which these interact to generate emotion, tension, and suspense. It spotlights, in particular, the role of the chorus, an internal audience that models a mode of reception for the external audience. Most importantly, it encourages students to interrogate the frames of reference that they bring to *Oedipus Rex*, whether or not they know the story in advance, and to consider how their perception of the play is an integral part of the play itself.

MEDEA BY EURIPIDES

Ellen Moll, Michigan State University

IN BRIEF

Compose live tweets from a particular audience member's point of view during a production of *Medea*.

PURPOSE

To help students perceive how individual audience members react to specific parts of a performance of *Medea* differently, particularly in an increasingly diverse polis; to more fully imagine or envision movement and gesture onstage, including the way these movements express characterization and themes; to identify the ways that *Medea* either reflects or subverts dominant Athenian attitudes toward women, metics, and lower social classes; to identify the place of art in larger conversations about identity and society; to identify how Euripides' portrayal of characters with outsider status (women, non-Greeks, servants) can be interpreted as a break with, or innovation in, more traditional Greek tragedies.

PREPARATION

Before this exercise, students should be placed into groups, and each group should create a Twitter account specifically for the class. Perhaps the Twitter handle and thematic nature of the account relate to the course or this play.

The instructor should introduce students to the role and status of individuals in ancient Athenian society: the role and status of men, married women, metics (resident aliens in Athens, sometimes translated as "foreigners"), slaves, non-Greeks ("barbarians" in Greek), and lower social classes. Instructor should emphasize the controversies concerning metic women who marry Athenian citizens, as well as Athenian citizens' stereotyping of the outsider status as emotional and impulsive, claiming that they are unable of reasoning and, therefore, less capable of handling the responsibilities of democratic citizenship. The instructor should also explain that Euripides diverged from the traditional myth that the audience would have known; as a result, Medea's deliberate killing of her children would have been a shocking twist to the audience.

MATERIALS

Students may use their own phones/computers/devices, but it is sufficient for one person per group to have a device. I find that it is effective for students to read the tweets aloud to the class. It is also possible, however, to have a class Twitter account that follows all group accounts, and, in doing so, the Twitter feed of all groups can be displayed with a laptop connected to the projector. This record of the activity could also serve as in-class notes for student reference.

Nuts and Bolts

1 Divide the students into groups. Prior to the exercise, have each group establish a Twitter account specifically for use in this class.

2 Students are told to imagine that they are an audience member seeing *Medea*.

3 In groups, students draw a piece of paper out of a hat or bag. Each piece has one of the following identities:

a You are an audience member who is an Athenian male citizen. You are concerned about the number of metics in Athens and how much influence they have. You do not see them as true Athenians, and you do not want them to pollute the Athenian bloodlines. You also think metics tend to be uncivilized and less ruled by reason.

b You are an Athenian female citizen. You are rarely allowed outside the home, but you are an important part of religious festivals. Tragedies often feature strong women who go against authority in ways that most women could never do in real life, but these female characters are usually punished by dying by the end of the play.

c You are the wealthy Athenian male citizen. As it so happens, you sponsored this play. You want this play to please the crowd and demonstrate your status in the polis. You hope that Euripides does not do anything that makes the crowd hate the play, ruining your chances to win in the process.

d You are a female Athenian slave who works in the household of a wealthy family. You are used to seeing slaves and servants portrayed in drama as less intelligent and wise, and less ruled by reason than people of higher social status.

e You are a female metic married to a wealthy Athenian man. You left home when you married your husband, even though your parents wanted you to stay. Your husband and children are well-to-do financially, but you are made to feel like an outsider, and your children and grandchildren will never be allowed to be Athenian citizens by law.

f You are a male metic. Your great-grandfather came to Athens when he was young, and your family has lived here ever since. Still, you are not considered an Athenian citizen. You work as a bricklayer and are known for the quality of your work, but you always worry what will happen if you offend some important citizen, risking your sponsor to turn against you. You also notice that non-Greeks are often portrayed as very uncivilized onstage; you don't agree that Athenians are more civilized than others.

4 After selecting their performance identities, students are given these instructions:

a In groups, discuss your given identity. What are you likely to want? What are you likely to fear? In what ways do you feel misunderstood or unappreciated? In what ways are you both harmed by social hierarchies in Athens (related to gender, class, metic status) and in what ways are you helped or privileged?

b For the purposes of this exercise, imagine that all people living in Athens could attend the theater, even though that was likely not the case.

c Imagine that you are in the audience watching this play.

5 Select a few scenes from the play. Either ask for student volunteers to read the lines aloud at the start of the activity or show film clips from a production of the play. The goal is to give the students some kind of performance to react to, even if it is quickly assembled. Have the students then "live tweet" their reactions to what they see and hear as they watch the example/listen to the lines. If a performance or clip is not possible, ask the students to go through the play and find at least eight things that they would tweet about if social media existed during the first performance of *Medea*. They must be sure to use the perspective of the audience member they have been assigned.

a Any scene wherein the nurse or another character of outsider status possess a wisdom and perceptiveness that other characters do not is a perfect example to illustrate the contrast between reactions. This includes the opening scene, Medea's speech at line 230 in which she laments the state of women, Jason and Medea's argument starting at 446, or the final scene starting at line 1280. Suggest that the students consider all of the following as they "live-tweet" the performance:

i What parts of the play would be most surprising to the audience member with your perspective? What would make this play seem different from other Greek plays?

ii In the early scenes, which characters in the play would evoke a negative or positive emotional reaction from this audience member? Recall that the audience would not likely be able to predict the ending.

iii Finally, choose one of the scenes viewed/heard and analyze the specific gestures, movements, blocking, and body language used in this scene (or that might be used in this scene if doing a reading of the lines). Tweet about this aspect of performance and what your audience member's reaction to this might be.

6 Students use their group's twitter accounts to publish their tweets and then groups read aloud their tweets to the class. Alternatively, the instructor shows the tweets on a screen. After each group's reading, a brief discussion occurs, drawing out the ways that the play resonates with tensions in Athenian society at the time and how we imagine the staging and physical movement of the actors onstage in conjunction. It is especially useful here to utilize social media as a way to perform the role of their particular individual. Students can be encouraged to utilize (non-offensive) memes, though they might be instructed also to compose some of their own tweets.

Note on social media use in the classroom: Generally speaking, students enjoy using social media and use it often, but it is obviously important to recognize that many students do not have the same relationship to social media as many of their peers. It is incumbent on instructors to model a mindful approach to data and privacy for our students, so work to be flexible. Perhaps offer students additional ways to submit their tweets that allow you to easily read all of their posts.

Reflection

Students are accustomed to the genre of "live tweeting," and this exercise helps them to understand the play as a live performance to be interpreted in varying ways by a heterogeneous audience. The exercise also encourages them to articulate how the play speaks to tensions over gender, class, and metics in Athens at the time, exploring how Athenian perceptions regarding foreigners, slaves, and lower social classes (e.g., uncivilized, less freedom-loving, less ruled by reason, more associated with the body and/or nature) are embedded in the dramatic content of the play. Finally, students see how *Medea* offers an unusual portrayal of a woman's agency, intelligence, and power; while she is seen as monstrous because of her murderous actions, she is not killed at the end as expected. The playwright offers both a misogynistic portrayal of women and a sympathetic representation of the character that is dependent on the perspective of each member of the ancient audience.

LYSISTRATA BY ARISTOPHANES

Jessie Mills, Pomona College

IN BRIEF

By performing dueling choruses, students witness the battle between the sexes.

PURPOSE

While a simple summary of the play suggests only an age-old patriarchal conflict between men and women, this exercise highlights *Lysistrata*'s satirical take on both sexes. It emphasizes the farcical premise of women attempting to curtail men's headstrong insistence on war by utilizing the most immediately powerful means available to them: withholding sex. One technique Aristophanes used was the dueling choruses of Old Men and Old Woman. As a divided chorus, it is unusual among Aristophanes' plays, and it showcases how the performed debate adds to both the comedy and underlying tragedy of the play—women mourn their fathers, brothers, husbands, and sons who are lost to the war. Even though the dueling choruses rarely come close to imitating the rational rhetorical debate between Lysistrata and the Magistrate, the energy behind the exchanges of insults symbolizes the frustration that led Lysistrata, the "disbander of the army," to call the sex strike in the first place.

PREPARATION

This exercise works best once students are familiar with Lysistrata, though instructors can also position this exercise as a precursor to reading the play. Before the exercise, students should understand the nature of the chorus—specifically the use of strophe and antistrophe—in Greek theater. The instructor may provide this information in lecture format or require students to research the movements, vocals, and rhythms of the Greek chorus as homework.

The instructor should select a short excerpt from *Lysistrata* where the strophe and antistrophe are split between the choruses of men and women, mimicking a call-and-response style. In the Dudley-Fitts translation, I recommend the first choral strophe and antistrophe in Scene 4. When chosen, photocopy the excerpt, making however many is needed for the size of the class. As this exercise can be a bit fast and furious, instructors may want to print and distribute the excerpt to each student ahead of time with the chosen strophe and antistrophe highlighted.

MATERIALS

As suggested, it may be helpful to have a one-page printout of chosen strophe/antistrophe for each student. It is also important to have a large, open space.

Nuts and Bolts

1 Split the class in half—one side becomes the chorus of old men and the other, the chorus of women. The class may split between gender identities or, by the discretion of the instructor, based on which part students feel most compelled to play.

2 Give the students ample time (at least 15 minutes) to create a fully choreographed short "battle" of their text. Both the movement and the lines should be synchronized. Encourage students to choose simple, contemporary gestures to punctuate their points and represent their chorus' perspective. Additionally, remind students to play with rhythm, movement, and volume.

3 Encourage the students to choreograph these group-battle pieces as synchronized, progressive movements; the strophe group should move stage left to center, and the antistrophe group, in response, should move stage right to center. That way, the exercise will end in a shared standoff.

4 Once students are ready to perform, position them in "battle mode," wherein they are encouraged to throw extemporized insults at their opposing chorus. As the prepared performances take place, the ad-libbed insults or comments should not interrupt either group's performance but may be used liberally before and after a strophe/antistrophe is completed.

5 Time permitting, students will be given a second chance to refine their battles. Offer a few notes on how to strengthen choreography, volume, and synchronization, then let them work for another 5–10 minutes. After round two is completed, lead the class in a quick discussion about how the contemporary reimagining of the dueling choruses contextualized themes and content of the play.

Reflection

Greek theater—specifically the chorus itself—can feel stilted and overly academic on the page; however, as a staged and animated piece, Aristophanes' text feels instantaneously alive and exciting with the choral inclusions. Moreover, placing the choral movement in the creative hands and direction of the students reveals truths about contemporary gender issues and conflicts.

I have found that this exercise highlights the immediacy and, perhaps most importantly, the fun and humor of *Lysistrata*. Not only is the content made relevant, but the large-scale performative debate is intentionally familiar. More often than not, students remark that this exercise links to a current movie/piece of media where similar thematic-and-performative battles occur (dance-offs, a cappella battles, rap battles, etc.).

This exercise builds emotional, intellectual, and artistic bridges into Greek theater, helping to illuminate the persisting relevance of its application from the past to the present, and vice versa.

THE TWIN MENAECHMI BY PLAUTUS

Michael Schwartz, Indiana University of Pennsylvania

IN BRIEF

This exercise explores properties that are symbolic of self, i.e., physical items that provide security for individual identity.

PURPOSE

Plautus was one of the first to make great sport of existential themes in drama and philosophy, seeking answers regarding the criteria of identity. Who or what determines it? This exercise introduces students to the farcical plot of mistaken twin-identity. Both of the Menaechmus brothers experience the ultimate "identity crisis" when everyone they meet insists that they are not who they know themselves to be. This knowledge is cast into question and doubt until the happy resolution. As a genre, farce allows for such preposterous situations as twins separated at birth, but, in this play, provides a more substantial and relevant commentary, heightening the threat of identity loss and our feeble hold on identity.

PREPARATION

Students should have read and discussed *The Twin Menaechmi*, and have a strong sense of the characters and the workings of the plot. The instructor can draw attention to some key scenes in the text, perhaps reading them aloud to emphasize the farcical elements while still ensuring to underscore the danger: the scene when Erotium invites Menaechmus 2 into her home, mistaking him for his brother; the scene where the suspicious, jealous wife accosts her husband (Menaechmus 1) returning from the forum; or when a doctor diagnoses Menaechmus 1 as insane. Reading about the nature of Roman comedy and identity (see Hardin in Resources on Companion Website) will also be helpful for students and the actors' relationship with the audience—i.e., how actors played to each other and directly to the spectators as well (see Christenson in Resources on Companion Website).

MATERIALS

No technology or specific props needed.

Nuts and Bolts

The exercise implores students to consider what constitutes their own identity; it asks them "how do you prove that you are you?"

1 Ask the students what methods of identification they have with them or have access to at that moment—driver's licenses, credit cards, social media, any other electronic data or records, etc.

2 Next, tell the students to do away with all modern methods of identification, asking them to place themselves in an earlier world where such documentation would not have existed. Prompt them to consider what kinds of documentation might have existed in Plautus' time. The students could dispense with their identification methods figuratively or literally. For instance, there might be an added element of group fun if all modern IDs were collected in a box to be retrieved at the end of class.

3 Brainstorm with the students ways by which they can conclusively prove to their classmates that they are who they say they are. Who or what can they rely on to show who they are? (Friends? Relatives? Telltale birthmarks?) This phase of public proof can be done in groups or individual presentations. Class contributions will either validate the students' attempts to prove their identity or will cast doubt upon their proof, and students should be asked to justify their reasoning in their response. This part of the assignment could be done extemporaneously by the students, or the instructor could provide class time for the students to write their proof strategies before presenting them to their peers.

4 Finally, invite the students to consider, or reconsider, how and why they know who they are in the here and now. Are the kinds of identification we have available to us definitive proof? Can we be absolutely sure that someone has not given us wrong or deceitful information and documentation? What, for example, does "identity theft" mean beyond the levels of inconvenience in dealing with credit card companies? To bring the discussion back to the specifics of the play, encourage the students to think about how much of identity is performed. How do the performance and improvisational skills (or lack thereof) of the twin Menaechmi affect how the other characters respond to them as the misunderstandings grow? This segment of the exercise can take the form of in-class discussion or be tweaked necessarily as an essay prompt.

Reflection

The exercise encourages the students to look beyond what might seem to be a silly and time-worn comic plot device and examines the nature of identity. Removing student's tangible forms of identity and asking them to prove who they are without it, most likely for the first time, will compel students to consider what makes them individually unique. The difficulty of this task displays how fragile the construct of identity can be. A good discussion or essay question might deal with how identity is performed: "How much of identity is performance?" Relating this question to the play, students could consider how and why Menaechmus of Syracuse fares better throughout most of the play than the local Menaechmus of Epidamnus: Menaechmus of Syracuse can improvise the wild situations to his advantage, whereas Menaechmus of Epidamnus gradually grows into his performance skills after a brutal learning curve. The students will not only begin to appreciate the social rituals and symbols designating who we are but will subsequently consider the performance of this farce with the earnestness required from the actors. While farce is often considered to be lightweight, the play illustrates the serious threat of having one's identity questioned or subsumed by another. Audiences should find the whole series of affairs to be funny, and their humor is heightened by the desperate plight of the characters. The exercise underscores the symbolic violence implicit in farce, and the students can witness how characters find no joy or relief until the final scene.

THE SECOND SHEPHERD'S PLAY BY THE WAKEFIELD MASTER

Nicole Andel, The Pennsylvania State University

IN BRIEF

Parallel stage two scenes to perceive the literal and symbolic tension within the play.

PURPOSE

Since undergraduate students often miss the comedy of the Mak/Gil plot in The Wakefield Master's *Second Shepherd's Play*, the goal of this exercise is to help them appreciate the humor in the scene at Mak's house when the shepherds discover the sheep disguised as Mak and Gil's baby. The exercise also opens up a discussion of the thematic relationship between the sheep, as a food source for unemployed or underemployed Medieval farmers, and the Christ Child who will be remembered as the Lamb of God. The analogous relationship in the play between the actual sheep and the Christ Child makes this play a true masterpiece for its theological import; for Medieval Catholics, the embodiment of Jesus begins at his Nativity and continues in the living sacrifice of his Body and Blood, thus the connection between the actual and symbolic lamb as Mak and Gil's pretend baby. Furthermore, the overlay of the family of Mak, Gil, and the pretend baby on the Holy Family demonstrates the didactic component of this play for Medieval audiences. For example, Joseph, the prototype for fathers facing problems providing for their families, is the person Mak should aspire to be like but cannot because of his very human frailty.

PREPARATION

Students must have advanced far enough into the play to get to the scene at Mak's house. It is worthwhile to have them prepare as they read short written character sketches of the three shepherds based on their opening monologues. They may also benefit from writing 5 to 10 sentences describing the differences between the shepherds and Mak.

> **MATERIALS**
>
> Students bring props to class: A manger/crib (a mail-order cardboard box), a prop cleaver or large knife (a ruler), a baby blanket or large scarf, a Sheep/Baby (suggestions: a large pillow decorated to look like a sheep or a child's stuffed toy—the fluffier the better as it is stuffed into the manger/crib).

Nuts and Bolts

Before Class: Assign students the roles of Mak/Joseph, Gil/May, 1st Shepherd, 2nd Shepherd, 3rd Shepherd, and Angel. Require students to bring the necessary props: a sheep stuffed animal, cradle, blanket, and gifts of cherries, a ball, and a bird, as well as the necessary costumes, although they may be abbreviated to simple iconic costumes: winter scarves for the shepherds, a hood for Mak, an apron for Gil, a silver (foil) halo for the Angel.

Ask them to read the play and focus on the last two scenes: first, where the Shepherds arrive at Mak and Gil's house and discover the stolen sheep, and second, where the Shepherds are directed by the Angel to visit Mary, Joseph, and the Christ Child. They should annotate the text as necessary with gestures, blocking ideas, and tone or emotional notes.

1 Students may wish to do a quick read-through of the scene together in order to discover how the scene should be directed (overall blocking of the scene, with special attention to the position of the characters and the timing of the discovery).

2 Call up the group for the in-class performance. Ask the class to provide directions regarding blocking, tension, vocal inflection, and gestures. Assist as necessary, specifically asking students to consider how they might increase the dramatic tension or physical antics conducive to comedy (e.g., double takes, "mugging" the audience, pratfalls) (35 minutes).

3 Once the students have acted the discovery scene, up to Mak's punishment of being tossed in a blanket (use the students' imagination here—with limits!), prepare the next scene, where the Angel directs the three Shepherds to visit the Christ Child.

4 Invite the class again to provide stage directions to the five characters; this time the students playing Mak and Gil are now Joseph and Mary and the sheep (stuffed animal) should be wrapped in a blanket so that it resembles an infant. It might help to read the passage from the Gospel of Luke on which this Mystery play is based (Luke 2: 8–20, "And there were in the same country shepherds abiding in the field, keeping watch over their flock by night …"). Again, the theological concept of Christ as the Lamb of God could be introduced or reinforced here.

5 Discuss the dramatic tension created by juxtaposing the Sheep/Child and the Christ Child at the conclusion of the play and ask students to assess the comedy with reference to the play's larger themes including the cold, taxation, and food scarcity as described by the Shepherds in the earlier scenes, their generosity, and the promise of hope brought by the Christ Child in this play.

Reflection

Two main hurdles exist for teaching British Medieval drama to undergraduates: a lack of knowledge about Catholic theological beliefs of the time period and a difficulty imagining how the lines of dialogue work in concert with timing and gesture to create the dramatic tension needed for comedy. Asking them to direct the piece for the comedic elements before directing the same characters in the Nativity scene raises questions about comedic tension and comedy's appeal. A good question might be whether the fake sheep-baby is a sacrilegious treatment of Christianity or does it serve to make Christ's message of salvation more accessible?

In my experience working with Duquesne University Medieval and Renaissance Players, I have had to provide theological background about the concept of Christ as the Lamb of God (Agnus Dei) from the Gospel of John 1:29, "Behold the Lamb of God who takes away the sin of the world," and of the importance of the shepherds as the first human visitors to laud Christ. Reviewing visual art of the "Visitation of the Shepherds" or the "Adoration of the Shepherds" from the web or the database ARTSTOR can provide ideas about the gravity of this event as visualized in the Medieval imagination.

I teach this play and Ben Jonson's "Christmas: His Masque" in a course centered on the theme of Christmas art; *The Second Shepherd's Play* is difficult for students to imagine because they are unfamiliar with the theological implications of the Incarnation or they come from a Christian tradition that resists visual depiction of biblical events. Medieval Catholics were very comfortable with putting on these stories in the community as an extension of their shared belief. Making the students read (or stumble through) the script in class together gives them a sense of shared difficulty and shared triumph when they finally comprehend how these plays work as art. It also becomes easier to talk about the focus on how the Christian message is meant to be accessible to common people, as both plays share the same focus on the lower classes, fettered economic markets, and deprivation.

A word of caution: The students will get loud while working on the blocking. It is often best to take them outside or be in a theater space for the blocking portion of the exercise.

ATSUMORI BY ZEAMI MOTOKIYO

Peter A. Campbell, Ramapo College of New Jersey

IN BRIEF

Introducing students to the basic movements of Noh drama in order to appreciate the physical aesthetic.

PURPOSE

My students read *Atsumori* as an example of Japanese Noh performance. This exercise focuses on the physical movement and space of Noh, which helps the students explore ideas of physical culture and context. The climax of Noh performance is not related to plot development but instead is an intense dance done by the lead performer, known as the *shite* (pronounced sh-tay); in *Atsumori*, it is a reenactment of the battle that caused Atsumori's death. The virtuosity of the performance parallels the power and strength of the idealized Japanese warrior, who even in his final defeat is graceful and dynamic.

PREPARATION

Students will read the play and also do some research on traditional Japanese homes. In the *Norton Anthology of Drama* there is also a useful introduction to Noh and the playwright, Zeami Motokiyo. They will also watch a short video that gives some visual context on Noh and another that is the 20-minute climactic dance of *Atsumori*. We will spend 30 minutes in class discussing the historical context of Noh before getting directly into the exercise. Make sure they wear socks to class on this day!

MATERIALS

You need a room with a smooth floor so students can slide on it in their socks.

Nuts and Bolts

1 Have the students share their observations of the physical spaces of traditional Japanese homes from their internet searches. I usually have some images to show them just in case they don't find good examples. Make sure to bring up the highly polished wooden floors and the walls of paper. Also note that the Japanese take off their shoes and wear cloth socks called *tabi* (tah-bee). Ask students to compare this with their own living spaces. What are the differences? Make sure to bring up that they may not take off their shoes in their home-socks elements and the fact that they don't have paper walls.

2 Ask them to remove their shoes. Have them walk around the space. How is it different from walking in shoes? Feel free to bring up that it is slippery and you have to focus a bit more on the actual walking than when you wear everyday shoes. As they continue walking, point out that if a person is walking on a slippery floor and the walls are made of paper, one needs to be careful to avoid losing balance; paper walls will only break if one tries to grab it for balance.

3 Now have them stop and line up next to each other. Have them try to get into the neutral stance of a Noh performer—I often have the video handy to refer to and might show a brief section of it again—but what's most important is that their feet are shoulder width, their knees are very slightly bent, their arms are at their sides, and they are leaning slightly forward with their chest while keeping their balance. One trick here is to get them to stand and then have them all lean forward a bit at the same time to give them a sense of the difference.

4 Once they've got a semblance of the stance, have them try to walk without lifting their feet off the floor and not allowing either foot to ever be fully ahead of the other. It's a kind of shuffle at the beginning. Coach them to keep trying and to make it as smooth as possible. They should also be trying not to bob up and down but to maintain the same vertical height as they move across the floor, as if they are gliding. Have them work on this for 5 minutes or so and move among them trying to help them.

5 Now have them get back in line. Tell them they are going to do a small piece of choreography that involves three parts—a slow part, a medium paced part, and a fast part. This echoes the aesthetic principle of the *jo-ha-kyu*, which is vital to Japanese Noh. The *jo-ha-kyu* is an artistic aesthetic that translates into "beginning, break or development, and fast," and students will be familiar with it from the contextual reading and lecture. The steps are very simple—this is not the climactic dance of Atsumori. Tell them to begin with their left foot and take three steps slowly, then six steps a bit faster, and then nine steps quickly. Have them practice on their own a few times, as you coach them, moving up and down the line.

6 Once you feel like most of them have the pattern, have them all line up. Then try to have all of them begin at the same time and do the steps in unison. This will be sloppy, but do it three or four times and they will start to feel each other's rhythms a bit. Once they've achieved a basic unified movement, have them take their seats and put their shoes back on.

7 Begin a discussion about what their bodies felt like. Ask what was awkward or different or physically uncomfortable. Likely there will be comments about sore legs and lower backs. Use these points as a way to talk about the quality of the walk and how physically demanding it is.

8 Next, ask them to compare their own movement with the work they have seen in the videos. What have they learned about the movement of Noh? Ideally they bring up the slowness of the walking and gestures, the smoothness of the movement, and the focus and concentration necessary to perform these aspects of the work. They might also make connections to the core of the body and the focus on the ground; in perceiving this connection of the grounded body and its difficulty they begin to appreciate the virtuosity of the performers and understand why the practice of Noh is a lifelong pursuit.

9 Finally, ask them to compare their movement to what they are used to seeing in contemporary theater. What is similar or different? What kinds of things might account for these differences? Here I try to move away from clichés about East and West to instead focus on the specific cultural behaviors that inform the gestures and stories. For example, the walking and its relationship to the traditional home create a specific kind of movement that is reflected in Noh walking, just as our own walking relates to our own living spaces and the learned gestural and movement behaviors they demand.

Reflection

The students should understand the rigor and virtuosity of the movement and its centrality to the Noh form. The importance of dance and movement as storytelling tools and the meditative quality of the performance are in stark contrast to action-based Western drama. Studying and performing the materials, movements, and particulars of another culture's performance in unfamiliar cultures help my students avoid the problems of generalization and essentialization that often occur when applying a Western model of discussing literary themes or analyzing character behavior through psychology. The attempt at performance, especially in another cultural performance tradition, creates for the students a sensory experience that reminds them of the difficulty of seeing the world from another perspective and provides them deeper appreciation of the complexities of another performance tradition.

Only by attempting to experience other cultures can we begin to understand these cultures and thus other perspectives on the world. Performing that which is unfamiliar, according to Peggy Phelan, is an essential way in which to make this attempt, as it involves an experience and an embodiment of another person, another self, and potentially another culture:

> It is in the attempt to walk (and live) on the rickety bridge between self and other—and not the attempt to arrive at one side or another—that we discover real hope. That walk is our always suspended performance—in the classroom, in the political field, in relation to one another and to ourselves.[1]

Performance avoids the certainty of the lecture or even the discussion by forcing the students to have an experiential relationship to an art form. By looking at the "other" of Japanese Noh, students can learn the vital critical skill of looking afresh at their own cultural perspectives and assumptions.

---

[1] Peggy Phelan, *Unmarked: The Politics of Performance* (New York: Routledge, 1993), 174.

EVERYMAN BY ANONYMOUS

Nancy M. Michael, The Catholic University of America

IN BRIEF

Everyman goes to college.

PURPOSE

One of the biggest challenges to teaching *Everyman* is that students find the allegory and didacticism not only unengaging and two-dimensional but also irrelevant to their daily lives. They read the characters as attributes and nothing more, the dialogue is little more than religious set speeches, and they question its relevance compared to other, more interesting plays. But one of the key components of the play is how Everyman acts in his community—how he shapes and is shaped by it. His very salvation comes when he redirects his relationships to almsgiving and restitution, thereby taking responsibility for himself in a network of interactions.

Despite the fact that the character Everyman must realize that he is alone on this pilgrimage toward Death, his surrounding community, in fact, is central to the play. This exercise helps students move past the didactic, allegorical aspects of the text, so that they can connect with the play's theme of community. By allowing students to focus on the community aspect of the play, they will find their way to the moral center of the text and will feel less disengaged.

PREPARATION

Students should read the entire play in advance. In the preceding class, discuss the historical context of *Everyman*, including its religious significance, evidence of performance, allegorical contexts, and literary characteristics.

MATERIALS

Copies of the text. If students wish to create minimal costume pieces, any in-class supplies can be made to work.

Nuts and Bolts

1 Choose two passages of *Everyman*. Have the students act these scenes out and discuss. Were they engaging? Boring? Why? For instance, the exchange between Everyman, Good Deeds, Knowledge, Beauty, Discretion, and Five Wits gives a good sense of a heavily didactic scene involving multiple characters, which gives several students a chance to participate. This underscores the problem that many students have with the play's heavily allegorical, theological tone. Another option is to use the exchanges earlier in the play between Everyman and Fellowship, Kindred, Cousin, and possibly Goods and Good Deeds. For this second choice to work, teachers may want to abridge the text somewhat for time; they may want to keep all of the actors onstage, ignoring the stage directions for each character to exit, allowing them to simply move off to the side, where they can interact with one another silently while the next character speaks with Everyman.

2 Now, reframe the play in the context of college. Ask the students to imagine the character Everyman is a college student and that the community is their own school.

3 Divide the class into small groups and assign characters to each. One group contains God, Death, Messenger, Doctor, Confession, and Angel; a second group should be formed for Fellowship, Kindred, Cousin, and Goods; a third group consists of Good Deeds, Knowledge, Strength, Discretion, Five Wits, and Beauty. It is also possible to allow Good Deeds, Knowledge, and Confession to form their own group, if you prefer, to work with four smaller configurations.

4 Students should work to determine what their relationship to Everyman is within their school community. In imagining Everyman as a college student, perhaps Cousin is a fraternity brother who likes to party too much or Goods is a roommate who supplies Everyman with things that distract him from his studies. Perhaps Discretion *et alia* are "good students" and part of his study group, and so on. The goal is to develop characters that would have the appropriate type of relationship to Everyman; in the example above, for instance, Discretion *et alia* as a study group would be preparing Everyman to succeed, but the final trial would still be Everyman's own.

5 Students should write out a short paragraph about their characters. If Discretion is a member of a study group, what's his major? How does he know Everyman? Are Kindred and Cousin actually related or do they have a different connection to Everyman here?

6 Students should share their characters with one another so that the class as a whole can offer feedback, critique, or further development, and the students can decide how the community functions as a whole.

7 Once the community has shaped itself, revisit the passages that were acted out earlier. Students may, if they wish, create rudimentary "costumes"—Cousin and Kindred could carry a small sign with Greek letters on it to represent that they belong to a fraternity, or Fellowship might carry around a phone and pretend to text the entire time, as college students frequently do.

8 Re-perform the scenes in the new community with the characters and relationships the students have come up with. Follow up with a discussion about how the students' reactions and understanding of the play may have changed. Ideally, the same scene will be used, so the contrast between the first reading and the second, when students have a fuller sense of how community and character relationships can function as allegory, is clearest. Notes: Feel free to be creative with the type of "community" Everyman is a part of. If your students will be more responsive to an alternate community-based setting (a circus, an office, a government, etc.), then let them explore those dynamics. However, I strongly caution against mapping *Everyman* onto another preexisting world students are familiar with, such as popular television shows or fictional worlds within novels. Students who have tried to place the text within the world of, for instance, *Mean Girls*, even if they do not use the specific characters from the movie, always have more difficulty with the exercise, because they end up trapped by the rules of the setting they are trying to use, and the analogy inevitably breaks down. Instead, have students focus on creating their own communities in their groups that are not building off a preexisting world.

Reflection

By reframing the characters as actual people and peers, and by grounding the story in a recognizable community framework, students are invited to engage with the play beyond its Christian allegory. Julie Paulson, in her analysis of *Everyman*, suggests that within the play "to recognize death fully is to recognize that one is both a part of one's community and therefore responsible to it, yet also separate from that community and therefore accountable for one's actions" (122–23). She goes on to argue that morality and individuality must be built from human relationships—from engagement with one's community—and that for Everyman, it is the performative act of penance that enables him to obtain absolution, being that it enables him to gain self-understanding through his interaction with the world. These interactions teach him about his own, individual accountability within a community, until he is able to go through penance and turn his goods into alms. By sacrificing the thing he once loved more than anything else—his worldly riches—because it is the right thing to do, and not through fear of hell but moral obligation, Everyman comes to understand his place in a wider nexus of community. At the same time, the allegorical, spiritual themes of the play come to their conclusion.

In terms of performance, an activity like this can help students develop their sense of ensemble acting and appreciate the integral role that an ensemble plays in its interactions with the main character. It can demonstrate to students of acting how, even in a seemingly didactic, heavily allegorical play, the ensemble of characters function as a dynamic unit of players, telling a story beyond symbolic representations. An ensemble of actors is, for the duration of a play, its own community, both onstage and off. Allowing students to explore deeper meanings and relationships between characters— whether these relationships are made explicit within a production or not— can only strengthen the ensemble and help students understand their place within a production community. The nature of this kind of work can extend beyond the classroom and give students a sense of their own place within a given community. Even if students cannot fully identify with the specifically Christian themes of the play, they can understand and relate to the struggles of figuring out where they belong within a community: which groups they should be a part of, which groups will not be beneficial to interact with, how they relate to a community as a whole, and who and what truly makes up a community. Beyond the scope of *Everyman*, by resetting the text within a familiar framework the exercise can help deepen how and why we foster community.

A *MIDSUMMER NIGHT'S DREAM* BY WILLIAM SHAKESPEARE

Edward L. Rocklin, California State Polytechnic University, Pomona

IN BRIEF

Students will use props to explore performative choices regarding the play's themes of love and law.

PURPOSE

A Midsummer Night's Dream consists of many themes, but ideas of love and law are fundamental to the play and central to its understanding. Two of the groups use a property—a rose and a book entitled *The Laws of Athens*—while the third group performs without a prop. By alternating the scene's props, students discover that the number of sublots is a choice made by the director. This activity also explores the themes of constancy in romantic love, as well as tensions created between arranged and romantic marriages.

PREPARATION

Students are expected to read Act 1 of *A Midsummer Night's Dream*, ensuring that the instructor may productively spend the opening moments of class asking, "What is the plot of this play?" One objective is to provide students with the necessary context in order to explore the challenges of articulating with coherency the design of a multi-plot play, especially a play that can be seen as having three or four plots.

MATERIALS

A rose and a book entitled *The Laws of Athens* (I print a large-font page with the title and tape it to a large, thick book).

Nuts and Bolts

1 Ask students how many plots are there in *A Midsummer Night's Dream*. You can point out that some critics answer "three," whereas some would contest that it's four. Write the three or four different plots on the board: Theseus and Hippolyta—the lovers; Hermia and Lysander and Helena and Demetrius; Bottom and the Rude Mechanicals; Oberon and Titania (15 minutes).

2 Divide the class into three performance groups: one group receives a rose, one group receives a book titled *The Laws of Athens*, and one group has no prop. Ask each group to read and rehearse aloud Act 1, Scene 1, lines 1–127. Each group has 15 minutes to explore the text, cast it, and rehearse their performance.

3 If students seem to have difficulty using their props, you can ask some questions to stimulate their creativity. Ask questions such as "Who enters holding the rose? Is the rose passed to one or more of the other characters? Does anyone do anything to the rose? Is *The Laws of Athens* onstage to begin with or does someone bring it to the scene? Who brings it? Does anyone attempt to cite a specific law or laws from the book? How many people do this? Is the book used in any other way?" Ask the group without a property to use voice, gestures, blocking, and address to create and project their interpretation?

4 Each group performs its version of the scene. Pause after each performance for students to take notes on key performance choices, observing how key choices prompt them to interpret the scene. After the three performances are completed, the students share their comments regarding the key choices, focusing on how the rose or the book was used to help create a specific interpretation. Conversely, discuss how the prop-less group projected their interpretation and the ways in which the outcome was effected through the absence of object (30 minutes).

5 You can also introduce several guiding questions when appropriate: What does an exit do? What can a prop do to help create and project an interpretation? What do these two properties do to focus attention on the themes of consistency in love and how the law regulates marriage in Athens? How do props help the audience in seeing the play as a multi-plot story structure?

6 At the end of the discussion, encourage students to write in their journals, reflecting on what they saw, beginning with the prompt: "One thing that is becoming clear to me from these performances is …" and/or "One thing that is still confusing to me is …." Remind students that they certainly can add a second, third, or more points to this reflection. These reflection points can form the basis of the next class's opening discussion.

Students may share these reflections in pairs or as a whole class, or the instructor may collect copies of them to help in future activities or discussion.

Reflection

The opening scene establishes the tension between love and law: that is, how the law tries to regulate lovers and their relationships, and how love tries to escape from the dictates of the law. Conversely, it can also show how love makes people act irrationally, and the law corrects for good behavior in society. The use of specific properties, or none at all, can work to emphasize these themes in ways that help students understand the play at a deeper level.

For example, traditionally, Theseus and Hippolyta have been played as a mature, harmonious couple; however, if accepted that the theme of law is emphasized through the use of the book, the ducal couple might exhibit disharmony, based on such lines as "I wooed thee with my sword." Here, there is an observable relationship between object and performance that goes beyond aesthetic.

In my experience, all three groups can produce vivid performances. For example, one performance saw Theseus give the rose to Hippolyta, who expressed her increasing unhappiness with his threat to execute Hermia on their wedding day. She plucked the petals, one by one, so that when Theseus turned to ask, "What cheer, my love?" he was stunned to discover her displeasure. But, if Hippolyta brings the rose, she can pass it to Hermia, creating a sense of female solidarity. The book is usually brought in by Egeus, who shows Theseus the specific law authorizing his control of Hermia. In interpretation, Theseus might either point to another paragraph on the same page or turn to another page, justifying his offer to Hermia of becoming a nun—and he can do so to placate Hippolyta. And either Hermia or Lysander might seize and slam the book shut. The group without a prop will have to invent other means of conveying their interpretation, and the contrast between performances with and without a prop itself can stimulate further insights into performance. The immediate, visible contrast between the performances—being apparent for the prop-less group from the very beginning of rehearsal—creates a visualization of creative potential through objects, displaying how ambience can be converted into possibility.

A MIDSUMMER NIGHT'S DREAM BY WILLIAM SHAKESPEARE

Ethan McSweeny, American Shakespeare Center

IN BRIEF

Use punctuation to explore playable moments.

PURPOSE

In many classical texts, especially Shakespeare plays, the punctuation we now have is a matter of editorial conjecture. We don't authoritatively know where he placed his commas or his end stops. Certain editions tend to favor more elaborate punctuation (Arden, for example, is usually heavy with semicolons) and certain are sparer (Cambridge tends to favor end stops). A fun way to explore the differences is to compare the punctuation in a couple of texts, particularly if one is working on a soliloquy. You can then engage in a debate over which punctuation works best for the performance that is being created. Sometimes a principle is best indicated by its absence, as in this wonderfully tortured introduction by Peter Quince to "The Tragedy of Pyramus and Thisbe."

PREPARATION

Since the exercise focuses on a passage from Act 5, ideally the students should have read the play in its entirety before this class. It is possible, however, to extract the brief passage and use it, depending on the context, as an introduction to the play since it drives home a performance element rather than an interpretation of the text.

MATERIALS

None.

Nuts and Bolts

1 Ask for a student volunteer to read the role of Quince.

2 Either give the students a photocopy of the prologue from Act 5 or direct them to that passage in their text:

i QUINCE

If we offend, it is with our good will.

That you should think we come not to offend,

But with good will. To show our simple skill,

That is the true beginning of our end.

Consider then we come but in despite.

We do not come as minding to content you,

Our true intent is. All for your delight

We are not here. That you should here repent you,

The actors are at hand, and by their show

You shall know all that you are like to know.

3 Direct the actors to take the text, hold it in their hand, and look at it. As they speak it aloud, walk in a straight line. At every piece of punctuation, change direction. Be rigorous. Include parentheses or quotation marks.

a The hierarchy of punctuation is not important, just marking the turn. Challenge the students to move as fast as they can without stumbling and to make distinct, sharp turns. Don't pre-plan, just experience it physically. If they miss a piece of punctuation, go back and do the line again. If they have a "long thought," i.e., a long phrase with no punctuation, and they run out of room, go back and see if they can find a route that lets them stay in a straight line for the whole thought.

b As a side coach, you might snap or clap at every piece of punctuation to subtly reinforce the turns.

4 Invite a second student to try, but ask him or her to remove all of the punctuation.

a What happens? Where do they simply run out of breath? How does punctuation help us know where to breathe?

5 Invite a third student to do the speech, only turning at the punctuation marks that correspond to the end of a line.

a Ask the class to compare the three versions.

b How does the punctuation in Shakespeare's text inform the character? In this example, Peter Quince is clearly very nervous, so he is gulping for breath before he has completed a thought. And at the end he accelerates and runs it all together so he can get finished more quickly.

6 Once completed, lead a discussion with the student actors as well as the student audience.

  a Where are there "long" thoughts (of more than 7–10 words)? This might suggest that a character "knows" more of what they are going to say or is comfortable articulating something larger. Where are there "short" thoughts (less than 7–10 words)? This might indicate very active thinking or an emotional state that is driving fast and contradictory thoughts. Where have we missed using the punctuation to experience the subtle change in specific thought? Often we will find where actors are racing over thought changes or are not being specific. Good ones will notice this for themselves.

Reflection

For the sake of clarity, the exercise is explained with a single speech from *A Midsummer Night's Dream*. But it can be used with almost any speech or scenes as well. The simplest conclusion to draw from this exercise with the students is that "Punctuation = Thought." The punctuation alone does not tell you what the "thought" is; one still needs to understand the vocabulary and motivation. But it does help show you where the thought shifts or how it changes with different punctuation. You can deploy this exercise at different points in the process of studying or rehearsing Shakespeare. With a relatively inexperienced group, it can be used early as it nicely complements table work with a physical component. You will find that vigorous walking and turning also influences the breath, and your actors will naturally start breathing where they need it and fitting it into the punctuation and thus the rhythm of the line.

In directing plays, I have had actors come up to me as late as during our preview performance periods and request removing or changing the place of a comma. Their doing so always makes me happy because it shows how much they have invested themselves in the specifics of the text and how closely they are listening to Shakespeare's language and to themselves. Perhaps as a written component of this exercise, your students could also be granted permission to reorganize any punctuation and compare their choices.

In rehearsal, a lot of ink is spilled on the phrases "moment to moment" and "thinking on the line." This punctuation work is a great way to distill a text down to its smallest constituent moments and then to activate thinking for each of them. The overall concept is that punctuation helps illustrate where a change in thought is occurring, but does not necessarily dictate what that thought or action might be. Remember, however, that eventually we want to perform the text at the speed of actual human thought. We want to involve the thinking process, but not necessarily have it be indicated or marked in actual performance.

ROMEO AND JULIET BY WILLIAM SHAKESPEARE

Jim Casey, Arcadia University

IN BRIEF

Use cue scripts to better understand Shakespeare's characters and early modern performance practices.

PURPOSE

In order to save money, reduce rehearsal time, and protect the plays from theft, actors during Shakespeare's time were not given complete copies of the play they were performing. Instead, they were given cue scripts (also called parts, lengths, rolls, and sides) that included only their own lines, the last word (or few words) of their cues, and any essential stage directions that were not already written into the text. The use of cue scripts introduces students to early modern staging and rehearsal practices; it develops careful listening habits and provides deeper insight both into the characters and into particular moments of the play (variations of this exercise may be adapted to other early modern plays, but cue scripts work especially well with Shakespeare and his collaborators).

PREPARATION

A complete copy of the brief scene to be performed, as well as cue script versions of the same scene where only the actor's lines appear (see Nuts and Bolts). If the instructor wishes to extend this exercise over several class periods, students can choose their own scenes, create their own cue scripts, memorize them, and perform them in class at another time. I usually have students copy lines from an online source such as *opensourceshakespeare. org* and then copyedit the lines to match our course text(s).

MATERIALS

Cue scripts, created by the instructor or students. If desired, these can be attached to pencils or short dowel rods on either end to create scrolls that can be rolled to the appropriate lines.

Nuts and Bolts

1 Introduce the concept of cue scripts before the exercise itself, explaining what cue scripts are and how they were used in the early modern period.

a Scholars believe early modern actors created their own cue scripts and memorized all lines before a very short rehearsal period (often consisting of hours rather than days) that probably did not include a complete run-through of the play. Cue scripts were created by gluing or stitching together several pages and then attaching them at either end to wooden rods in order to form scrolls or rolls (the origin of an actor's "role").

b Actors of the time were often not given complete scripts, for several reasons: there were no copyright laws to prevent an actor from passing the work off as their own at another theater; it would take too long to handwrite complete copies of the play for every actor; and ink and paper were simply too expensive.

c As a solution, cue scripts were prepared. A cue script consists of only *one* to *three* cue words (aligned right) for each set of lines, followed by the character's own lines. Stage directions, if included, are kept to a minimum (no "asides" or editorial instructions should be included). Actors, therefore, discovered what the other characters would say or do either in rehearsal (if possible) or on opening night (as usual).

d These cue scripts were often presented to an actor as a scroll, or roll (giving us the origin of the term "role"), so if possible, present the lines to the students in the same way.

2 Cue scripts may be created for any scene that the instructor wishes to explore, but lines around 1.3.18–60 (when the Nurse tells a story about Juliet as a toddler) and 1.4.206–19 (when Romeo and Juliet first speak) can be particularly effective. For the first of these, the Nurse is speaking to Juliet and Lady Capulet, telling a story that lasts 40 lines. The cue for both Juliet and her mother to speak is "said 'Ay,'" so the cue scripts for the mother and daughter for this particular portion of the scene would look like these:

a Lady Capulet

said "Ay."

Enough of this; I pray thee, hold thy peace.

my wish.

Marry, that marry is the very theme [...]

b Juliet

said "Ay."

And stint thou too, I pray thee, nurse, say I.

be married?

It is an honour that I dream not of.

3 Ask for volunteers to read the roles of Nurse, Lady Capulet, and Juliet. Distribute their rolls. Give them a moment to review their own lines and familiarize themselves with their cue: "said 'Ay.'"

4 Invite the actors to the front of the classroom. Since Shakespeare's company performed on a thrust stage, with some patrons sitting in the balcony behind the stage, have the students who are not acting surround the actors on three (or four) sides as the audience. Have the actors speak directly to the audience when they feel it is appropriate.

5 Have the Nurse begin the scene (instructing the actor to keep going regardless of any interruptions), and instruct the other actors to really listen to what their scene partner says and to "jump" their lines when they hear their cue words. Since Lady Capulet and Juliet have only one line, and if time allows, it is possible to ask those students to memorize their line and attempt to recite it without looking at their scroll. Have a prompter available in case they forget their lines, but ask the students to try to muddle through the scene even if they have difficulty.

6 Unbeknownst to the actors, Lady Capulet and Juliet both have the same "cue" that is spoken four times and the homophone "Ay/I" is said five times. Actors listening carefully for cue words will try to speak several times before finally delivering their lines. On stage, these false starts will make it appear as if Lady Capulet and her daughter are both unsuccessfully trying to interrupt the Nurse, who never pauses in her recollection of the inappropriately sexual anecdote.

7 Run through the scene at least twice and then ask the actors to discuss their experience, both in terms of the use of cue scripts itself and in terms of what they discovered about the scene, characters, or lines.

8 Then have the audience members comment on the scene. Have some of the audience watch the scene while looking at their books and have others view it without looking at the full play script. Then have them switch. After several scenes, have everyone comment on the different experiences and understandings of the play—as actors with only cue scripts, as audience members with no play script, and as readers of the full play.

9 If possible, repeat the same process with Romeo and Juliet's first encounter at 1.4.206–19 or choose any other scene. If assigning work in advance, students, in groups, can select a scene, create a cue script, then exchange it with another group (so as to avoid familiarity with the scene).

10 After all the scenes have been acted and the students have all commented, ask them questions about the process. For example, if more than one actor was on stage, how did they decide which person to address? How did they know when to perform an action or to use a prop when they had no stage directions? How did using the cue scripts change their "reading" experience of the play? What might such a rehearsal practice mean for a performance (Shakespeare's company had an extensive repertoire and very limited rehearsal time, so they often performed a play with only hours rather than months of rehearsal)?

Reflection

The American Shakespeare Center's Blackfriars Playhouse in Virginia regularly uses cue scripts during their spring Renaissance Season. Actors there report revelatory experiences using cue scripts (especially for parts they have performed before). For example, the actors' sense of their own characters will change if all they know is what they say themselves and what they hear on stage. In Romeo and Juliet's first encounter at 1.4.206–19, for example, the actors may notice a lyrical exchange between the characters in their first words to one another, with their cue words often rhyming. The actors may feel that this suggests some kind of innate connection between the two characters, but they probably will not describe the lines as stale or rehearsed. By contrast, those reading the play may notice that the young lovers' first words form a perfect sonnet when read together, perhaps suggesting a conventional performance of Petrarchan "love." Students often report that reading these lines on the page can make them appear contrived or formulaic, but reading them aloud from cue scripts makes them seem more playful and spontaneous. Unlike the stale, conventional love that Romeo professes for Rosaline at the beginning of the play, the budding romance between Romeo and Juliet is impetuous and exciting. It is vibrant, and dangerous, and surprising, not merely the boring cliché that many students might expect.

Similarly, using cue scripts can change an actor's understanding of "Shakespeare" from a stilted, formal museum piece to a raucous, instinctive living work. For instance, in the cue scripts for Juliet and Lady Capulet above, the characters are responding to the Nurse, who is recounting a racy story that predicts how baby Juliet will fall "backwards" into bed when she is older (with obvious sexual innuendo). It also questions whether the Nurse is oblivious to the attempts of others to speak or if she simply refuses to be interrupted. If we believe that moments such as these are not merely incompetent stagecraft, then we can see how Shakespeare's characters speak over one another often, providing vibrant, tumultuous dialogue that is at odds with the typically artificial delivery of lines spoken either in unison or with a ritualized, unnatural progression. Using cue scripts helps restore the vitality to Shakespeare's lines and attunes students to the freshness and staged spontaneity of the performance. Such immediacy is especially important for *Romeo and Juliet*, a play where characters repeatedly engage in lively, often chaotic, verbal battles. Using cue scripts highlights how ineffectively most of these characters listen to one another, as opposed to the two young lovers, who connect so well that they literally and figuratively rhyme.

THE MERCHANT OF VENICE BY WILLIAM SHAKESPEARE

William Hutchings, University of Alabama at Birmingham

IN BRIEF

Create an in-class debate to demonstrate an inherently dramatic form: the public trial.

PURPOSE

This exercise enhances students' understanding of the complex issues that surround Shylock's fate, especially the common societal values of justice and mercy. By means of an actual, formal debate among the students, the exercise distinguishes and defines the role of these values as they pertain to the trial of Shylock. Finally, students will become more aware of divergent possibilities in the enactment of the trial scene.

PREPARATION

The exercise occurs after a close reading of *The Merchant of Venice* during the final phase of teaching the text. The instructor prepares 4" x 6" cards for students. Each is labeled under one of four categorizations (see below).

MATERIALS

None.

Nuts and Bolts

1 Provide each student a single 4″ × 6″ card. From these options, students will select one of four thesis statements:

a "Shylock receives mercy but not justice."

b "Shylock receives justice but not mercy."

c "Shylock receives both justice and mercy."

d "Shylock receives neither justice nor mercy."

2 Encourage the students to think carefully about the choices; after they hand in the signed cards, they cannot change their thesis, and they will have to justify their stance to classmates who do not agree with them. They may review significant passages in the text, but they may not consult classmates or know the choice that any of their fellow students are making. They are allowed up to 10 minutes to make up their minds, after which they hand in the choices they have made.

3 Divide the students into four teams based on their choices and move them to separate corners of the room, as far apart as space will allow. For the remainder of the class period, they are to (a) discuss the best arguments and the most relevant evidence from the text that will support their views, (b) consult/"brainstorm" with each other to identify the best strategies for persuading others of their validity, and (c) choose a spokesperson from within the group to present their case. Advise them to keep their voices down when discussing their planned arguments so that the other teams will not overhear them strategize. Each discussion group is restricted to those on its own "prosecution or defense team" only.

4 During this part of class, I visit/"sit in on" the conversation of each group, making sure that the discussion stays on topic and, if the discussion seems to lag (which it very rarely does), I suggest various issues that may complicate/problematize the thesis that they have chosen to assert. I also make sure that they carefully define both "mercy" and "justice," and question if and how they know these qualities when they see them. Regardless of their chosen position, they soon find that such definition is not as self-evident as they may have assumed.

5 Instruct them to continue their discussion via exchanged emails, a newly formed Facebook group, via an online learning management system, or in a study area outside of the classroom.

6 On the second and third class days, the students present their arguments in the order that they are listed above, presenting at a rate of two "cases" per class day. In a 50-minute class, each team gets approximately 20 minutes, with 10 minutes for questions from students on the other teams. Any student may reply on behalf of the group, and any student from the other three groups may ask a question. The instructor presides over the debate, preventing any digressions and overruling any inappropriate comments if necessary. A gavel is sometimes helpful to keep order in the court.

Reflection

Often, the students quite aggressively assert support for their group's thesis, secure in the company of the like-minded; the percentage participating in the "team" discussion is unusually high in each group, and students are eager to present their arguments and strategies—including those who are usually rather reticent in class—when the time comes. On the rare occasion that any of the four perspectives may not share their side, it can either be omitted or the instructor can summarize the argument later (although it is best to avoid the "teacher said" syndrome). If only one student chooses a side, reassure him or her in front of the class that there is a *very* valid argument to be made in order to encourage a strong presentation.

Among the issues that should be raised are:

1 What would be a "just" punishment for Shylock, under the circumstances?

2 What would be a "merciful" judgment for Shylock?

3 Does Shylock's repeated refusal to accept an amount of money that is many times the value of the bond affect your opinion of whether he receives justice or mercy? Would rewarding him with vast "windfall profits" for sparing Antonio's life, as Portia and Bassanio propose, really be an appropriate settlement of the case? Would it make a good precedent for other cases?

4 Is Portia's eloquent definition of mercy (4.1.185–204) actually applied in Shylock's case? If so, to what extent? If not, does that alter your judgment of her speech—and/or of her character?

5 To what extent does the overt anti-Semitism expressed by certain characters (including Antonio, the play's title character) affect the judgment that Shylock receives? Do characters who are involved in delivering and administering the verdict (the Duke, Balthasar/Portia) ever express any anti-Semitic views?

6 How does Shylock's forced conversion to Christianity affect your judgment about whether he does or does not receive justice and/or mercy?

7 Does it matter that the case is presided over by someone who is not actually a judge?

8 Or are justice and mercy qualities of the decision itself, regardless of the identity of the decider? Would the same verdict have been any more just or merciful if it had been issued by Bellario, the actual doctor of laws with whom Balthasar (actually Portia) "turned o'er many [law] books together [and who] is furnished with [the doctor of laws's] opinion, bettered with his [actually her] own learning"? (4.1.156–8).

9 Does it matter that both the judgment and the person doing the judging have the approval of the Duke, who is the play's supreme political authority?

10 Is mercy automatically given to Shylock when the Duke "pardon[s Shylock's] life before [he] ask[s] for it"? (4.1.368). Does this, as the Duke claims, show Shylock "the difference of our [Christian] spirit"? (4.1.173).

11 Is Shylock right in claiming that, by bankrupting him, "You [the court] take my life / When you do take the means whereby I live"? (4.1.475–76). If so, is mercy being granted? Why or why not?

As a final point, ask the students to consider Shylock's exit line—one of the most problematic in all of Shakespeare's plays. Consisting of only three simple words—"I am content" (4.1.393), the actor bears the responsibility of interpreting the tone. Are Shylock's parting words sincere? Sarcastic? Resigned? Ironic? Angry? Or something else? Note that Shakespeare provides no stage direction about how this line should be said, so each actor and director must decide for himself or herself, creating potential for every production to be different in this regard. By emphasizing the problem of Shylock's exit line, an instructor can provoke an extraordinary discussion of textual indeterminacy and choices that must be made in any production.

Ask an actor in each of the four groups to deliver the line as they think Shylock would say it. The actor's variant possibilities in Shylock's tone as he departs are practically limitless, and they exemplify the innumerable choices that any actor and director must make for any role.

The effects of such questions are, of course, to destabilize students' certainties, problematize their initial reactions, encourage critical thinking, and sharpen their arguments in the debate. After the debate, their written assignment over *The Merchant of Venice* asks them to present their own individual argument in response to the initial question, regardless of the debate team they were initially on.

THE TRAGEDY OF HAMLET BY WILLIAM SHAKESPEARE

Joseph Kidney, Stanford University

IN BRIEF

The students will perform the same soliloquies as found in different versions of the text, with particular emphasis on the so-called "Bad" Quarto of 1603.

PURPOSE

If *Hamlet* is, as Olivier's movie announces, about "a man who could not make up his mind," then it is fitting that the playtext itself exists in a state of uncertainty. When we read Hamlet's soliloquies in conjunction with the sometimes comically different "Bad" Quarto, we can defamiliarize the most famous speeches in English literature by experiencing how the canonized Shakespearean text facilitates and frustrates both performance and interpretation.

PREPARATION

The students should come to class having read no more than a conventional text of *Hamlet*. The instructor may advise the students in advance to pay particular attention to the soliloquies, but the speeches in their isolated nature should manage to draw attention to themselves regardless. Any earlier assignment of the "Bad" Quarto extracts will detract from the spontaneous intrigue of the exercise. The instructor should consult the recommended resources (see Resources on Companion Website) to familiarize themselves with the critical tradition surrounding the "Bad" Quarto.

MATERIALS

Handouts with the two soliloquies (see the Appendix on Companion Website).

Nuts and Bolts

1 Handouts with two soliloquies from the "Bad" Quarto will be distributed to the students: "To be, or not to be—ay, there's the point" and Hamlet's soliloquy on the First Player's recital of Priam's death: "Why, what a dunghill idiot slave am I!"

2 The instructor will deliver aloud Hamlet's speech to the players: "Speak the speech, I pray you," as an invitation to the two students playing Hamlet to perform in front of the class. One student will act out a soliloquy in its more commonly encountered form— from either the Second Quarto or the First Folio—after which the other student will act out the same soliloquy from the "Bad" Quarto.

3 The students will exchange copies and then perform whichever version of the speech their fellow student had just performed. They should attempt to elicit from the class whichever reaction their previous performance provoked—if the first reader of the "Bad" Quarto was met with laughter (as is most likely), they should try to elicit the same response with the more familiar text. The student tasked with delivering the "Bad" Quarto speech should attempt to present it convincingly as a moving piece of serious drama (15 minutes).

4 The foregoing exercise will then be repeated with the other soliloquy.

5 The instructor will then enumerate a few theories about the nature of the "Bad" Quarto—perhaps it is a rough draft of the play, or a poorly remembered bootleg copy, or a version abridged for performance—and invite the students to speculate, according to their experience as both actors and audience of the two texts, upon the relation of the "Bad" Quarto, the first extant text of *Hamlet*, to the play as it is more often encountered.

6 The students should discuss how the Shakespearean text is and isn't an improvement upon the "Bad" text; do we as audience members find something more believable about the unpolished, limping, at times anticlimactic text? Do we as spectators feel closer in sympathy to the less articulate, less rhetorically sound prince? Moreover, in the canonized version, Hamlet opens the soliloquy upon the performance of the First Player with the statement: "Now I am alone," but in which of the texts does he sound like he is actually by himself? If Hamlet is about incurable delay, how does the more streamlined quality of the "Bad" Quarto text better prepare us for the Act 5 Hamlet, who seems to transform into an action hero so unlike the leisurely musing prince of the bulk of the play?

7 The actors will then be asked to reflect upon the experience of performing the two texts. Shakespeare, as an actor himself, is often thought of as a playwright with a particular insight into the rhythms of spoken verse, but which of these two versions do we find easier to perform? Hamlet's lines are so crammed with complex imagery, so powered by abrupt leaps of imagination, that it can be difficult for an actor or an audience member to keep up with the very speed of thought. By engaging with a Hamlet reduced in breadth and depth in the "Bad" Quarto, do we find ourselves more immediately drawn in to the character and his circumstances? Could the students, as hypothetical directors of Hamlet, see themselves incorporating anything from these examples of the "Bad" Quarto?

Additional Discussion Questions

1 How does this exposure to the fact of multiple Hamlets modify our feelings with regard to the notion of a performance's fidelity to its source-text?

2 The existence of alternate texts necessarily complicates interpretation. Is this particular kind of complication a blessing or a curse for a prospective actor? Is it liberating or just additionally confusing? Do you think an actor or director has a certain responsibility to channel this textual ambiguity in a performance or should he or she aspire to convey the sense of a unified drama?

3 Among literary forms, do plays uniquely resist the idea of a definitive presentation? After all, the first Hamlet on film was portrayed by legendary actress Sarah Bernhardt, and Ethan Hawke, in a Hamlet from 2000, delivered "To be or not to be" while pacing the aisles of a Blockbuster. T. S. Eliot accused Goethe of turning Hamlet into Werther, and Coleridge of turning Hamlet into Coleridge, but doesn't a play compel us, as readers, interpreters, and performers, to transform given characters into creatures of our own making?

4 In a conversation with Rosencrantz and Guildenstern, Hamlet (though not until the First Folio!) says: "There is nothing either good or bad, but thinking makes it so." Could we not follow in saying: there is no quarto good or bad, but thinking makes it so?

Reflection

The point of the exercise is to ask the question: What do we talk about when we talk about *Hamlet*, or any play for that matter? Most students who encounter Shakespeare have never been exposed to any other Renaissance drama, but by reading a canonical play like *Hamlet* beside a premature or potentially mangled version of it, students can engage with Shakespeare's drama in a way that makes it seem more alive, more as something divided between alternative possibilities than solidified in one unalterable, perhaps fossilized, state. This is a play that we know as opening with the question: "Who's there?," but by encountering a wildly different Hamlet, students can come to understand how the questioning of identity undertaken by the drama is embodied in the language and text of the play itself. To teach a play as literature is to build a bridge between creative writing and creative reading, and by allowing ourselves as performers to inhabit and scrutinize the relative merits of two differing playtexts, we come to see how acting can be like editing and directing, in that it turns a participant of the text into just that, one who collaborates with the author in delivering an art form to the world.

One of the glories of a live, unrecorded play performance is its utter singularity; even the same actors will fail in replicating exactly the Hamlet of the night before. Yet we may feel inclined always to judge a given performance according to some master-predecessor, whether it be the first or best *Hamlet* we saw or have seen, or even the text itself in its immutable authority. But *Hamlet* not only lends itself, like other plays, to a condition of multiplicity through contrasting methods and styles of performance but exists already, by nature of its textual variants, in a state of indeterminate variety. This frees up the play as a site of inquiry where students can begin to question how performance can turn a single play into multiple plays or, conversely, multiple plays into a single play. "Doing justice" to a classic text might, after all, involve harnessing its invitation to be reshaped and reimagined.

THE TRAGEDY OF HAMLET BY WILLIAM SHAKESPEARE

Desi Cameron, Pepperdine University

IN BRIEF

Students illustrate the dramatic tension of Hamlet's monologues through the use of ropes.

PURPOSE

Many of Hamlet's soliloquies illustrate what Matthew Arnold referred to as "the dialogue of the mind with itself." Rhetorically, the soliloquies establish a tension between two valid arguments that Hamlet weighs, moving back and forth between options as he decides what to do. In this exercise, students will tie ropes onto Hamlet and pull him back and forth to demonstrate physically how divided he is mentally. Specifically, they will use the ropes to designate the tension Hamlet experiences in his seventh and last soliloquy (Act 4, Scene 4) as he debates whether or not to take revenge on Claudius for murdering his father. This is a vital soliloquy as he finally makes up his mind to take action and no longer has any further soliloquies in the play past this point. As the soliloquy traces his decision of whether or not to avenge his father's death, participants will map the tension between Hamlet's religious and moral beliefs on his mind and his body.

PREPARATION

Students should have read through Act 4.

MATERIALS

Two pieces of rope per group of four. The rope should be thick enough to grab onto. I recommend the student playing Hamlet grab the rope and wrap it once around each hand for a better grip, as it is not intended to be tied around the wrists.

Nuts and Bolts

1 First, brainstorm all arguments in favor of Hamlet avenging his father.

a Why should he do it? Write down all student ideas. Make sure to bring up Hamlet's duty to his father. He made a promise to his father's ghost—should he keep his promise? How should Hamlet kill his uncle? Should it be easy or should it be an "eye for an eye," or should he truly suffer?

2 Next, write down all the arguments against Hamlet avenging his father.

a Bring up Hamlet's religious beliefs—what would stop him from murdering his uncle? What are the benefits of not killing someone?

3 Put students into groups of four. You may choose to assign a part to each student below:

a Person 1 will play Hamlet and will hold a rope in each hand.

b Person 2 will grab the rope in Hamlet's left hand and will represent "religion" and play the viewpoint that murder is a sin.

c Person 3 will play Hamlet's father's ghost and grab the rope in Hamlet's right hand. This person will represent "honor/duty" to avenge his father. Holding onto the ropes, Hamlet is stretched into a vulnerable position.

d Person 4 will play Hamlet's uncle, Claudius, who faces Hamlet but is just "out of reach." This person acts as the one who taunts Hamlet.

4 Hamlet's goal is to move forward to "reach" his uncle with his soliloquy but the two actors on either side of Hamlet are literally pulling him back and forth, making it challenging for Hamlet to get what and where he wants. Claudius taunts and teases Hamlet. When Hamlet gets close enough to Claudius, Claudius falls to his knees and prays. Hamlet must stop in his tracks as he will not kill Claudius while he is praying. It's only at the very end of the soliloquy, where the ropes are let go by players 2 and 3 and Hamlet will finally be released. Hamlet should literally feel exhausted and physically pulled apart just as his mind is torn apart by the end of this soliloquy.

5 In groups, have the students read through the soliloquy and discuss its meaning and interpretation.

6 Next, have the students highlight or underline key words that they believe would pull Hamlet in one direction or the other. See Appendix on Companion Website for an example. Each group will then be asked to perform the soliloquy and pull in the appropriate direction at the decided upon times.

7 Now, engage in the rope pulling activity.

Reflection

By engaging in this physical tension exercise, students can physically feel the tension in Hamlet's body as he's literally being pulled in opposite directions while trying to reach his end goal. The tug-of-war over Hamlet reveals Hamlet's tortured pain and suffering, while the close attention to the competing ideas in every line reinforces his indecisive nature. Students come to the realization that Hamlet is torn throughout the production. He isn't just infected by revenge in his mind, but his body should feel the repercussions as well. Students frequently reference this activity while they rehearse for this production to help them understand the constant struggle Hamlet experiences in all his soliloquies.

Reflect on this experience together as a class. Ask the following questions:

1 What did you discover about the tension in Hamlet's mind and body?

2 What was frustrating?

3 What was exhilarating?

4 What was surprising?

5 What did you discover about Hamlet's character?

6 What did Hamlet finally decide to do by the end of this soliloquy?

7 Why is this soliloquy so vital for us to understand Hamlet?

8 Being quartered was a form of torture. Here, Hamlet refers to being quartered while also physically being torn apart. What connection can you make between physical and mental torture?

9 Hamlet is motivated by Fortinbras' willingness to go to war over a small piece of land and to sacrifice so many men. Does this example of commitment make Hamlet realize he too can rise up and take action, finally, over avenging his father's murder?

THE TRAGEDY OF OTHELLO BY WILLIAM SHAKESPEARE

Katheryn Bilbo, Northwest Missouri State University

IN BRIEF

Using choral performance with Shakespeare's poetic language to explore how Iago's words become Othello's jealous "inner voice."

PURPOSE

Jealousy is critical to Othello's story; without this key element, there is no play. Unlike Shakespeare's other tragedies, following the epic tales of royal figures, Othello is a highly personal psychological study of one man who succumbs to an eminently universal emotion: jealousy. His feelings of jealousy and suspicion are the catalyst that turns this moral, respected man into a killer. Without Iago's poisonous words in his ear, Othello would have never stooped so low as to kill his wife despite his insecurity about his place in Vienna. Although Iago's calculated cruelty often manifests itself as no more than whispers, his words become a cacophonous, unrelenting inner voice from which Othello cannot escape. Iago doesn't even need to say the words "Desdemona has been unfaithful"; by simply planting the seed of doubt, Othello's jealous mind does the rest.

PREPARATION

Students will read *Othello* prior to the exercise. In a separate class, discuss the theme/motif of Othello's "tragic flaw" of jealousy and watch a clip of the scene in which Othello and Iago refer to the "green-eyed monster" (3.3.217–56) (see the Appendix on Companion Website).

MATERIALS

Copies for each student of Act 3, Scene 3, beginning with Othello's line "I prithee, speak to me as to thy thinkings ... " and end with Iago's "... to grosser issues nor to larger reach than to suspicion."

Nuts and Bolts

1 Begin the class with a discussion of Iago's manipulation of Othello. Describe how the scene to be analyzed is short, yet appears inexplicably to move Othello from a relatively sane person into one so consumed with suspicion he eventually murders his wife. How is it possible that one short conversation can inflame someone's jealousy? Explain they will experiment with the power of Iago's words by working collectively as one voice.

2 Pass out scenes and read through Act 3, Scene 3, of Othello as a class, beginning with Othello "I prithee, speak to me as to thy thinkings …" (l. 131) and end with Iago "… to grosser issues nor to larger reach than to suspicion" (l. 220). The first student will read the first full sentence ("I prithee, speak to me as thy thinkings as thou dost ruminate, and give thy worst of thoughts the worst of words"), the next will read the following sentence ("Good my lord, pardon me, though I am bound to every act of duty, I am not bound to that all slaves are free to"), and so on around the room. Reading the scene aloud as a group will give students the opportunity to ask questions about any unfamiliar references and words and/or practice pronunciation. (This exercise can work with the dialogue between Iago and Othello in Act 4, Scene 1, lines 1–53, 72–107, and/or 185–226 as well.)

3 Take a look at the language of the scene together. As a group, have students collectively determine the operative words in both Othello and Iago's lines, such as "beware," "jealousy," "monster," "mock," "cuckold," "dotes," "doubts," "suspects." Point out that by using verse, Shakespeare manages to include all of these provocative words in six short lines! As the words are noted, have all students circle the same words so everyone has a script that is identically marked.

4 Give them clues as how to say these words most expressively: extending the vowels "a" or "o," such as in the word "beware" or "monster," and hitting the sharp, percussive consonants of "mock," "cuckold," and "dotes." Practice doing this as a group.

5 Divide the class into 2–3 groups: one person as Iago, one as Othello, and the rest as a "chorus" in each group. Explain the chorus will surround Othello and Iago, repeating and whispering these operative words immediately after they are spoken by the characters in the scene. Demonstrate what you want them to do. An example is given below; chorus lines are in all caps:

  a Iago: O, beware, my lord, of jealousy; (JEALOUSY)

  It is the green-eyed monster (MONSTER) which doth mock (MOCK)

  The meat it feeds on (FEEDS); that cuckold (CUCKOLD) lives in bliss (BLISS)

  Who, certain of his fate (FATE), loves not his wronger; (WRONG)

  But, O, what damned (DAMNED) minutes tells he o'er

Who dotes (DOTES), yet doubts (DOUBTS), suspects (SUSPECTS), yet strongly loves! (LOVES)

Othello: O, misery! (MISERY)

6 Instruct the chorus to begin in a wide circle and eventually close in on Othello himself. Prompt them from the audience to become louder and closer to Othello as the scene progresses. If they are unable to move in this way around the actors due to space constraints, rearrange students in desks around Othello and Iago.

7 When all groups have completed the exercise, debrief with them on their experience. Discuss how persons acting together as a group can increase the intensity of emotions—for better or for worse. You might provide examples of such vocalized group conformity, such as protest marches, choirs singing in unison, angry mobs in the street, or a lively family reunion. Ask for their thoughts on how easy it became to amplify poisonous speech into a dangerous emotion such as jealousy. Discuss the effects of the exercise with the person playing Othello and Iago. Pose the question of whether the ideas and emotions they observed or experienced were more effective by being communicated in verse, rather than standard prose. Ask them to support their opinion by using examples of figurative language, imagery, or alliterative diction from the text.

8 At the end of class, have students write a paragraph or two detailing their experience, new perceptions of Othello or Shakespeare's language, and/or any discoveries they may have made.

Reflection

The biggest complaint I hear from students while studying *Othello* is condemning his downfall by minimizing his emotions, saying, "I would never do that." It is effective to point out how feelings and actions can be spurred by the collective, amplified voice of social media, memes, television, video games, and so on for contemporary students. The exercise itself, incorporating choral repetition and chanting, demonstrates how a suspicious mind is like an echo chamber of false beliefs.

Invite the students to consider examples of their own where their inner voice was exaggerated out of proportion by the emotion of jealousy or the insidious nature of suspicions. Many examples will come from social media, such as "I'm not as pretty as her selfie" or "He got more 'likes' than me on his Instagram post." Point out that if an Instagram post can alter their self-image as their inner voice shouts repeatedly these negative comments, how easy it is to imagine how one or two conversations with a particularly well-trusted, convincing "friend" could feed on one's insecurities, as occurred with Iago convincing Othello. The more closely students can relate the exercise to themselves, the more likely they are to better understand Othello, even if they do not condone his ultimate act of jealousy.

MEASURE FOR MEASURE BY WILLIAM SHAKESPEARE

Nicole Sheriko, Rutgers University

IN BRIEF

Highlight the play's surveillance culture and its uneven economies of knowledge and power.

PURPOSE

In all of Shakespeare, but especially in *Measure for Measure*, monologues are interpersonal. They reveal something about the person speaking as well as the person listening.

The exercise aims to stress the ubiquitous presence of the Duke as a shaping force for characters' actions in the play. His disguising and eavesdropping often enable him to collect knowledge and then leverage it like a playwright or director to script dramatic events—a bed trick, a head trick, and his own unmasking—to produce himself as the events' hero.

PREPARATION

Students should have read at least up through Act 2, Scene 4, before class, preferably the entire play.

MATERIALS

Cell phone.

Nuts and Bolts

1 Assign the parts of Angelo and the Duke. Have these students stand at the front of the room. The Duke should have a cell phone.

2 Angelo will read a soliloquy twice. The best choice thematically for this exercise is his speech at the beginning of Act 2, Scene 4, before Isabel returns (see the Appendix on Companion Website).

3 For the first read-through, as Angelo speaks, the Duke should eavesdrop on him and record his actions with a cell phone camera (no actual recording is necessary). It is most effective if the Duke walks around Angelo, scrutinizing and filming him silently from all angles. Throughout, Angelo should deliver his monologue as if the Duke is not there, just as the original script suggests. This first round aims to suggest that the Duke is always watching and gathering information, even when he is not physically present in a scene.

4 Ask the students about the power dynamic between the Duke and Angelo. How does Angelo's ignorance of the Duke's spying impact his behavior? It can be useful to point to Angelo's interjection to himself, "let no man hear me." How does the Duke's awareness of all Angelo's actions shape his relationship to Angelo? How and why does the Duke record action in the play even when he doesn't witness it?

5 After this brief discussion, the actors will perform a second read-through. This time, the Duke should stand in front of Angelo, facing him (slightly off to the side so both readers can be seen). The Duke should feed Angelo his lines one sentence at a time, like a stage director directing an actor: the Duke will read a sentence and Angelo will repeat it.

6 Ask students again about the power dynamic between the Duke and Angelo. How does dictating Angelo's speech differ from simply observing it? How are spectating and directing related in the Duke's role more broadly?

7 Use these questions to lead a discussion about the relationship between knowledge and power and the Duke's leveraging of both to create political theater. How does the Duke leverage his position as a spectator to facilitate major actions in the play, behaving like a kind of playwright or director? Linking this moment to other scenes where the Duke is physically present to eavesdrop can be a helpful transition into thinking about the Duke's surveillance in relation to his project to observe the city's affairs in his absence (e.g., Act 3, Scene 1, when he has "overheard what hath passed" between Isabella and Claudio in prison). You might also connect this exercise to the broader surveillance culture at the Renaissance English court if the course is invested in the play's historical context.

Reflection

This exercise doubles as an opportunity to focus on a key speech in the play and to understand personal crises as related to the Duke's larger project for the play as a whole. It can precede or follow a close reading of the speech's arguments. Repeating each sentence in the second round offers a second benefit of slowing down the language and attending to the passage's shifting moods. In addition, highlighting the fact that even private speeches do not occur in a vacuum also invites students to think about Angelo's long and complex speeches as actions and reactions rather than stand-alone poems. In addition, when performed early in discussion of the play, the exercise helps to illuminate some of the Duke's early expository speeches about leaving Angelo in charge to take the fall for his own failure to enforce strict laws and his existing sense of Angelo's hypocrisy. Though the Duke actually performs neither direct observation nor directing in this scene, inserting him here helps students to see his surveillance and social experiment hanging over the entire play. Using a student's own cell phone to "record" Angelo encourages students to draw parallels between the play's complicated sense of privacy and surveillance and similar cultures in their own digitally mediated lives.

Understanding the Duke as a playwright-figure helps students to see how he manipulates events for heightened drama, as in the final act when he withholds the information that Claudio is still alive in order to heighten Isabella's joy when she discovers he was not in fact dead and for personal gain as he scripts himself as the hero undoing injustice. Students become increasingly attuned to the power dynamics of interpersonal relationships in the play and how they overlap with differences in knowledge. They raise questions of agency and recognize the play's coercive forces as coming from more than Angelo's lechery. More broadly, the exercise's attention to the relationship between the Duke and Angelo lays the groundwork for ongoing comparative conversations about the characters framed as the hero and villain of the story. At the end of the play, students can draw parallels back to this exercise as they wonder whether the Duke's proposal to Isabella is any less problematic than Angelo's.

In my experience, students also learn to think about theatricality as not just a feature of the play but an approach individual characters can take to shaping the world around them, considering theater as a social and political tool. Thinking about a theatrical sensibility as something that can animate a character expands their sense of how plays think about their own theatricality beyond more obvious metadramatic tools.

THE TRAGEDY OF KING LEAR BY WILLIAM SHAKESPEARE

Nicole Sheriko, Rutgers University

IN BRIEF

Highlights how larger political hierarchies are reflected in interpersonal relationships.

PURPOSE

From the moment King Lear divides up his kingdom at the beginning of the play, his once-powerful position begins to degrade. As the new rulers increasingly deny his authority as a former king and their father, Lear finds himself with few loyal companions. The Fool, who serves Lear as the kind of household court entertainer often kept by wealthy families, is one of the characters who stays by his side. The power dynamics of Lear's relationship with the Fool function as a microcosm of the larger play, manifesting Lear's shifting social position in personal interactions. This exercise presents two differently hierarchized versions of their relationship and offers a range of models for how each character sees his place in the world.

 The exercise also efficiently illustrates a key variation between the two *King Lear* texts, pulling apart versions of the Fool often collapsed together in conflated versions.

PREPARATION

Students should have read up through Act 1, preferably the entire play.

MATERIALS

A chair (the taller, the better).

Nuts and Bolts

1 Place a chair at the front of the room. Assign the parts of King Lear and the Fool. (The three very short lines by Kent can be read by the instructor so as not to distract from this duo.) Lear and the Fool will read through their dialogue in Act 1, Scene 4 twice, positioned each time in a different configuration. They will begin reading from the Fool's first line in the scene ("Let me hire him too. Here's my coxcomb," line 81) and end at the arrival of Goneril ("Here comes one o' the pairings," line 164).

2 For the first read-through, the Fool should be positioned higher than Lear. The Fool can either sit or stand on the chair and Lear should sit or kneel on the ground. This first read-through loosely approximates the Fool's character in the earlier quarto version as a satiric fool criticizing Lear.

3 Ask students how this spatial configuration shapes their sense of Lear and the Fool as characters. What does it suggest about their relationship to one another?

4 After this brief discussion, the actors will read the scene again. For the second read-through, they switch positions so that Lear is higher than the Fool. This second read-through loosely approximates the Fool's character in the later Folio version as a gentler companion under Lear's care.

5 Ask students how this new spatial configuration shifts their sense of Lear and the Fool as characters? How does this hierarchy suggest different possibilities for their relationship to one another? Ask the performers how swapping positions changed their experience of reading for their characters.

6 Use these questions to lead a discussion on Lear's shifting social position in the play. How does Lear's treatment of the Fool (or the Fool's treatment of Lear) relate to Lear's fall from power? Discuss what function this relationship serves in the play. Why do these men stick together? More broadly, how do small shifts in performance suggest important differences in how the play uses these characters?

Reflection

Focusing on just two men who remain together through the play helps students to locate larger themes of power, loyalty, and service in interpersonal conversation. In this way, students understand the play as not a political tragedy about Lear's fall from rule but a human one about the changes power effects in personal relationships. Representing the hierarchical relationship between both men in a visual way with the elevating chair and the (often uncomfortable) floor draws students' attention to the subtler ways that uneven power dynamics manifest themselves in the play. The students who performed the two characters sometimes find that having to look up or down at their stage partner unintentionally shifts their delivery of the same lines. In the text, students begin to notice small markers of relationships embedded in the dialogue, such as terms of address like "my boy," "sirrah," or "nuncle." Reading through the scene twice in two different configurations also helps to establish early on that Lear's status and his relation to other characters are highly unstable. Even within this single exchange, Lear and the Fool assert themselves to different degrees at different points.

Paying close attention to the Fool in particular also facilitates conversation about a question consistently raised by both students and critics of *King Lear:* How does a joking clown fit appropriately into such a dark world? Resisting the centuries of productions that left out the Fool entirely, this exercise offers students a way of exploring the stakes of his involvement. Playing with the power dynamics between the two men helps students to understand the wider role the Fool has to play and raises larger questions about the role of comedy in tragedy—is the Fool a comfort or a violence to Lear in his tragic moments?

For a performance-oriented classroom, one of the challenges and pleasures of teaching *King Lear* is that it has no single definitive text and thus an even wider range of possibilities in performance than most single-text plays. In particular, the Fool's character and relation to Lear are meaningfully different in each, shifting broadly from a bitingly satiric fool (with an extra song critical of Lear's political choices) to a more childlike figure of pathos under Lear's care (with an extra prophecy like those attributed to "natural" fools with "simple" minds). By loosely suggesting the different models offered by different *King Lear* texts, the exercise also allows me to talk about how plays evolve in print without bogging the class down in a comparative textual study, skipping ahead to discussing how shifting one character slightly can reshape a play in major ways. More broadly, the exercise illustrates a complex textual tradition in a way that attunes students to the ways that dramatic texts can also be reshaped by different emphases in performance.

THE TEMPEST BY WILLIAM SHAKESPEARE

Miriam M. Chirico, Eastern Connecticut State University

IN BRIEF

Provide a food offering and then take it away in order to highlight a broken ritual.

PURPOSE

In *The Tempest*, the thematic progression of the play moves from Prospero's desire for vengeance to his ultimate forgiveness of his brother and conspirators for taking his dukedom. The initial shipwreck that opens the play signals his attack upon three men in particular: his brother, Antonio; the King of Naples, Alonso; and Sebastian, Alonso's brother who plots against him.

Prospero separates the members of the crew in order to discipline these three "men of sin" separately. He punishes them by conjuring pleasant music, whimsical fancies, and a table laden with food, only to remove it cruelly from their view. In other words, he stimulates the desire of these starving, shipwrecked men and then takes away the foodstuff before they can begin to eat. However, the cruelty of the trick is never obvious from reading the play; the only indication of the appearance of the table and its subsequent dismissal are character commentary and stage directions.

This exercise will draw students' attention to the "theatrical" component of the text, emphasize the power of spectacle and how to read visual semiotics, and lead them to understand how visual emblems correlate to the themes of vengeance and forgiveness.

PREPARATION

Students should have read at least up to Act 3 of *The Tempest*, if not completed the play. Instructor should bring in baked goods/candy to offer to students.

> **MATERIALS**
>
> None other than making cookies or buying treats ahead of time.

Nuts and Bolts

1 Provide your students with some food—either a dish of homemade cookies or a bag of candy that can be easily passed around the classroom, the sweeter and more appetizing the better.

2 Instruct them not to take a bite until all of the students have received their share.

3 Wait until it gets passed among at least half of the class. Note: If students are reluctant to eat the food, encourage them to at least place one on their desk anyway.

4 Once several students have one, act as if you have changed your mind. Express, matter of factly, that you have decided you would like the cookies (or foodstuff) back. You do not know why you are offering goods when the occasion does not really warrant it, etc. In other words, the students do not deserve your treats.

5 After you received the food, pause a moment and then explain that this has been a teaching exercise to explain the dramatic spectacle at the climax of *The Tempest*, 3.3 – Prospero's cruel trick or his social violation of the host obligation.

   a Draw their attention to the text, specifically the following stage directions that appear in the *Norton Facsimile of the First Folio of Shakespeare*:

   i "Enter several strange Shapes, bringing in a banquet; they dance about it with gentle actions of salutation; and, inviting the King, & c. to eat, they depart" (3.3.24 s.d.). Then, later, "Thunder and lightning. Enter ARIEL, like a harpy; claps his wings upon the table; and, with a quaint device, the banquet vanishes" (3.3.69 s.d.). Later, "Then, to soft music, enter the shapes again, and dance, with mocks and mows, and carrying out the table" (3.3.101 s.d.).

   b Next, focus on Ariel's speech where he suggests the moral behind the spectacle, "You are three men of sin / .. . Being most unfit to live. I have made you mad / ... But remember– / that you three / From Milan did supplant good Prospero" (3.3.58–87).

6 Lead the students in a discussion beyond the words on the page. The spectacle itself is the physical torment of these men: having food taken away is a symbolic parallel to the way Prospero's dukedom was usurped; having people yearn after food hungrily corresponds to the vice of greediness; and Prospero's breaking the host bond—a serious deviation of social convention set into place since ancient times—signals the moment that Prospero achieves his revenge or retributive justice and can move toward forgiveness.

7 Ask the students to explain the experience from their own perspective: What did they think or feel when asked to give back the food item? How did this action differ from normal social practice? Also, ask if they noticed the stage direction and how they interpreted it initially. How has their interpretation changed?

8 If there is time, ask the students to consider a time when they felt wronged by someone. How did playing a trick on the person or "getting even" help move them toward letting go of a grudge?

9 Don't forget to offer the students the cookies in the end as a reward.

Reflection

From antiquity, the practice of giving food to another is an expression of community and fellowship; it is a gift that is an extension of the donor's self. Furthermore, classical Greco-Roman civilizations had specific rules for protecting travelers, such as the obligation a host had toward a stranger in his house (cf. custom of Xenia, "guest-friendship") that was sanctioned by the gods. Anglo-Saxons also practiced a kind of compulsory hospitality of providing food, shelter, clothing.

The particular actions of this scene, equivalent to a court masque, has its origins in both classical mythology and traditional folklore, such as Arthurian legends where worthy knights eat at tables laden with food, but those who have transgressed see nothing but emptiness. One could explain to students how the motif of illusory banquet scenes appear in many sources, where characters are initially offered food as an expression of fellowship, only to be reminded once the food is retracted that they are undeserving or immoral (see Resources on Companion Website).

Prospero practices a particularly mean trick upon the shipwrecked men by offering them a banquet table laden with food and then abruptly taking it from them, making them feel as if they were delusional and crazy. In effect, Prospero punishes the "three men of sin" by arousing their desire to eat and drink, starved and fatigued as they are, and then leaves this desire completely unfulfilled. He violates both the host-bond and basic tenets of humanity. In order to help the students gauge the impact of such a gesture, the instructor acts like Prospero, the benevolent power who offers food to starving men, and then asks for it back, encouraging students to analyze their own astonishment at the violation of a social norm.

LIFE IS A DREAM BY PEDRO CALDERÓN DE LA BARCA

George Drance, S.J., Fordham University and Magis Theatre Company

IN BRIEF

Through the use of lighting and properties, students understand how appearances can be deceiving or how one's perceptions can be transformed.

PURPOSE

The text of Pedro Calderón's Life Is a Dream examines how appearances and truth are often blurred in complex circumstances. This exercise encourages students to witness how reality can be perceived in multiple ways through the deliberate manipulation of shadows. Through the use of shadow play and asking classmates to guess what they see, the exercise demonstrates how the artful manipulation of lighting, setting, and stage properties can affect what the audience sees in performance. The hiding and revealing of the projected object also reinforce the play's larger point regarding the subjective nature of reality.

Using a light source, students will cast a shadow of a specific "form" onto the back of a viewing screen and ask audience members (i.e., classmates) to guess what the silhouetted object is: "What do you see?" Students will work to create a silhouette that first appears to be something that it is not. After hearing the audience's interpretations, the screen is moved to show the actual form that cast the shadow.

PREPARATION

Students should read the whole text of Life Is a Dream ahead of time or at least the first half. Ask them to read with attention to the direct references about appearance and reality and be ready to identify the moments of the text where appearance is taken as reality. They should list any pairings of things that seem to be one thing but are later revealed to be something else. The instructor may wish to familiarize students with Plato's "Allegory of the Cave" from the Republic (Books VII and VIII, lines 531d–534e).

Students must prepare their shadow form at home.

MATERIALS

A translucent screen or a sheet, or a fabric.
    A light source: high-powered flashlight, or overhead projector, or clip light.
    Each student's "form" will be assembled behind the screen and must not be shown to the audience until after the shadow is viewed.

Nuts and Bolts

1 Homework Assignment: Ask the students to find or construct a "form." This can be a single object that exhibits different properties when it casts a shadow from a light source, such as a common household item that, when brought close to the light source, casts a shadow of a small part of itself that looks like something else. On the other hand, it can be an assemblage of disparate objects that creates a silhouette strikingly different than its original component parts. Refer them to the shadow animals we make with our hands as an illustration. Students should practice assembling the shadow form at home in front of a light source.

2 Presentation: In class, rig the sheet or white fabric like a screen so that the form can cast a shadow on it. You can use a clothesline, or a rolling pipe clothes rack as a frame, or just have two students hold it. The light source should be positioned behind the screen at a distance for optimal effect. Students present their shadow forms.

3 Response: The "audience" indicates their first impression of the shadows created. It is important to capture their first impressions as well as later ideas, which may vary among the class members. When the audience has finished saying what they see, the screen is moved so that they can see the form itself.

4 Discussion: The most important part of the exercise is for the student audience to reflect upon their own recognition of what the form really is. Allow students to discuss the experience of being deceived by the appearances and the moment of understanding the form as it is.

Reflection

Optical illusions occur when the eye perceives something that is different than reality. This exercise works on the same principle as an optical illusion in order to remind students that the mind may draw erroneous conclusions based on what the eye "sees." The Magis Theatre production, in fact, used multiple, movable cubes as part of the stage's set. During the performance, the characters would rearrange them at different times, so that their shadows projected against the scrim became at different times clouds, mountains, and a tower. In this way, the production underscored the play's theme of reality being an illusion.

Students should apply their experience of the exercise to a discussion of these dynamics in the text of the play. Invite them to consider: What are the moments of the play when characters have similar realization about reality as it truly is? Which characters have these realizations? How does their perception determine character choices that affect the dramatic action?

Calderon's play taps into an ancient theme of reality as a dream, which allows him to explore other ideas implicit in aristocratic rule, such as the behavioral or moral qualities that befit a king. Through this motif of life as a dream, Calderon questions whether absolute certitude is attainable. What point is Calderon making about life in general? About leadership and ruling? In what ways could a director, an actor, or a designer employ shadows to emphasize the ambiguity in truth and reality?

TARTUFFE BY MOLIÈRE

Véronique Flambard-Weisbart, Loyola Marymount University

IN BRIEF

The use of costumes to illustrate the theme of hypocrisy.

PURPOSE

In *Tartuffe* (or *The Impostor*), Molière denounces religious and political hypocrisy, the plague of his time. Tartuffe's comeuppance occurs in Act 4, Scene 5, when Elmire reveals Tartuffe's identity as an impostor to her gullible husband Orgon who has turned his whole household to Tartuffe's (fake) devout or noble gregarious practices. Students perform the famous "table scene" in alternatively two different costumes (first as a priest, second as a gentleman) to reveal the abyss between Tartuffe's appearance as a devout or noble man and his true opportunistic motivation. Orgon will hide silently under a table while Tartuffe reveals his true self and feelings to Elmire. Only the audience will see Orgon's reactions while learning the truth. The exercise also helps students understand Molière's motivation to denounce religious and political hypocrisy—the plague of his time.

PREPARATION

Students should read the play in its entirety before class or at least through Act 4. The instructor will either request students bring in their own costumes or will need to provide them for the exercise. See below for examples. Also, as an historical and cultural background, I sometimes show Belgian filmmaker Gérard Corbiau's film *The King Is Dancing* (2000)—a costume drama presenting libertine and pagan Lully as a natural ally of the early Enlightenment figure Louis XIV of France in his conflicts with the Catholic establishment. The film focuses on Lully's personal relationship with the King, as well as his camaraderie with Molière. A portion of Tartuffe's crucial Act 3, Scene 3, between Elmire and Tartuffe, which directly leads to Act 4, Scene 5, that students will perform, is represented in the film.

MATERIALS

Table. Tablecloth. Priest's costume. Gentlemen's costume. There are, however, many options and variations. For the table, simply use what is already in the classroom. Ideally, an actual table, or a desk large enough for one actor to hide beneath it, or a few student desks pushed together. The tablecloth can be any kind as long as it covers three sides. For costumes, I suggest:

1. Tartuffe (as priest): all black clothes. A black or solid color graduation gown is an option. Perhaps even the instructor's regalia or robe if appropriate. White collar (made from a strip of paper). Perhaps a Bible. He must look austere.
2. Tartuffe (as gentleman): colorful clothes. A wide-brimmed hat with a feather. Perhaps a walking stick. He must look elegant and respectable. Fabulous even.
3. Orgon: an ascot or neckerchief scarf. He must look wealthy.
4. Elmire: a long ruffled skirt, a ruffled blouse, and a simple headband with a flower. Her appearance is very decent and does not attract attention, so that Tartuffe cannot use Elmire's manner of dressing to justify his actions; therefore, the focus of the exercise remains on his hypocrisy.

Again, depending upon time and resources, the students can go "all out" with costumes in advance, or the instructor may supply the minimum to make a point.

Nuts and Bolts

1 Create groups of three students and assign the three students in each group one of the roles (Tartuffe, Elmire, or Orgon). Also assign to each group whether Tartuffe will wear a priest or a gentleman's costume. If performing this exercise in the same day, the students will read lines from their textbooks. If the instructor wishes to enhance this exercise and turn it into a project, then the students may be responsible to learn their lines by heart and to rehearse them with the group before the day of the performance in class. If you have a large class, you can assign different portions of the lines to different groups.

2 Have the students perform the table scene based on the props and costumes suggested above, first with Tartuffe as priest, then with Tartuffe as gentleman. Each performance takes approximately 10 minutes.

3 Guide the performers to accentuate playing their roles, especially Tartuffe. As priest, he should play austere and sanctimonious. As gentleman, he should play elegant and rakish.

4 Within the context of these different depictions, discuss the impact of costume on performance: Does the costume sometimes make the man? In other words does the costume confer status on the character or determine audience perception of a person? If "the suit does not make the man," does the text make the man? Or is it the contrast between the costume and the text that indicates hypocrisy? What does this contrast add to the performance? Can students imagine a better/different way of transcending appearances to make the man? What about the clothes making the woman? What impact did costuming have on Elmire? Does the tablecloth make Orgon? How did that material provide secrecy, transparency, comedy?

5 Discuss each group's performance and how successful it was to convey Molière's intended meaning. The discussion can range from 10 to 20 minutes.

Reflection

This exercise helps bring to light Molière's comedic talent at denouncing and making fun of the most pernicious evil: the hypocrisy inherent within the religious and political climate of his time. Here, he seems to depict the Jansenist stronghold of Tartuffe over Orgon and his house's pleasures and social life. However, Molière's joke is not so much on the true ascetic rigor displayed by Jansenists such as Orgon but rather on the false rigorism used by Tartuffe to literally and figuratively cloak his cupidity and self-indulgence—traits associated with the caricature of Jesuits at the time Molière wrote the play in 1664. But if in *Tartuffe*, Molière does not pitch the rigorist praxis of the Jansenists against the casuistic values of the Jesuits, he decries the impostors' hypocritical behavior that empowers them to make people serve their self-interests.

Students' performance of the two versions of Act 4, Scene 5, reflects the temptation to judge a character/person by their appearance. I try to convey to students that jumping to conclusions based on appearances can have drastic consequences and that they need to take the time to look beyond appearances to make their own judgment and act wisely. Indeed, the goal of the exercise is for students performing in the role of Tartuffe to express the abyssal contradiction between the devout/noble appearance expressed through his costume and behavior, and the dishonest feelings and cynicism expressed through his words, in short to incarnate Tartuffe's hypocrisy by showing that "the suit does not make the man."

THE MISANTHROPE BY MOLIÈRE

Daniel Smith, Michigan State University

IN BRIEF

Performing various versions of a poem to expose character hypocrisy.

PURPOSE

The Misanthrope is understood as a critique of a pretentious and superficial court society, where everyone is hypocritical and no one knows the truth of anyone's heart. Oronte's love sonnet to Célimène is so replete with clichés and hyperbole that it stands as another example of insincerity. Comparing various translations of Oronte's sonnet reveals its lack of meaning and enables students to grasp the play's aesthetic conflict about style and substance. A comparison between the two poems written by Oronte and Alceste furthermore indicates Oronte's empty posturing in the face of Alceste's idealistic love.

PREPARATION

Students would ideally have read the play before doing this exercise in order to have a sense of character relationships. However, the exercise is self-contained because the instructor provides all necessary text on the handout. It could, therefore, serve as an introduction to the play as well.

MATERIALS

Before class, the instructor should gather several English translations of Molière's play and copy the different translations of Oronte's sonnet on "Hope" and Alceste's song/poem "If the King." In French, the entire play is in verse and most textbooks are likely to include a rhyming verse translation, either Richard Wilbur's or Constance Congdon's. Prose translations are also available, but Oronte's sonnet is likely to be in verse even if the rest of play is in prose. Also, it might be helpful to have some greeting cards on hand (e.g., Valentine's Day cards work well) to discuss the contemporary mode of sharing of sentimental emotions.

Nuts and Bolts

1 Give students a handout with several selected translations of Oronte's sonnet on "Hope." Ask them to work in groups to compare the translations. (Four translations are a good sample size.) What word choices are the same? Where do the translations differ? What examples of clichés, flowery language, and hyperbole do we find? Has each translator prioritized rhyme? Meter? Content? How does the translator address the theme of hope? Most importantly, whom does the poem talk about more: the lover or the beloved?

2 Have the students look at the same number of translations of Alceste's poem. Ask them similar questions. The analysis of this more direct and heartfelt poem should be different from the analysis of Oronte's poem. Point the class to understand the differences between superficial, meaningless language and language that has integrity.

3 Ask the students to read aloud Oronte's poem. This can be done in the context of the scene, with other students listening to the poem as the characters of Alceste and Philinte. Another possibility is to perform the poem out of context and have Oronte read it to Célimène while Alceste watches. Translators have a tendency to exaggerate the poem's bad qualities in English for comedic purposes, but as students listen to several versions of this poem, ask them to identify whether it's good/bad, earnest/pretentious, or loving/empty of meaning and how they know this. How do the translators achieve the effect of pretension and superficiality in English?

4 Next, ask the students to read aloud Alceste's poem. You may provide a context similar to step number two. Do the translations differ as with Oronte's sonnet or do all the versions replicate similar language? How does Alceste's poem sound when read aloud and what does it convey?

Reflection

I tend to introduce Molière within the historical context of seventeenth-century France, where court decorum dictated that people act with such proscribed, stylistic manners; Molière's play has long been understood as a satirical critique of the hypocrisy originating from such artificial behavior. The basic plot of the play, a man competing with many other courtiers for the love of Célimène, is heightened by the challenge of experiencing and expressing love within such a superficial and insincere society. As Philinte remarks about Célimène, "Her heart's a stranger to its own emotion." Instructors may wish to bring in particularly sentimental greeting cards to discuss whether ready-made commercial phrases increase or diminish feelings toward the sender.

Oronte's poem is useful because its pretentious style tells us a great deal about Oronte as a character as well as the kind of language required of a courtier. Alceste, on the other hand, is considered an idealist for his strong commitment to standards of honesty, often at the expense of hurting another's feelings. Oronte's superficial pretension contrasts with Alceste's serious simplicity, so they don't get along as characters. But for an actor the conflict of objectives is crucial, and the poem's position as the inciting incident of the play can lead to a rich discussion of the layers of dramatic conflict. Both Alceste and Oronte are pursuing romantic relationships with Célimène. Oronte's poem addressed to Célimène is a gift intended to demonstrate his love for her. Alceste, who is asked to provide feedback, wants to be in an exclusive relationship with Célimène and thus will hear the poem with cynicism, as much as he believes he is being "honest." What does this poem tell us about Oronte as a character? To what extent do translators' choices help the poem to inflame Alceste's jealousy? (Congdon, for instance, raises the stakes of the poem's carpe diem theme by incorporating "receive me" as a sexual metaphor.)

Furthermore, comparing translations of a short passage gives us a sense of the style of the play and particularly how English-language translators make choices that can help or hinder actors performing a role. During their small group discussion, students should decide which translation is the most effective version, based on whatever criteria they consider most important. I speak French, so I am also able to read the original to the class in order to allow them to hear the rhythm of Molière's verse. But reference to the original French text is not necessary for this exercise.

RESTORATION THEATER AUDIENCES

Kerri Ann Considine, University of Tennessee, Knoxville

IN BRIEF

Create an in-class Restoration audience experience to deepen awareness of late seventeenth- and eighteenth-century performance dynamics.

PURPOSE

Theatergoing during the Restoration was a boisterously social experience. The audience in the Restoration playhouse was primarily, although not exclusively, upper class. In addition to the noble and titled members of society, one might also find wealthy members of the rising merchant class hoping to see and be seen, servants waiting on their masters, and orange sellers and prostitutes there to ply their trade. The playhouse offered an opportunity for gossip, intrigue, assignations, and displays of social status. Audiences were not passive spectators focused on the theatrical performance; instead, actors on the Restoration stage had to contend with an audience that would exuberantly respond to both successes and failures. Happy audiences might cheer, laugh, or even loudly request an actor repeat a favorite song or speech. Should an audience be displeased with a performance, however, they might boo, hiss, or even throw rotten food at the stage. This social environment had an impact on the content and comedy of Restoration plays and the performative style of the actors. The goal of the exercise is to help students see how the acting style, the performance, and the humor of most Restoration comedies are shaped by the audience and theatergoing experience of the Restoration playhouse.

PREPARATION

Students should read an assigned Restoration play in its entirety before class. The exercise works best if students have already been introduced to some basic information about Restoration comedy and the Restoration playhouse as well as the post-1660 sociocultural political moment.

Copies of a key scene, such as the "china scene" in William Wycherley's *The Country Wife* or the encounter between Don Pedro and Don Antonio outside Angellica Bianca's window in Aphra Behn's *The Rover*.

Some scrap paper to crumple into soft balls for throwing and fake "oranges" (or real oranges if you like) for the "orange wenches."

Nuts and Bolts

1 Assign parts and pass out copies of the chosen scene to those who will be reading.

2 Send the actors out into the hall or away from the rest of the group to read through the scene and plan for their staged reading. It can be useful to assign someone in the group to be the "director."

3 When the actors have left, explain to the remaining group how you will "stage" them as an audience. Reiterate, if needed, ideas about the culture and atmosphere of the Restoration playhouse.

4 Arrange them into a thrust configuration so the actors will have audience on three sides.

5 Assign some students to be "orange wenches," and give them some balls of paper to wander around and sell. Assign the rest of the students roles in the "audience" as well. Some might be members of the aristocracy, some might be young sparks out on the town, some may be members of the rising merchant class hoping to see and be seen, some may be servants there to wait on their masters, some might be ladies of the night there for an assignation. Depending on the level of initiative in the class, it can be fun to allow the students to make up their own backstories here within a framework you provide.

6 Next, provide the student audience with directions about their comportment during the scene. Encourage them to have side conversations and comment on the performance. They can cheer, laugh, boo, or react—vocally and loudly—in any way they feel appropriate to the scene. Their goal is to make the actors work for their attention. If the actors miss lines or get confused or are just standing there reading, they can, for example, talk among themselves or boo. When the actors are doing something interesting, they should allow the actors to have their attention and cheer or laugh when appropriate. Provide the student audience with some paper to make into little balls and allow them to throw this at the stage when the scene is not going so well.

7 When the audience is ready, invite the actors back in and begin the staged reading—without warning the actors about how the audience has been prepared. There will inevitably be some chaos, and the actors may be confused for a bit, but they will find ways to catch the attention of this audience. As the instructor, engaging in the activity along with the student audience (loudly booing or cheering early on) will help students feel permission to also engage in this way.

8 After the reading, ask the actors and the audience how they felt about the experience. Discuss how the scene changed for actor and audience alike when forced to contend with the experience of the theater in this way. What did the actors have to do to get the audience to pay attention? When did the audience feel the actors best captured their interest?

Reflection

The first time I taught *The Country Wife*, I realized that the students recognized that it was funny, but that they were reading the play as though it were a contemporary play-going experience and the humor as though it were contemporary humor. Through a firsthand engagement with the text and its performance, this exercise allows students to better understand the style of the play and how the humor and its performance are rooted in an interactive theatergoing experience of the Restoration. Because a Restoration play's content addresses the way different members of society shape their performances to their own advantage in accordance with the social expectations of the time, beginning with this exercise allows us to situate the style of the play and its content in the historical moment of the Restoration. Since the actors will often begin to mimic the declamatory styles of seventeenth- and eighteenth-century England in their attempts to capture the attention of this audience, the exercise can also spark a good discussion on acting styles and how they proceed from a sociocultural moment.

THE COUNTRY WIFE BY WILLIAM WYCHERLEY

Erik L. Johnson, Stanford University

IN BRIEF

Drawing attention to the functional use of asides as a performance technique for communicating characters' private thoughts.

PURPOSE

The theatrical use of asides is a unique technique within drama for letting characters communicate directly with the audience. This exercise prepares students for discussion of *The Country Wife*'s notorious "china" scene (in Act 3) by sensitizing them to the role of asides—remarks that one character makes directly to the audience that by convention go unheard by the other characters on stage. Asides can also be spoken to another character and in that case are sometimes called aparts. Furthermore, focusing on asides encourages students to see how these devices allow characters to communicate their private thoughts and relationships differently than in fiction or cinema.

PREPARATION

Students should arrive in class having read most of *The Country Wife*; no other advanced prep is required. I do find this exercise helps students to relate themes in Eve Sedgwick's essay "'The Country Wife': Anatomies of Male Homosocial Desire" to formal aspects of the play. I assign Sedgwick's essay for the subsequent class, but the piece could also be pre-read alongside the play.

MATERIALS

Instructor should prepare index cards, depending on the number of groups, indicating the passage to work with (keyed to pages in your text) and the task assigned (performing asides or rewriting them).

Nuts and Bolts

1 Separate students into two, three, or four groups. Assign each of the groups one of these scenes. Each group will work with asides from one of the play's two establishing scenes: the introduction of Horner's impotence ruse in Act 1 (from the opening to Sir Jasper's exit, that is, up to Horner's line "Your servant, Sir Jasper") or the argument between Pinchwife, Mrs. Pinchwife, and Pinchwife's sister Alithea early in Act 2 (from Mrs. Pinchwife crying to the entrance of Sparkish and Harcourt, that is, from Pinchwife's line "You're a fool" to his line "But here comes Company, get you in, get you in").

2 Give them time to reread the assigned scene silently, paying special attention to the asides, and give each group written or oral instructions on one of the two possible tasks below.

3 One group will choose part of the assigned scene with asides they consider crucial and think creatively about how to deliver the asides differently from the rest of the dialogue so that they stand out. They should send volunteers to the front of the room with texts in hand to perform their chosen bit. Ask the audience to pay attention and describe the effects this has and how the scene feels for them watching.

4 The next group working on the same scene should choose one or two crucial asides to convert into regular dialogue, changing the grammar as necessary. For instance, Pinchwife's aside in a later scene "Death, does he know I'm married too?" would become "Death, do you know I'm married too?" They should also consider how the scene might proceed differently if this aside were delivered as a remark the other characters can hear. They should send volunteers to the front of the room with texts and/or notes in hand to perform a bit of the scene centered around one or two significant converted asides and improvising what happens differently when the aside is merged into the regular dialogue. Ask the audience to consider not only how the substance of the scene now differs but whether they feel differently watching it.

5 Depending on the size of the class, length of the period, and how many days you are spending on this play, you can run this activity rapidly with a single scene, focusing only on how the asides are delivered differently, or you can give more students time on their feet by working with both scenes and having four groups perform: straight bit from Act 1; tweaked bit from Act 1; straight bit from Act 2; tweaked bit from Act 2.

6 After debriefing on students' responses, you can segue directly to the famously bawdy china scene in Act 3, if you wish. I manage the transition by showing a clip of the scene in performance from the 1977 BBC production, prompting students to pay special attention to the rapid multiplication of asides and asking them how the performance frames the asides and if it handles different types of asides differently.

Reflection

Asides are an especially prominent formal feature of *The Country Wife*; the play includes, by some counts, more than 100. They are a formal manifestation of its focus on secret relationships. Besides the fact that Horner carries on affairs under the noses of jealous husbands, only some of the male characters know that he is allegedly impotent and only some of the female characters know that his feigned impotence is an elaborate ruse.

This warm-up exercise makes students aware that plays have their own devices, and their own grammar, for establishing intimacy between characters and audience. Although the discipline of literary studies still tends to consider the novel the genre that offers readers the fullest access to its characters' thoughts and feelings, drama can bring different types of information into sharper relief, in particular information about character relationships and social networks. I teach *The Country Wife* in a course covering different genres and find this exercise's attention to the form and grammar of the aside prompts students to make helpful comparisons to novelistic devices like free indirect discourse.

In Act 3's china scene, asides multiply rapidly, and the distinction between different types becomes crucial. The cuckolded Sir Jasper demonstrates his isolation from the play's active sexual networks by addressing his rationalizations to the audience directly, whereas Horner and Lady Fidget speak apart in front of him (and in front of another mistress). These devices thus make different communities of knowledge in the play visible on stage and invite the audience to identify with some sets of characters more readily than others. Double entendre, another formal device prominent here, also sorts characters into "in" and "out" groups based on who understands the joke and who does not, and my students have fruitfully compared or contrasted it to asides.

I like to drive the importance of these theatrical elements home by showing, near the close of discussion, a corresponding clip from the 1975 Warren Beatty film *Shampoo*, a comedy inspired by a performance of *The Country Wife*. Beatty's character, a glamorous hairdresser, is often mistaken for a gay man. Under this cover he freely carries on an affair with the wife of a wealthy businessman. In a remake of the china scene, when her husband nearly walks in on them, Beatty and the wife retreat into the bathroom and pretend that he has been doing her hair. Absent asides, the effect of this still-comic cinematic scene differs from Wycherley's—as does the more staid morality of the film, which insists on the Horner character's eventual punishment.

THE ROVER BY APHRA BEHN

Joanne Cordón, University of Connecticut

IN BRIEF

Demonstrating how portraits are stage properties than the commodification of women's bodies.

PURPOSE

Written in 1677 after Charles II and his Cavaliers had defeated Cromwell's Puritans, but set during their pre-Restoration exile, *The Rover* explores the tensions between Puritanical beliefs regarding women's sexual freedom and the libertine ideology that pervades the stage. While the men are allowed the freedom to roam and go on adventures, the women can do the same only when they disguise themselves during Carnival. The opening scene speaks to the patriarchal intent to control women's sexual behavior: Sisters Florinda and Hellena discuss their family's plan to marry the elder off to a wealthy suitor while sending the younger to a convent. Though the sisters challenge these directives, the woman in the play who attempts to fully control her sexuality is the courtesan Angellica and only because she ignores romance in favor of the economics of sexual exchange.

Newly arrived from Padua, the renowned courtesan Angellica Bianca advertises her availability by posting a picture of herself outside her residence. This exercise, through the viewing and handling of portraits of women, illustrates the ways women can be objectified as their portraits are viewed, circulated, or owned. It also illustrates a more complicated idea behind managing women's sexuality.

PREPARATION

Students should read at least the first two acts of the play. I encourage students to consider the dynamic of the three main couples of the play as they read: Florinda and Belvile, Hellena and Willmore, and Angellica Bianca and Willmore. Laura Mulvey's "Visual Pleasure and Narrative Cinema" underlines the topic of the male gaze, but you can choose to read the essay with or as a continuation of this exercise.

MATERIALS

Classroom computer capable of projecting images from the internet; magazine advertisements of women, one illustrating the sale of a product, another from a movie. Optional: put four prints together of Nell Gwyn's portraiture for a concise handout.

Nuts and Bolts

1 The Scene: Ask several students to read aloud the scene where Angellica Bianca places a portrait outside (Act 2, Scene 1). Help students understand the painting's function: that the picture serves as a kind of advertisement as well as a vacancy sign. In other words, when the image hangs outside her door, interested men may drop by to engage her services.

2 Draw their attention to key lines from the text that indicate the value of the painting as well as her value as a courtesan. For example, the stage directions note that Angellica sets out three pictures of herself all together, and she leaves two paid guards to watch over the trio of images: "Enter two Bravoes, and hang up a great Picture of Angellica's, against the Balcony, and two little ones at each side of the Door." Point out Belvile's immediate reaction to the portrait: "See there the fair Sign to the Inn, where a Man may lodge that's Fool enough to give her Price." Also, this moment in the play literalizes what Frederick reveals to his curious male friends: "she's exposed to Sale, and four Days in the Week she's yours—for so much a Month."

3 The Image: Next, show students how the portrait outside Angellica's door selling herself and her services might have appeared. A good example of Restoration portraiture is Nell Gwyn's portraits at London's National Portrait Gallery, where thirty pictures of her are held (available online). Note also the black-and-white prints of Gwyn inspired by her portraits. Optional: put four of the prints together for a concise handout. Have students consider which image might be closest to the picture that Angellica Bianca would choose for her own advertisement. How do the different prints illustrate diverse aspects of Nell's personality?

4 Comparison: To what extent is the portrait a stand-in for Angellica? Discuss with the students Pedro's evaluation of Angellica's portrait: "I have seen the Original, nor is there one Charm here more than adorns her Face and Eyes; all this soft and sweet, with a certain languishing Air, that no Artist can represent" (2.1). Draw attention to both the differences between the real person and the artist's rendering. When is a person similar to her portrait, and how is a human worth more—or less—than the object? Why are portraits considered so valuable? Draw attention to the value behind this portrait at the National Gallery: Who has access to a portrait? What is the difference between viewing and possessing? What various aspects of Nell's personality do the painters highlight? Is this Nell's choice or the painters' choice?

5 Contemporary Comparison: Next, show the students advertisements collected from magazines. If possible have them circulated around the classroom to illustrate circulation of women's bodies as commodities. Open up any publication and you will find an ad that uses a woman's body to sell all kinds of products: beer, cars, or protein powder (e.g "Are you beach body ready? Controversial weight loss ad sparks varied reactions," *The Guardian*, 25 June 2015). Contrasting the ad for protein powder with the portrait, for example, makes the point of ownership very clear. While Angellica Bianca chooses to use her own image to advertise her availability for sex, the Protein World ad uses the female body to suggest that uses of its product will perhaps result in sex. While the portrait is open and deliberate with the woman in charge, the woman in the ad is an agency-less object on display.

6 Further Comparison: If available, offer the students a movie poster of an actress. In advertisements for new movies the picture is hung outside the theater to advertise the film, which suggests a talismanic access to the actress/character equivalent to Angellica Bianca's portrait. While going to see the movie is less costly than the thousand crowns necessary to secure the companionship of Angellica Bianca, fans do collect movie posters as if to secure a tangible piece of the visual experience. How does Wilmore both possess Angellica and not possess by stealing one of her smaller portraits (Act 2, Scene 2)? What does he say?

7 Scene Work: Finally, ask the students to read through the scene again, this time pointing to the portrait projected on the overhead, the image of Nell Gwyn on a handout, or even the advertisement from the magazine. How does their interpretation of the scene change with the presence of an image? Does it matter which image is used?

Reflection

Like their male libertine counterparts, all three women strive to pursue lovers and fulfill their own sexual passion. Radical by seventeenth-century standards, the three women chafe at different restrictions: Hellena desires a freedom equal to a libertine's, Florinda wants a man of her own choosing, and Angellica asks for a man who can engage her "virgin heart." However, while the play illustrates the topsy-turvy freedom of a carnivalesque celebration, the larger message indicates keeping women located in three possible destinations: house, convent, brothel.

Showing students portraits of Nell Gwyn and sharing some of her background deepen their understanding of the cultural context of this play. Students are interested in learning about this "orange wench" who became a successful, working actress and later Charles II's "Protestant Whore," as she once described herself to an angry anti-Catholic mob. In the 1680 portrait by Simon Verelst, Nell Gwyn appears as a woman with a knowing look, luminous skin, demure pearls at her neck, and a choreographed décolletage. In fact, Nell's work in comedy during the period led to a widespread misattribution of her as the originator of the role of Angellica Bianca in Behn's play, a part actually played by Anne Marshall Quin (cf. introduction to Anne Russell's Broadview edition of *The Rover*).

In order to show students how women's bodies are categorized by their sexual destiny, circulated for public pleasure, or commodified to earn money, this exercise indicates the different uses of women's illustrated and photographed bodies to suggest various kinds of freedom or limitations the women experience in the play. The exercise uses students' abilities to read visual messages to understand the importance of the portrait as a symbolic stage property: understanding who possesses it, how it is read and viewed, and ultimately the way in which the real woman associated with the portrait can contest cultural constructs.

THE WAY OF THE WORLD BY WILLIAM CONGREVE

Erik L. Johnson, Stanford University

IN BRIEF

String characters together in different ways to consider how groups and networks function in performance.

PURPOSE

This exercise helps students to get a handle on a play known for its complex plot by tracing the competing layers of connection between its characters. In the process, it highlights drama's unique capacity to show how characters function in groups, as well as individually. Because our understanding of the character networks in *The Way of the World* changes radically as the play progresses, this exercise prompts students to consider how visible groupings of characters on stage can bring out different relationships. Juxtaposing characters' public and private relationships also makes students aware that there are many ways to present characters with complicated, nuanced motives, even without extensive use of soliloquy or narrated thought.

PREPARATION

Students should arrive in class having read *The Way of the World* through once. Before their first reading, prompt students to be able to explain the primary motivations and relationships of Mirabell, Fainall, Millamant, and Lady Wishfort. No other advanced prep is required. I do, however, assign excerpts from Eve Sedgwick's *Epistemology of the Closet* for subsequent classes, which could also be read in advance of or alongside the play.

MATERIALS

Prepare one set of the following materials for each of 2–4 groups: 10–12 index cards with character names written in marker; yarn or string in at least two different colors; scissors; and Scotch tape. At least two colors are needed to contrast public and private networks. Depending on time allotted, you may want to use anywhere from two to four colors of yarn or string so students can discriminate between different kinds of public and private relationships.

Character names are Mirabell, Millamant, Fainall, Mrs. Fainall, Lady Wishfort, Mrs. Marwood, Waitwell (a.k.a. Sir Rowland), Foible, Petulant, Witwoud, and Sir Willful Witwoud.

It is interesting to see what students make of minor characters, though, depending on length of class time, the instructor may wish to omit some of these to keep the exercise shorter and more straightforward.

Note: No act and scene numbers are cited in this exercise because they vary across editions. D. F. McKenzie's authoritative edition follows Congreve's 1710 act and scene divisions, but others (like Scott McMillin's text in the *Norton Critical Edition*) follow the quartos of the plays as truer to the texts brought to stage.

Nuts and Bolts

1 Start from a simple foundation, writing the names of main players—Mirabell, Millamant, Fainall, and Lady Wishfort—on the board. Ask the students to remind us of each one's principal motive and of one of his or her key relationships (e.g., Mirabell is in love with Millamant; or, Lady Wishfort is Millamant's aunt and guardian, but more interested in getting married herself).

2 Once students show their grasp of these basics, explain that they are going to build their own versions of the play's character networks, in two phases. Divide the class into two, three, or four groups of two to five students each, depending on size. Each group receives eleven index cards with character names already written on them in marker, as well as access to a pair of scissors, a roll of Scotch tape, and yarn or string in at least four different colors. My classes are small, so I get a handful of sample stools from a fabric store and set them in the middle of the table with scissors and tape for groups to grab as needed.

3 Hand out the eleven cards in each set: Mirabell, Millamant, Fainall, Mrs. Fainall, Lady Wishfort, Mrs. Marwood, Waitwell (a.k.a. Sir Rowland), Foible, Petulant, Witwoud, and Sir Willful Witwoud.

4 In the first phase of network building, tell the students to choose one color yarn and link characters who have a strong public connection. Such connections might include relations by blood or marriage, or other forms of open alliance such as employment or formal courtship. Students can arrange the cards in whatever layout suits the shape of their network and attach the connecting strings with Scotch tape. Allow up to 10 minutes for them to discuss the connections among themselves while doing this; often, they remind one another of forgotten points from the play. Then allow about 5 minutes for groups to mingle and debrief. The instructor could walk around looking at the cards, asking who has the most connections in each network and whether or not any characters seem, on this perspective, marginal, linked to only perhaps one or two others. Record some results for each group in brief annotations on the board. (You may want to suggest, or leave the option to students, to use different colors of thread for different categories of public relationships, e.g., one color could be used for family relation by blood or marriage and another for other kinds of public relationships.)

5 Now comes the second phase. Ask the students, working in the same groups and with their preexisting networks, to choose a new color of thread and, using it, to add secret relationships to their evolving network models. At this point, for instance, Mirabell's affair with Mrs. Fainall and Mrs. Marwood's affair with Fainall would be added. Students may need to rearrange the layout of their cards. Allow 7 to 10 minutes for this. Then debrief for about 5 minutes, as the groups mingle to view one another's sets of cards and share their findings. Instructor should reformulate the questions: Who, now, appears the most connected in each network? Do characters become prominent who were previously marginalized? Again, record results on the board.

6 For the remainder of the period, the discussion opens into one about performance. Which scenes would be central to an interpretation that emphasized the public networks, such as the courtship of Mirabell and Millamant? Which scenes would be central to an interpretation that emphasized the private networks? How might a production reflect these conflicting interpretations?

Reflection

This exercise encourages collaboration, as students help one another master the plot and develop shared interpretations. One of the challenges of teaching this work is to move beyond simply explaining the plot and to focus, rather, on the complex interplay of open and secret relationships. Although discussions of The Way of the World often focus on the proviso scene (in Act 4), in which Mirabell and Millamant negotiate marriage conditions, what is remarkable about Congreve's play is the web of relationships that complicate and affect this marriage plot. By constructing different possible networks and actually seeing them superimposed, students put Mirabell and Millamant's union into a social and psychological context.

On one view, the play is about couples. Some students take it, conventionally, as centered on Mirabell and Millamant. Others find the truly central alliance to be between Mirabell and Mrs. Fainall, who as Mirabell's co-conspirator against her husband is a linchpin of the play's secret networks. On the former interpretation, the proviso scene is central and sincere. On the latter interpretation, it is an interlude that might be acted cynically, with Mirabell interested in Millamant's estate for financial purposes. The proviso scene sits, after all, alongside a second contract scene in the play's denouement, when, in Act 5, Mirabell reveals a financial agreement between himself and Mrs. Fainall that predates the Fainalls' marriage.

On another view, *The Way of the World* is about rivalries. Some find the rivalry between Mirabell and Fainall at its heart, with the women their pawns. Others see Lady Wishfort and Mirabell as two competing centers of power, with public power centered on Lady Wishfort, whose fortune is the object of so many schemes, and private power concentrated in the hands of the ascendant Mirabell. Students discuss how such competing allegiances could be signaled by costumes, by the positioning of characters on stage, or by the acting of certain scenes. In a Team Mirabell vs. Team Fainall staging, visual parallels might be created between the two men's opening card game at the start of Act 1 and the contest of female wit in the scene introducing their female co-conspirators, Mrs. Fainall and Mrs. Marwood, at the start of Act 2. If, on the other hand, the play records a struggle between matriarchy in Lady Wishfort and patriarchy in Mirabell, the older widow's first appearance at the start of Act 3 may be played as the climax of a long arc of introductory scenes.

Tracing these variable networks opens up a variety of conversation topics suited to different kinds of courses. If you have a historical focus, for instance, understanding the role of women in the play can launch discussions of the role of royal women in the Glorious Revolution and Hanoverian Settlement, major political events around the time of writing. If your focus is textual, a conversation might ensue about how the act and scene structure of plays can prioritize different relationships. Congreve redivided his plays into scenes in the French neoclassical style (according to which the scene changes every time the group of characters on stage changes) for his collected works in 1710, so interested students could compare versions. For my part, I have used the play to introduce queer reading as a means of reading that is not necessarily about labeling certain characters queer but rather about considering the power of invisible networks and the unknowability of other people's desires.

THE SCHOOL FOR SCANDAL BY RICHARD BRINSLEY SHERIDAN

Helen Williams, Northumbria University, UK

IN BRIEF

Understanding the role of public slander in early print culture using current tabloid newspapers as stage properties.

PURPOSE

Sheridan's play *School for Scandal* is a comedy of manners satirizing contemporary society, mainly its aristocratic and most wealthy citizens. Two of the main targets of Sheridan's satire are closely related: the love of gossip and the concern for reputation. Sheridan draws upon the increasing popularity and circulation of newspapers to establish his comedy about reputation. He explicitly calls upon the gossip column in his repeated reference to "paragraphs," by which he means pithy, almost slanderous, announcements about people's personal lives that were printed as short paragraphs in the major London newspapers. They broadcast to a national reading public the bawdy and unbecoming behaviors of well-known figures in society. The print world of mid-century London, therefore, fed a market of rumor-mongers who enjoyed tarnishing one another's reputations through gossip.

The School for Scandal opens with a scene that draws attention to print publication: Lady Sneerwell asks Mr. Snake if he has had her "paragraphs" inserted into the gossip column of the newspaper. The slanderers entertain themselves with wild speculation about the lives of others, in the same way that society today enjoys celebrity gossip gleaned from tabloid news, magazines, and social media. One question that Sheridan raises is whether reality or fiction is the more powerful tool for making and/or breaking reputations. This is an issue also raised in the prologue to *The School for Scandal*, written by David Garrick. This exercise focuses on the prologue as a gateway to the play. It draws upon close textual analysis, prop-based performance, and historical context to invite students to consider *School for Scandal* as an inherently textual play and to reflect on reputation as a printed as well as performed social construct.

PREPARATION

Photocopies of David Garrick's prologue to *School for Scandal*, lines 9–25 (see the Appendix on Companion Website).

MATERIALS

Students bring a paper copy of a popular newspaper or magazine featuring celebrities.

Nuts and Bolts

1 Distribute, or write on the board, the following extract from the *Gentleman's Magazine*, 39 (Dec. 1769): "An assignation at the White Hart at St. Albans between L— G— and a certain great D-e, was disconcerted by the forcible intrusion of my lord's gentlemen."

2 Treating the above piece of news as a riddle, challenge the class to attempt to fill in the gaps. (Lord/Lady/Dame/Duke might be possible— what does that say about eighteenth-century society?) Divulge that this is a piece of gossip about Lady Grosvenor and the Duke of Cumberland and that their identities would have been obvious to most readers from the period.

3 Invite students to compare the *Gentleman's Magazine* with the newspaper or magazine that they have brought to class. Do they share any similarities?

4 Give out photocopies of David Garrick's prologue to *School for Scandal* (see the Appendix on Companion Website). Compare the prologue to the extract from the *Gentleman's Magazine*. How does Garrick present newspaper reading? What is he doing here with newspaper conventions? Why? If the students need help, instructors may wish to point out the following:

    a The passage is punctuated with "sips," indicating that Lady Wormwood reads her gossip with her morning tea (though she rises at noon). The alignment of "Strong tea and scandal" as "refreshing" suggests that gossip had become a ritualized part of London life.

    b For Lady Wormwood, gossip is only enjoyable when it concerns someone else. Her rapid turn from rapture to anger suggests the hypocrisy of the gossip column and its readers.

c Both the *Gentleman's Magazine* and the prologue use dashes to "censor" proper names. Garrick's reference to "that dash and star" highlights the typographic idiosyncrasies of the eighteenth-century gossip column, strewn with dashes or asterisks to preserve against libel. Quite often, the number of dashes or asterisks was equal to the number of missing letters in the "censored" name, which made for a sort of challenge. For many readers, puzzling out the targets of the paragraph was part of the fun, and surviving copies of newspapers from the period have manuscript annotations filling in the gaps.

d As in the extract from the *Gentleman's Magazine*, the line "Last night Lord L—was caught with Lady D—" implicates two people together in a seemingly amorous encounter.

e Instructors may also wish to note that the use of puns was common and added to the entertainment. For example, "draw"/"undraw the curtain"; "Wormwood is bitter."

5 Invite students to annotate the text, distinguishing between Lady Wormwood's lines that are her own and those spoken by her servant.

6 In groups of three, direct one student to read Lady Wormwood's lines and another to do a voice-over for the newspaper text (and Lisp's short interjection). Invite them to experiment with voice (some students may enjoy attempting a "radio" style journalistic impression to identify the newspaper text as "news").

7 Now, as individuals, present the lines as they were originally intended: as a monologue. How does thinking about voice help us shape the comedy of these lines through delivery?

8 Now ask students to redeliver the above lines using their newspapers or magazines as props. Has their use of voice and gesture changed? Does using a prop alter the way they wish to deliver the lines?

9 Feedback to class: What happened to the performance when we included a voice-over? Does the "printedness" of certain lines affect their delivery? How does understanding the material culture of the period help us to (a) better perform the prologue (b) better understand the play more broadly?

Reflection

Sheridan himself had been the subject of "paragraphs" in newspapers before he wrote *School for Scandal*. But very few students have ever encountered this kind of journalism before. This exercise provides a print historical context for the gossip, which dominates the play at the level of motif. In being unable to understand the "paragraphs" of the opening line of *School for Scandal* or grasp the historical context, students often find the play initially difficult to access. Through helping students visualize print matter from the eighteenth century as material artifacts, this exercise shows how far the dialogue and humor of this play depend on print for their full effect.

Bringing newspapers and magazines to class allows students to see the relevance of the eighteenth-century gossip column or "paragraph." Because print is material, working with newspapers and magazines as props facilitates their performance of the play while also allowing students to better understand its meaning, historical context, and comedy. The physicality of the newspaper in the prologue, for example, encourages students to identify the ways in which Sheridan's text is multivoiced, how it references print artifacts, and how, for Sheridan, as for us, identity and reputation in the age of print culture is often textually constructed. Through this attention to the physicality of print and its effect on performance, students develop their skills in close analysis, growing more confident in identifying the satire in *School for Scandal*, improving their understanding of the print historical context in which Sheridan's play was first performed (see References on Companion Website), and becoming more acutely aware of the conventions that governed the establishment and perpetuation of celebrity reputation in the eighteenth-century press.

WOYZECK BY GEORG BÜCHNER

Christopher Wixson, Eastern Illinois University

IN BRIEF

Students reorder scenes to perceive how plot sequence correlates to theme.

PURPOSE

The play *Woyzeck* is often considered the foundation of Expressionist theater because of its episodic structure and unsettling depiction of reality. The thematic content of the play can shift depending on how the episodic scenes are ordered, from jealousy and a crime of passion, to poverty and exploitation of the lower classes, to mental illness. This exercise will introduce the students to the collaborative nature of authorship in the theater, particularly with a text whose plot is available for interpretative sequencing. By working together to create a sequence in which the scenes should occur and offering explanations for their choices, students will gain a deeper appreciation of Büchner's play and its experimental prescience at the advent of modern drama.

PREPARATION

Students number each scene in their text 1–29. Provide each student with a unique number sequence and instruct them to read the scenes in the sequence given. After reading each scene, ask them to write a one-sentence summary of it.

MATERIALS

No specific technologies are needed for this activity, although electronic copies of the script can be used in lieu of hard copy.

Nuts and Bolts

1 On the day of the exercise, students should have already read the scenes in the unique sequence given to each of them and written their one-sentence summaries of each scene. Again, no two students have read the same order of scenes.

2 Break the students into groups of three to five, depending on preference and class size.

3 Within their groups, assign the students the task of collaboratively producing a definitive "ordering" of the scenes and to articulate a rationale for the choices they make with their version.

   a The instructor may invite them to imagine they are a producing committee for a theater, and they must determine the best possible order of scenes to illuminate a particular theme, performance, experience, etc.

4 Once they have decided upon their sequence of scenes, ask the groups to next reflect upon these questions, via discussion/collaborative in-class writing:

   a What factors led to their decisions?

   b What are the key scenes, in their opinions, and how did those determine their choices?

   c How does their ordering influence the play's meaning?

5 Finally, have the students each informally reflect on the process of this activity in a short individual in-class writing. What was most challenging aspect about the process? Least? What connections can be made between the process of this activity and Woyzeck's journey through the play? What discoveries about *Woyzeck* or modern drama occurred during the activity?

Reflection

Initially, students feel very overwhelmed by the fact that there is no definitive order for the scenes and that each student first reads a different random ordering before joining the group. Like Woyzeck, they struggle with "authority" as they strive toward autonomy over and clarity in their version of *Woyzeck*. Also, like the character Woyzeck, their process of ordering the scenes is a complicated interweaving of the individual and the social.

Savvy (as well as intimidated) students may gravitate toward published versions of the play as possessing a kind of "authority," something instructors should work to discourage. I always let students know that I am fully aware of published versions but encourage them not to compromise their authority by mimicking the choices of other scholars and practitioners. That is to say,

I remind them repeatedly that, as there is no definitive ("correct") ordering of the *Woyzeck* scenes, the project is a unique opportunity for immense creative freedom. The early moments of the group activity are the most unsure for the students, and strong reassurance and some guidance by the instructor in how to move forward are usually needed.

Ultimately, in constructing their script, students must determine the play's central thematic focus (i.e., is it a love story, about murder, about biological determinism, a social critique?), through-line of action, and the objectives and challenges of its central protagonist(s). The challenge forces them to read very carefully and think in dramatic and theatrical terms.

The activity may also be expanded with additional components and divided up over multiple class sessions. The students can be put into groups, each tasked with assembling a "definitive" order to the scenes and, through presentation and/or informal performance of selected scenes, justifying their decisions for the rest of the class.

A DOLL'S HOUSE BY HENRIK IBSEN

William Boles, Rollins College

IN BRIEF

Underscoring the influence of the bourgeois setting on Nora's dilemma through images of dollhouses.

PURPOSE

To help students understand how the visual construction of Ibsen's set as a theatrical space echoing a dollhouse corresponds to the characters as doll-like in nature. The exercise allows students to understand how the physical setting of the play reinforces the spatial, economic, social, and cultural controls over the central dolls in the play, Nora and Torvald.

PREPARATION

The students are expected to read the entire play before coming to class. The instructor should familiarize himself or herself with Oortman's web site or another web resource illustrating dollhouses and prepare a cutaway drawing of a house, with a large space indicating the drawing room of the Helmer household. Faculty could also consider bringing an actual dollhouse to the classroom.

MATERIALS

Black board/white board and computer capabilities to project images in front of classroom.

Nuts and Bolts

This exercise has two parts—a visual and textual element.

The Visual Element

1 Spend some time looking at Oortman's creation of a dollhouse—or other similar reproductions. Although it represents an earlier century, it reflects the opulence of home interiors and can suggest to the students the Helmer family's class aspirations.

2 Give all students a copy of the cutaway drawing house. Let each student start to position the characters in the space, by using either post-it notes or small figures, blocking the initial scene like a set designer or director would. Ask for a student volunteer. As you read the stage description of the Helmer household, have the student fill in the house set-up on the board or an overhead projector (doors leading to the study, outside, etc., as well as windows, furniture, stove, etc.). The rest of the students fill in their copies as well.

3 Now ask the students to look at Ibsen's set from a perspective of space. How much furniture is in the room? Where do the doors lead? Which characters pertain to which rooms? They should try to imagine the other rooms in the house, such as where the kitchen, children's rooms, and nanny's room might be.

4 Ask the students about their own experiences playing with a dollhouse when they were kids. What happened in those experiences? Try to get them to think about their own perspective (things falling over, furniture too big for the space) as well as the dolls' perspective (never leaving the house, being manipulated, never being able to sit on the furniture).

5 Turning back to the set design images they have in front of them, ask them what is missing. If they have thoroughly read the play, other objects from later scenes may be included, but above all, remind them of the mailbox. Why does Ibsen not include the mailbox in his description? If you were the set designer/director of the play, would you need to reorganize the set to draw attention to the mailbox?

The Textual Element

1 Having discussed the set and its various levels of representation when it comes to the Helmer family, turn to the text and have students read the first page or two of dialogue to see how the characters incorporate reference to the set or their environment in their dialogue.

2 Next, embark on a close analysis of the language used by Nora and Torvald, mirroring the close reading of the set. Ask the students to focus on how the subject matter of discussion is tied to money and debt, and how the set can reinforce the importance of money for social standing. Focus also on the various diminutive terms used by Torvald for Nora, which connects to the larger theme of a dollhouse and playing with dolls.

3 Finally, bring to the student's attention who and what is seen or not seen. Where is Torvald when the scene begins? (He is in his office and they talk through the wall at each other.) Visually, what does this use of house space say about their relationship and the events that occur later in the play? How does this mirror Torvald's control over the mailbox and, in turn, Nora? Furthermore, what objects does Nora have to hide somewhere on the set in the first scene? Her first phrase is "Hide the Christmas tree," and she also hides the macaroons she is eating. "Hide" is a crucial key to unlocking her character, especially when one begins to count the number of instances where she "hides" things from Torvald throughout the play. Encourage the students to think about how houses hide information from the outside world, as well as how family members hide secrets from one another.

Reflection

The discussion of the set appearance is a valuable tool to get the students to analyze how a setting underscores a play's meaning, and in this case, echoes the dollhouse of the title. Specifically, I try to get them to see that the sitting room, the one room Nora frequents the most, is an extension of her situation. While everyone else seems to be able to come and go throughout the play, Nora is almost exclusively trapped in this space. How much room— or liberty—does she really have? It becomes a defining element of her limits, but we also end up noting that the multiple entrances/exits of Christine and Krogstad into this space allow Nora to see the world with far more social opportunities and legal rules than she had previously understood. Furthermore, the letter in the mailbox that Krogstad slips inside becomes a miniature representation of Nora's own situation in the house. She is trapped in this living room, marriage, and societal role, just as the letter is trapped in the mailbox. The letter is a reminder to Nora (and the audience) of the danger she and her family faces of losing their reputation and thus losing their material footing in society. Since only Torvald has the key, he is the only one who has the power to "free" it and her from being contained. But her ability to lie and hide objects from Torvald also allows for a larger consideration of the role of women and family dynamics within such legal limitations that society imposes.

Essentially, what I have found with this exercise, which I have done for over twenty years, is that this exercise is a great way to introduce students to the multileveled way they need to read a play, starting with the stage directions for the set.

MISS JULIE BY AUGUST STRINDBERG

Aleks Merilo, South Kitsap High School

IN BRIEF

Use of stage properties to demonstrate power relationships between characters.

PURPOSE

Strindberg's play *Miss Julie*, often considered in Darwinian terms as the survival of the fittest, depicts a contest between the aristocratic Miss Julie and the status-seeking servant, Jean. Their interaction is fraught with sexual tension and competitive desire, as Jean tries to rise above his servitude and Julie admits to ancestral degeneracy. Physical and psychological ownership plays a large role in Strindberg's play, and this ownership is personified by a series of props and objects. This exercise emphasizes the properties either mentioned in the script or used by the characters that symbolize status, role, or wealth, depending on how they are used. By drawing attention to these "objects of power," students can more readily witness which character holds influence and social authority at any given time.

PREPARATION

This lesson is best performed after students have viewed or read *Miss Julie* in its entirety.

MATERIALS

Instructor should prepare (or invite students to bring to class) "objects of power," such as a coat, a toy canary, an engagement ring, a riding whip, a rose, a bag of money, a suitcase, or a servants' bell. Each of these items either makes a literal appearance in the play or is mentioned symbolically in the text. Instructor can also choose a handful of scenes to perform of approximately 10 lines per scene.

Nuts and Bolts

1 Guided Practice: Start the lesson by selecting two students to perform a cold reading of the following scene (from *Project Gutenberg Ebook of Plays*):

> **Julie** Oh, shame! We don't behave as you do when we are engaged.
>
> **Jean** [*Eyeing her*]   Are you sure of that? It isn't worthwhile to play the innocent with me.
>
> **Julie** I gave my love to a rascal.
>
> **Jean** That's what they always say afterward.
>
> **Julie** Always?
>
> **Jean** Always, I believe, as I have heard the expression many times before under the same circumstances.
>
> **Julie** What circumstances?
>
> **Jean** Those we've been talking about. The last time I— —
>
> **Julie** Silence. I don't wish to hear any more.

Once the scene has been performed, introduce one of the play's objects of power into it. For example: Reread the previous scene with Julie holding her "engagement ring." Ask the class to observe how this changes the performer's voice and physicality, and interaction with Jean.

2 Next, try the same scene, but this time with Jean holding the engagement ring. How does this change the dynamic? When observed, the first scene with Julie in power might be boastful, condescending. However, when Jean is in control of the ring, often Julie's performance becomes vulnerable, even uncomfortable.

3 For the last run-through, ask both of the actors to physically take the object of power when they feel their character might see a chance to take control. Once again, ask the audience how this changes the dynamic.

4 Group Work: Next, break the students into groups of two, and ask them to pick out one of the above-listed "objects of power" as well as a scene of approximately 10 lines. Alternatively, the instructor can determine these lines in advance to save on class time. Remember, the object itself need not be referred to in the scene for it to be used. For example, Julie placing Jean in his coat, or wearing it herself, could illustrate powerful relationship changes at nearly any point in the play.

5 Give students time to practice and rehearse their scenes, choosing a variety of props with which to experiment. While this activity could work with nearly any scene in the play, some favorites include Jean being invited to dance, the moment Jean kills the canary, the moment after the implied sex scene, and, of course, the notorious ending.

6 Ask groups to perform their selections with their designated objects.

7 Conclude with follow-up questions: What objects fit each of these scenes the strongest? Where there any that surprised you? How did negotiation over the object influence the voice, physicality, tension, and symbolism of the performance? Which character had power at any given moment?

Reflection

So much of the power dynamic between Miss Julie and Jean is played out symbolically. If we consider one of the accepted ideas that this play is about status and power, we notice Strindberg has, in a beautiful and economical fashion, filled this play with objects that are given enormous symbolic weight. For example, roses and money bags might buttress our perception of the luxury items and wealth that Jean dreams about acquiring, his need to "climb–climb, to plunder the birds' nests up there where the golden eggs lie." While at the same time, symbols such as the yellow canary in a gilded cage could show Julie suffers at being exposed as a near "degenerate" woman. This drill could also be used to explore class conflict, idealization and gender issues; students tend to discover new symbols and interpretations even mid-performance.

I have found in using this lesson that students' investment in their character, as well as their stake in the scene, increases dramatically, regardless of what object is used. Some objects that might seem to border on the ridiculous (such as a riding whip) all encourage students to make bolder physical and vocal choices that they otherwise would not.

HEDDA GABLER BY HENRIK IBSEN

Shadow David Zimmerman, University of California, Santa Cruz

IN BRIEF

An exploration of domestic setting as both realistic and symbolic space.

PURPOSE

Hedda Gabler, one of the great tragic heroines of modern drama, found herself trapped inside a marriage and a dream house that she supposedly wanted. Ibsen used newly innovated production techniques to deliver information about its titular character quickly and effectively. This exercise will help clarify the central conflict that Hedda Gabler experiences based on the information found in Ibsen's realistic setting.

PREPARATION

While students do not need to have read the play ahead of time, they should have the opening stage directions in front of them and come to class with a mental image of their "dream home." An alternative exercise would ask them to create a collage of their dream home on paper, using images from the internet or magazines, but this is not necessary.

Instructors wishing to do Exercise One (optional) should create two stacks: one of words and the other of corresponding images of valuable material items associated with wealth and luxury, e.g., mansion, money, tuxedo, jewelry, yacht, golfing/tennis equipment, or other item. These images can come from magazine advertisements or clip art/Google Image search.

MATERIALS

Paper for students to draw on.

Nuts and Bolts

Exercise One (Optional)

Studies, like those done by Lightspeed Research, show that images carry the same amount of meaning faster than text, thus the importance of a well-designed set. This point is easily demonstrated in action.

1 Ask for two volunteers to come to the front of the class. Give one student a marker and a numbered list of words; give the other an ordered stack of printed images of material items (see above, Preparation).

2 When you say "Go," it's a race: the first student writes the first word, while the second reveals the first image. Tell the class that they are to call out both the term associated with the image/written word they see as soon as they understand it and any connotative terms associated with the image/word. See which method is most effective at generating associations.

3 Repeat this with the other words/images.

Exercise Two

1 Supply each student with a piece of blank paper on which to draw a schematic design of a house—or photocopy this design ahead of time.

2 Invite students to close their eyes for a moment to picture their "dream home."

3 Inside this design, they should create their dream house. They could draw the items they wish to possess inside the home or simply write the words where the item should be (sub-zero refrigerator, plasma TV, Jacuzzi, etc.). Give them 5–10 minutes to complete this. Encourage them to achieve the highest level of detail possible, but remind them this activity is designed to reveal their vision of a "dream home," not test their artistic ability.

4 Taking another piece of paper, ask students to rip it into 20–25 scraps and to write on each piece of paper one of their current hobbies, interests, and future aspirations.

5 In the style of a mosaic, have students rearrange the pieces of paper into the form of their "dream home." Ask them to determine which hobby or aspiration should be inside of the home and which one should be outside. Tell them that they are only to use the domestic scraps to build their homes. So, for example, "painting, video-game playing, hanging out with friends, cooking" would be inside the house, but "travel, X-country running, work" would be outside the home.

6 Finally, ask the students to consider the following hypothetical: If they could have anything they ever wanted in their dream home at the cost of never being able to leave it, would they agree to this condition?

Reflection

Before the onset of theater technology in the mid-nineteenth century, theater-makers relied mostly on textual descriptions to figuratively paint a scene. All changed, however, when the Duke of Saxe-Meiningen and his Meiningen Ensemble developed methods for creating intricate, realistic settings for the stage, allowing playwrights to dive into the psychology of the characters within the stage space. Ibsen's later works were influenced by these productions, as the Ensemble toured thirty-five European countries during the 1880s. As such, productions of *Hedda Gabler* would have centered around hyper-realistic depictions of luxurious Nordic lifestyles, most notably the house itself, which served as both Hedda's prison and her only expressive outlet. The effect of this technology on Ibsen's text is apparent.

Explain to the students that the constant background image of the play carries very specific information about its titular character. Encourage the students to suggest the insights such a setting could reveal about Hedda, as well as any other aspects of her character revealed during their reading. Read the opening stage directions aloud and write on the board the list of decorative items, such as the piano, the curtains, and the painting of General Gabler. Examples include her wealth, her attention to detail, her willingness to devote time to such decoration, her protectiveness of belongings, but also her romantic desires, her potential career aspirations, her urge to travel. In the play, Hedda is unable to express herself or exercise control of anything but her home, mostly due to the constraints of her gender and societal expectations. Essentially, the setting represents Hedda's identity, the Victorian social restrictions in her day, as well as the material goods she was conditioned to want. The setting is a shorthand device to represent "her."

Ask the students about their own experience creating their "dream homes" and the shortcomings and sacrifices involved. How big was the unused pile of scraps that remained outside of the home compared to the usable pile? Similarly, in the confines of her perfect home, a large portion of Hedda's identity atrophied from disuse. Once the students start reading the play, you may wish to ask them how the exercise impacted their understanding of Hedda, who initially appears to be a mean-spirited character. Are they more or less sympathetic to her? Do they feel closer to her struggle?

Encourage students to then discuss any additional ways in which the intricate setting can help inform their understanding of the play, the conflicts therein, or the characters. Read aloud, for example, the scene in Act 2, where Tesman and Brack discuss Tesman's home. How does this understanding of Hedda inspire our understanding of Tesman? Ejlert? Or, perhaps most intriguingly, Mrs. Elvsted? Exploring the setting of *Hedda Gabler* will help students new to dramatic analysis appreciate the depths this play gains in performance.

THE IMPORTANCE OF BEING EARNEST BY OSCAR WILDE

Jessie Mills, Pomona College

IN BRIEF

This exercise employs the technique of "turn-outs" (spoken or silent comedic asides) to illuminate the subtext of the play.

PURPOSE

The Importance of Being Earnest often heightens comedy through the juxtaposition of characters' social façade versus their true intentions. In a society that places great emphasis on required upper-class behavior and fulfilling social niceties, Wilde's characters reveal their hidden thoughts and desires through the use of asides or physically "turning out" to the audience. A turn-out is a tool where an actor turns her face outwards toward the audience and reveals her thoughts aloud or via facial expressions. This contrast between the façade and the genuine thought creates a comedic moment between performer and spectator.

Using a scene between Jack and Algernon (the beginning of Act 1 upon Jack's arrival) or Gwendolen and Cecily (the middle of Act 2, upon their first meeting), students witness how performing a comedic turn-out conveys Wilde's larger examination of superficial society.

PREPARATION

Students should read the full play beforehand and/or think about the ways in which they, in their everyday practice, reveal subtext in conversation. Subtext can refer to one's underlying but unspoken thoughts, feelings, and motivations, as well as implicit understandings between people. Inquire if students, for instance, ever turn away and roll their eyes mid-conversation or exasperatedly make eye contact with a friend while annoyed. Many of these silent instances of subtext mimic the mechanism of a turn-out.

Nuts and Bolts

1 Begin standing in a circle. Pair students together and hand out the short scenes mentioned above. Ask students to either read the passages silently or solicit volunteers to read the text aloud for the class.

2 Give instructions on how to perform the speaker's turn-out. The actor should turn-out at the end of her line; her attention should begin with her scene partner and finish toward the audience just as she hits her final word. Implicit in the turn-out is the speaker's true feelings—she should reveal the subtext of her line to the audience through her facial expression. For instance, on Gwendolen's line "bread and butter, please. Cake is rarely seen at the best houses nowadays," Gwendolen can turn-out on the word "nowadays" to reveal that she is truly feeling contempt rather than courteousness. Allow pairs, all working at once, to take turns trying lines with a speaker's turn-out reaction.

3 Give instructions on how to perform the listener's turn-out. The listening actor should turn-out after her scene partner has completed their sentence; her listener's turn-out is a reaction to the full line. Again, the actor should silently (i.e., through physical and facial expressions) reveal how she really feels to the audience. For example, after Gwendolen has finished her line about what is "seen in the best houses nowadays," Cecily can turn-out to reveal that she is truly feeling wrath rather than warmth. Allow pairs, all working at once, to take turns trying lines with a listener's turn-out reaction.

4 Remind students of the fourth wall in Wilde's work. Both in the speaker's and listener's turn-out, it is important that the actor not make eye contact with the audience to uphold Wilde's form. Keeping the fourth wall in place, the actor should look beyond her audience, allowing the full room of spectators into her emotional world. Wilde, indeed, writes in moments for actors to reveal their truest selves to the audience while keeping the fourth wall intact (from *Project Gutenberg Ebook of Plays*):

   a Gwendolen: [*With elaborate politeness.*] Thank you. [*Aside.*] Detestable girl! But I require tea!

   b In Gwendolen's spoken turn-out, the "thank you" is delivered politely to Cecily, and the "Detestable girl! But I require tea!" is delivered indignantly and desperately toward the fourth wall.

5 Once students have a grasp on the mechanisms of a turn-out, have them craft four turn-outs—each actor should have one speaker's and one listener's turn-out, using no more than four lines of dialogue. On any given line, there should only be one turn-out, be it the speaker or listener. I allow approximately 10 minutes for groups to stage their turn-outs before presenting their work to the class. If time permits, I'll guide the student pairs in refining and strengthening their turn-outs (this usually consists of clarifying the subtext and smoothing out pacing).

6 Discuss with the class how comedic subtext works within the structure of the intellectual farce. You may wish to consider the differences between how an actor might perform dramatic subtext versus Wilde's comedic subtext.

7 While not required, I often conclude by playing a few short episodes from the YouTube series "Jersey Shore Gone Wilde," in which stars from the 2011 Broadway production of *Importance of Being Earnest* read dialogue from "Jersey Shore," the reality television series, in the style and tone of intellectual farce. I have students shout out any moment where a turn-out occurs in the video. This final activity continues to drive home the immediacy of Wilde's comedic form.

Reflection

In my experience, this exercise highlights and clarifies the subversive humor of Wilde's intellectual farce. Students are able to discover and perform the comedic subtext, which naturally ties into Wilde's larger theme of deception, or keeping a secret within the constraints of high society. Once this connection is made, students often remark on the performative nature of the text; in Wilde's work, form and function run along parallel lines.

This activity also helps students understand the sharpness of Wilde's wit and makes the text and character dynamics feel more relevant and relatable. Recently, while teaching this activity, a student burst into a fit of giggles upon seeing another student perform a turn-out, remarking that he didn't understand why the play was considered a comedy until he saw how mean the characters were to one other and how much they truly enjoyed their insults.

More often than not, subtext is relegated to the dramatic canon, most notably in psychological realism. As students discover the comedic form of the assumed dramatic technique, their reading of the text changes completely. Jokes are unearthed and the play quickly moves from a dry, academic reading to a laugh riot.

THREE SISTERS BY ANTON CHEKHOV

Janna Segal, University of Louisville

IN BRIEF

Perform "snapshots" of nostalgia, longing, and hope.

PURPOSE

All of the figures in Chekhov's *Three Sisters* articulate a need for the illusions afforded by nostalgia and hope in order to endure the disappointments of life. This theme is introduced at the outset of the action, when Olga expresses "a longing to get back home to Moscow!" Olga and Irena fantasize about a future return to Moscow as Masha "whistles a tune under her breath." Masha's musical underscore undermines the sisters' hopeful plans for a future escape from the present by suggesting that the plot to return to a past they shared in Moscow is a storytelling ritual routinely enacted in the Prozorovs' home. This theme carries forward throughout the action, which culminates with the sisters "huddled together," clinging to the past and to hope in the future as the life with the soldiers that they have known exits to the musical accompaniment of a military band. Irena fantasizes about a purposeful "Tomorrow" "somewhere" other than the now soldierless town, and Olga imagines that their present "sufferings may mean happiness for the people who come after us" as a band plays in the background. Like Masha's whistling in the play's opening scene, the military musical soundtrack signals to the audience that the sisters are again weaving a fiction of an alternative reality in order to "go on living" in the moment.

While this theme is perhaps most overtly evident in the actions of the titular siblings, the ensemble-driven play is populated by characters longing for a past or hoping for a future alternative to the present. This exercise encourages students to identify this unifying theme, or main idea, to examine how it applies to all of the play's characters and to experientially explore how such longing can be made active through performance with other actors.

PREPARATION

Introduce students to terms from Stanislavski's terms beforehand (see Nuts and Bolts below).

MATERIALS

None.

Nuts and Bolts

1 Review (or introduce) the key terms and components of Stanislavski's system. To assist the instructor, here is a brief overview of three key terms:

a The **ruling idea** is defined for the class as the play's primary theme, its main idea or message.

b **Given circumstances** are defined as all of the facts about each character that are given in the script.

c The **super-objective** is defined as the main objective that, consciously or unconsciously, guides each character's actions in the world of the play from the start of the action to the conclusion. It is explained to the class that each character's super-objective should be a goal that carries the character from the start of the action to the conclusion. It is also emphasized that the super-objective must serve the play's ruling idea.

2 Give the students the following instructions (in a handout, orally, or written on the board):

a "Cast yourself in the role you would most like to perform in Chekhov's *Three Sisters*. (Alternatively, the instructor can assign each student a role so as to ensure all of the play's speaking characters are addressed). First indicate the play's 'ruling idea.' Having identified the play's main theme, state your selected character's 'given circumstances.' After listing the character's 'given circumstances,' state your interpretation of the character's 'super-objective.'

b Provide one quotation spoken by your character in the play that supports your interpretation of their 'super-objective.'"

    i Students usually take about 20 minutes in class to complete this written portion of the assignment. Alternatively, you can make this portion of the exercise a take-home assignment.

3 To start the exercise, begin a discussion of the play's main theme by having the students share their interpretation of the play's ruling idea.

a During the discussion, look for points of contact between the students' responses that lead to the play's ruling idea regarding the function of nostalgia and hope.

b Lead the class to discover how the realistic play purports that a vision of an alternative reality is a means by which to endure the disappointments of one's current reality.

4 Having come to a consensus regarding the play's ruling idea, have the students share the name of the character each has selected or been assigned, offer the given circumstances they have identified for that character, and identify that character's super-objective.

   a If students' super-objectives do not relate to the play's ruling idea, ask them to retool them. Their super-objectives should serve the play's main message regarding the function of longing for an alternative past or future to endure the present.

   b If a student needs some coaching to select a super-objective that supports the ruling idea, ask them how their super-objective serves the play's primary theme and how the character strives for that goal from the start of the action to the conclusion.

   c If a student needs a more active super-objective, probe further by asking, "Why?" or "From whom?" For instance, if a student says, "Irena's super-objective is to find meaningful work," ask them, "Why does she need to find meaningful work?"

5 After hearing from all the students, have each student, as the selected or assigned character, use his or her selected quotation to act upon their character's super-objective. Invite them to the front of the room to perform a selection from a scene with at least one scene partner.

   a Other students in the class should take on the roles of other characters in the scene in which the chosen quotation can be found. Depending on the student's background and major, some light coaching may help to lead students to connect their textual research to live performance in what can be described, to borrow from the play's cameraman Fedotik, as "snapshot" scenic moments from the play. Creating a snapshot of the scene with nonspeaking students allows the student with the speaking part to discover how their character's super-objective is a longing for an alternative to their present circumstances that is acted upon with every utterance and yet never fulfilled. Acting upon their character's yearning with other characters in a scene leads the students to discover that in this ensemble-driven play, all the characters are united by unfulfilled desires that they cling to in order to endure their daily lives.

6 After all the students have performed their selected quotations in "snapshots," conclude with a class discussion during which you ask the students to share what they learned about Chekhov's play through this application of Stanislavski's system.

Reflection

This application of Stanislavski's system leads the students to a deeper understanding of the play's themes, characters, and plot, and it ignites their performative imaginations. The students realize the ways in which the characters' collective hopes serve the play's indirect action and its themes. They also discover how the approach to acting used for the Moscow Art Theatre's premiere can animate the drama's subtle plotting. The students often report in the concluding discussion that they found the early twentieth-century Russian play static and the characters "boring" until they were asked to select or were assigned a character with whom to identify, analyze, and then perform with others. Identifying their character's given circumstances and super-objective in relation to a ruling idea helps the students to determine the play's primary theme, leads them to discover how that theme is activated by performing with a scene partner(s), and serves to close the historical gap between the play's realism and the students' reality.

The students come to appreciate how the play's indirect action is enlivened by the ensemble-based approach to realistic acting that Stanislavski devised partly in response to the demands of Chekhov's theater. They come to conceive of the characters with their "funny, foreign names" as a collection of individualized people, all of whom are braving their daily lives by clutching onto tenuous illusions of a better reality. Scouring the text for the facts of the character and then playing those circumstances in "snapshot" scenes with others lead the students to make discoveries about the characters' relationship to the play's major theme regarding the need for illusions and hope to endure the disappointments of life. Further discoveries are made when the students embody their character and activate their super-objective in relation to the other characters in the world of the play. Hearing, seeing, and enacting each other's interpretations of their characters and the play's main theme lead to even more revelations about the realistic play's interrogation of how withstanding reality requires imagining life in different circumstances.

THE CHERRY ORCHARD BY ANTON CHEKHOV

Kelly Younger, Loyola Marymount University

IN BRIEF

Trick students into experiencing the lack of connection in Chekhovian dialogue.

PURPOSE

This exercise allows students to experience the monologic quality of Chekhovian "dialogue" by listening to a student speaking randomly in the classroom about a personal, troublesome issue and witnessing others ignore that student. Conversely, in observing their own unwillingness to connect with one another as identical to the characters' lack of responsiveness, the class perceives the relational nature of Chekhovian dialogue. That is, even if the page seems dominated by monologic speeches that are greeted by the silence of others, the dialogue is deeply relational because of the persistent and universal desire to be heard and acknowledged.

PREPARATION

Instructor prepares an in-class writing prompt about loneliness in Act II as well as an instruction sheet for an individual student (see Materials below); students should read Acts 1 and 2 in advance.

MATERIALS

Prepare the following note to place on a student's desk:

Dear Student: Today we will do an in-class writing exercise where I ask everyone to write about loneliness. A few minutes into this writing assignment, when it is quiet, blurt out so everyone can hear you: "I'm so lonely. I don't have anyone to talk to." Try to do it without laughing or without seeming like this was planned. Expect the whole class to be surprised, and most likely look at you. I will, however, act as if nothing has happened, and let everyone just continue in silence. You should do the same. The hardest part will be the few minutes after when the rest of the class is asking themselves, "what?" My advice is, turn back to your own writing and do not make eye contact with anyone. Act like nothing happened. And don't worry. I promise before class ends, I will admit that I put you up to this. I will also explain the reasoning behind this exercise in the context of the play. If you are NOT up to it, simply bring this piece of paper to me right now and I will hand it to another student. Thank you!

Nuts and Bolts

1 At the beginning of class, simply place the instruction sheet on a student's desk. Do so as casually as possible. Once the student has read it, make eye contact for silent agreement that he or she understands and is willing to do the activity.

2 When it comes time to discuss Act 2 of *The Cherry Orchard*, give the students a writing prompt about loneliness, but make it about the students, not the characters (e.g., "Define loneliness in your own terms" or "Describe the loneliest time you have ever experienced"). The goal is for these students to be thinking about themselves, not the characters right now, and to get a little lost in their own worlds.

3 During this time, the instructor should be writing notes on the board or doing something that prevents him or her from facing the class. This way, when the student blurts out her line, the instructor does not react but simply continues doing the chosen activity. Once it happens, let the writing continue for a few minutes, then begin your discussion of Act 2 as if nothing has happened.

4 Lead the students in a discussion of the opening of Act 2. Talk about Charlotta's opening monologue where she discusses her loneliness, yet she is on stage with other characters who do not respond or even acknowledge her. Ask the students how "realistic" this is (in the context of "Realism"). Why don't the other characters acknowledge her? Are they all lost in their own worlds? Is there any true dialogue in this opening? Is this unrealistic? What do you think Chekhov is dramatizing in this moment?

> **a** During this discussion, attempt to keep the conversation rooted in the text and the characters before opening it up to speculation as to whether or not the students might encounter a situation like this in "real life." Then ask them if situations like this happen in real life? By

this point, students usually agree that Chekhov's depiction is completely unrealistic and that it would never happen that way off-stage. Here is where you, as the instructor, draw attention to the fact that it just did. A fellow student expressed her loneliness out loud in a room full of others and yet no one acknowledged the student or responded to them. You also confess that you set the student up to do so.

b The class is immediately relieved and eager to share what they felt in that moment, what they heard, what they wanted to say but didn't, how they wanted to act but didn't, etc.

5 Now that the instructor has fessed up, revisit the discussion about Chekhovian dialogue, monologue, Realism, etc., and see how the students' opinions may have shifted.

Reflection

Most times, the students conclude Chekhov's portrayal is completely unrealistic, untrue, and unrelatable because the dialogue does not seem to be about any topic in particular, nor does it develop or resolve any conflicts. It is here you point out that they all experienced a moment in class when their fellow student spoke out loud about his or her own loneliness yet none of them responded to or even acknowledged the outburst. At this point, a general sense of relief is expressed and they all begin sharing the internal monologue that was going through their mind even while their external dialogue choice was simply silence.

For students who struggle to connect with one another in an authentic, interpersonal, dialogic, and non-tech mediated way, this exercise not only deepens their understanding of Chekhov's play but also increases their empathy toward characters who, prior to class, were written off as old, outdated, and unreadable.

PYGMALION BY GEORGE BERNARD SHAW

Rebecca Cameron, DePaul University

IN BRIEF

Directing students to use movement, gestures, and voice to offer two different endings to a play.

PURPOSE

This exercise increases student awareness of how stage directions illuminate different performance possibilities that lie within a script and helps students to understand the importance of movement and gesture in performance.

PREPARATION

Instructor must locate and photocopy the ending to the 1916 version of the play without the revisions Shaw made to the ending in 1939 and 1941 (see the Appendix on the Companion Website).

MATERIALS

Instructor should also prepare two sets of instructions as handouts (see below).

Nuts and Bolts

1 All students receive the photocopy of the 1916 ending to *Pygmalion*. Students divide themselves into groups of three, and any remaining students can be assigned the role of group director. Within the groups, students decide who will take on the roles of Higgins, Eliza (Liza), and Mrs. Higgins.

2 Students next receive two distinct sets of instructions:

Half of the groups receive written instructions telling them to imply that Eliza and Higgins will get together romantically after the end of the play. These groups are told that they may take liberties with Shaw's stage directions, but not with his lines.

The other half of the groups receive written instructions telling them to make it clear to the audience that Eliza and Higgins absolutely do not get together at the end of the play. These groups are encouraged to interpret Shaw's stage directions to make that point emphatically.

3 Students then rehearse the scene for 15 minutes, incorporating movement and gesture to correspond with the romantic or the severing intention of the scene. I let them know two sets of instructions have been given to the class to follow.

4 As the groups rehearse, I circulate, helping them to work out their movements and gestures. I ask several prompting questions, e.g., "Is there a gesture you could use with that line to help reinforce the romantic/ non-romantic relationship?" As I circulate, I make a note of groups on each side who are doing a particularly good job of finding gestures and movements to support their interpretation.

5 I then reconvene the entire class and invite two or three of the groups to perform their scenes in front of the entire class, with at least one group representing the romantic ending and one group representing the non-romantic or separating ending. Afterwards we hold a discussion about the two endings.

Reflection

These diametrically opposed interpretations of the ending highlight one of the key issues the play raises: the possibility of women's independence, both in early twentieth-century British society and in theatrical convention. Written at the height of the suffrage movement, the play repeatedly questions what will become of Eliza after the experiment ends. The two older women, Mrs. Pearce and Mrs. Higgins, recognize the problem early on, and Eliza eventually protests that all her hard work has done little more than equip her to "sell herself" in marriage. At the end of the play, Shaw actively resists both the societal expectation and the theatrical convention of ending with a marriage, preferring a more open ending in which Eliza asserts her independence and determination to set her own path, which may include marriage to Freddy, but also involves earning her own income. However, in performance, the convention of the romantic ending along with the expectation that Eliza marry the strong male figure who has played a key role in her class advancement proves powerful, as evident in the long-standing temptation to imply a romantic ending for Eliza and Higgins—in the original production, the 1938 and 1964 film versions, and the musical *My Fair Lady*.

During the class exercise, I let the students find their own gestures, but if they need some assistance, I draw from the play's production history. After opening night, Shaw complained in a letter to his wife that the actor playing Higgins, Sir Herbert Beerbohm Tree, insisted on playing the role romantically. Rather than following Shaw's directive that he "occupy himself affectionately with his mother, & throw Eliza the commission to buy the ham &c. over his shoulder," Tree "shov[ed] his mother rudely out of his way and woo[ed] Eliza with appeals to buy a ham for his lonely home like a bereaved Romeo."[1] Later in the run, Tree took further liberties, including throwing flowers to Eliza just before the curtain dropped.[2]

Taking cues from Shaw, the "non-romantic" groups might be encouraged to place Higgins close to his mother, with Liza at some distance, behind his back, so that he can deliver his request over his shoulder. Liza might walk out of the room briskly without any hesitation, while Higgins, left alone on stage, might remain standing tall, head held high with hands in his pockets, or might sit on the couch, comfortably spread out, with no signs of regret.

The "romantic" group, on the other hand, might be encouraged to place Higgins close to Liza, looking intently into her eyes and perhaps even touching her arm as he makes his final request as he moves away from his mother's kiss. Liza might pause at the door and turn toward Higgins before she leaves, or perhaps even remain at the threshold, while Higgins might follow her toward the door or stare at it after she leaves. Some groups might even want to borrow Sir Herbert Beerbohm Tree's move of having Higgins grab some flowers from a vase and toss them toward Liza. Students are sometimes uncomfortable touching one another, and I allow them to set their own boundaries. If they do not want to perform a gesture that would require intimate physical contact, they may simply describe what they would do at a given moment.

This exercise usually leads to a lively discussion about the end of the play and about dramatic form more generally. We discuss the expectations of romantic comedy and the difficulties of moving against generic conventions, which I sometimes illustrate further by showing them the end of the 1938 film adaptation. We consider the ways in which Shaw attempted to resist such romantic interpretations of the play and discuss why he was so insistent that Eliza and Higgins could not become romantically involved. Comparing the handout they used for the exercise to the edition they brought for class (with the 1941 revisions) provides one example of how Shaw attempted to revise the ending to remove ambiguity about the relationship between Eliza and Higgins.

[1] Bernard Shaw, *Collected Letters: 1911-1925*, ed. Dan H. Laurence (New York: Viking, 1985), 227–28.

[2] Charles A. Berst, *Pygmalion: Shaw's Spin on Myth and Cinderella* (New York: Twayne, 1995).

TRIFLES BY SUSAN GLASPELL

Noelia Hernando-Real, Universidad Autónoma de Madrid

IN BRIEF

Weave together props to understand the performance of oppression.

PURPOSE

In this exercise students focus exclusively on the stage properties and on how they are handled to explore by themselves how these props establish build the theme of female oppression. Additionally, the names of the props written on the cardboard strips will form a log cabin quilt pattern that helps readers to understand visually the reasons that have led to John Wright's murder and to appreciate the compact way in which Glaspell wrote this play.

PREPARATION

Students should read the play in its entirety before class. I also recommend the instructor offer some context in advance, including background about Susan Glaspell as a playwright, the Hossack murder case, the Provincetown Players, and women's limited civil rights at the time.

Before the day of the exercise, the teacher divides the class into eight groups and assigns a few props to each one—bread and pans, towels, preserves, stove, rocking chair, apron, log cabin quilt pattern, and birdcage and bird—and gives students these instructions:

1 Read the play carefully and note down when the prop you've been assigned is mentioned (in stage directions or main text). Pay special attention to the ways in which male and female characters refer to and/or handle the prop.
2 Discuss and come to an agreement as to what the prop reveals about Minnie's life and how it provides evidence in support of or against Minnie.
3 Ask the students to bring their props to class. Note: Miniatures or photos are welcome for more difficult ones (for example, the stove or the rocker).

> **MATERIALS**
>
> Props (provided by the students): Bread, pans, towels, stove, rocker, apron, birdcage, (toy) bird, log cabin quilt pattern. A photo of the stage design of *Trifles* can be shown in class (see the New York Public Library Digital Collections). Strips of cardboard or construction paper of eight different colors (two of each color) plus a red square to make the form of a log cabin quilt pattern (see the Appendix on Companion Website). Tape.

Nuts and Bolts

1 First, the teacher reads aloud the first stage direction to help students visualize the set and to emphasize that the setting is the kitchen, a traditionally female space. The 1917 photo shows most of the stage, the position of the pieces of furniture, and some of the props ... Note also how the male characters seem to be ready to act and find the motives for murder—so they look readier to handle props—while the women seem paralyzed.

2 Then, each group presents the prop they have worked on. They present it visually to the class, read from the play what is said about it, and mimic what is done with/to it. Additionally, they share what they think that prop means.

3 Next, the teacher gives the students two strips of cardboard/construction paper that are to be taped to the wall, making a right angle (follow the log cabin quilt pattern). On the one to be pasted horizontally, the group writes the name of the prop. And on the one to be pasted vertically, they write its meaning(s) telegraphically.

4 The order of the presentation of props is bread and pans; towels; preserves; stove; rocker; apron; quilt; bird and birdcage (see the Companion Website for a detailed discussion of the symbolism of each prop).

5 As the groups have been writing the name and meanings of props on the strips of cardboard stuck to the wall, these props and their symbolic meanings complete a log cabin quilt pattern, whose central red square, pasted at the end by the teacher, reads FEMALE OPPRESSION, indicating the reason Minnie kills John in *Trifles* (see the Appendix on Companion Website for a sample image).

Reflection

This exercise trains students to pay close attention to props and to what's said about them in the stage directions and main text. This exercise invites discussion of the main themes of the play, which are embodied symbolically in the props, and at the same time fosters the "detective" work of students, quite in tune with the plot of *Trifles* itself. Furthermore, students learn how the meanings of props are created in performance, as they are handled, looked at, or talked about by the characters. By focusing on these aspects, students find out the theatrical means Glaspell employed to bring to the stage the theme of female oppression. They discover the kitchen as a female area where female characters feel safe and free to be themselves only when the men are not there. They are able to see that the men disregard women's work and that they move imposingly around the farm, while the women are confined to the kitchen and its props. On the whole, students learn step by step what Glaspell wanted to communicate: that women had been treated as second-class citizens and denied basic rights such as the vote and the right to a jury of one's peers. Students more readily understand the need to legislate on domestic violence and that women had to join forces to move forward. Most importantly, they witness how political ideas are conveyed through the props in performance.

SIX CHARACTERS IN SEARCH OF AN AUTHOR BY LUIGI PIRANDELLO

William Hutchings, University of Alabama at Birmingham

IN BRIEF

The use of a simple cube demonstrates the problems of perception.

PURPOSE

The exercise is intended to enhance students' understanding of the complexity of Pirandello's radically destabilizing ideas regarding "the problem of knowing"—more specifically, solipsism and epistemology. It provides an accessible introduction of these concepts on which Pirandello's play depends. Condensed for classroom use, the play's fundamental question becomes "How do you know what you think you know?"

The short answer is, of course, "You don't."

PREPARATION

A six-sided cardboard box with the name of one of the six characters written on each side (see step #6 below). This exercise also follows an introductory discussion of Pirandello's innovations in dramatic form, including, but not limited to, its metatheatricality and its deconstruction of traditional forms—such as the absence of both traditional exposition and any form of "ending"/closure for the plot.

MATERIALS

The image of the Necker cube (see the Appendix on Companion Website). This can be drawn by the instructor on the board at the beginning of class or projected on a screen from an online site. A cardboard box, any size (see Preparation).

Nuts and Bolts

This exercise demonstrates how the relativity of truth can be illustrated in the classroom with simple eight-line box-like drawing known as a Necker cube.

1 The instructor can either draw the Necker cube on the classroom's whiteboard or use an overhead projector to provide the image from an internet website. If drawing the cube on the whiteboard, the instructor has the option to lightly shade in one square for ease in discussing which panel is at the forefront or the back.

2 Once it is drawn on the classroom's whiteboard, tell the students to stare at it and concentrate on the image until "something mysterious" happens. Before long, they will see the "box" suddenly change perspective: the panel that seemed to be foremost now suddenly seems to be the background panel, and the formerly background panel now seems to be the front. As they continue to stare at it, it will probably "change back," seemingly involuntarily.

3 Next, ask the students about their experience seeing one box or the other. Eventually, most will be able to control the illusion by their own focusing on it. But that is not the point. Ask if they know which box their classmates are seeing, and if they can be certain of any one of their classmate's perspectives.

4 The point is therefore proven: the box that any individual sees is "true" *for* that particular student, but it may *not* be the same as the box that any given classmate is seeing at the same moment while staring at the same box. The box is therefore a ready example of solipsism: what you see is what you see, but it is not necessarily what anyone else is seeing at the same time.

5 A further complication: remind the students that regardless of whatever box they see at any given moment, there is really NO BOX THERE! There are only eight lines that the instructor drew on the whiteboard. Accordingly, whatever they claim to be seeing and however ardently they are sure they are right, they are actually right and wrong at the same time. Or, as Pirandello phrased it in the title to another play, *Right You Are—If You Think You Are*!

    a If time allows, introduce other examples of this phenomenon, such as the 2015 viral "What color is this dress?" or the 2018 viral "Do you hear Laurel or Yanny?" (See Resources on Companion Website.)

6 Now that the students have discussed perception in the abstract, it is time to introduce the cardboard box.

    a Again, place the name of one character on one side of the box (including top and bottom). Like a board game die, each side should have written on it one of the following: The Father, The Mother, The Son, The Stepdaughter, The Boy, and the Child (a girl).

b Inform the students that you, the instructor, know the name of the "Author" the six characters are searching for and that you have written that name and placed it inside the box.

c Select a scene with the six characters (or more, if desired), and ask for volunteers to perform it before the class. It can be brief and unrehearsed. Simply have them read the lines.

d After this first performance, have a classmate/audience member roll the cardboard box like a board game die. Whichever name lands on top will be the character who becomes the "lead role" in the same scene.

    i In other words, repeat the brief scene again, but have this character take the forefront, act with more importance, speak more loudly, "steal the scene" if you will. Tell this actor that their character is 100 percent certain they know who the "Author" is, and they should act accordingly regardless of their lines.

    ii Repeat the above as many times as you wish, where another classmate rolls the die/cardboard box, and that new character acts with the same confidence and certainty of perspective that the student had with the Necker cube, The Dress, or Laurel and Yanny. They are certain they know the name of the author that is written inside the cardboard box.

7 Once the scene has been performed three or so times, allow one of the actors to open the box and share the name of the "Author" with the class. Of course, the box will be empty. Each character is convinced that his or her story is the correct one, and that the author (once found) will be the authority of this truth. The students are led to believe that there is an authority in the box and then the professor shows them that there is no final authority of the truth.

Reflection

Like the refrain of a far-too-long ballad, a baffled chorus of "This is weird!" starts class discussion of many post-Ibsenian realist plays when students express their initial reactions to that day's assignment. Not for nothing, they discover, was the course subtitled "Outraging the Audience"—though they never imagined that the phrase might include themselves.

Epistemology and solipsism (which are entirely new concepts to many college students) cannot better be introduced than through Pirandello's masterpiece. The playwright's idea-content is no less radical in its dismantlement of supposedly "common-sense" understandings of the self in relation to society. Often his plays dramatize that there may be no single ascertainable truth, that we all contain multiple personalities, and that we can never truly know another person if we scarcely know ourselves.

This fragmentation of the supposedly unified self seems quite baffling to students—until examples from their own lives get raised (again, The Dress, Laurel vs. Yanny, etc.). Remind the students of the fragmentation of self they engage in daily: "You are not the same person sitting in English class that you are when you are at work, are you? Or at a fraternity party on Saturday night? Or in the church choir on Sunday morning?" Students themselves may be all-too-willing to address the different personalities their friends have on social media and in real time. So each of those is a mask, and *you* are wearing a mask right now! And if you are always wearing a mask, then so is everybody else—and all the time! "So how can you ever claim to know anyone else? Even your best friend, even your roommate, even a relative, or even a spouse?" Herewith, "Alarums," a Shakespearean stage direction would say.

JUNO AND THE PAYCOCK BY SEAN O'CASEY

Ryan Sheets, University of Arkansas

IN BRIEF

Create a confined performance space to illustrate how setting affects the characters' family tension.

PURPOSE

This assignment reinforces a critical fact about early twentieth-century Dublin tenement life—the milieu of O'Casey's *Juno and the Paycock*—that most performances cannot or do not emphasize: that the play is set in a very confined space. The dramatis personae of *Juno* are thus always sharing space, being intruded upon, jockeying for more space, or simply seeking solitude.

PREPARATION

View images of the Tenement Museum Dublin at 14 Henrietta Street, a social history "time capsule" that documents the 300-year history of a Georgian house built in 1748 by Luke Gardiner (see Resources on Companion Website). After introducing the play, we discuss the detailed stage directions O'Casey provides to readers, actors, and directors. Discussing the function of stage directions and O'Casey's keen sense of space and place serves as a preamble to the activity.

Providing students with data from the 1901 census, as well as news clippings discussing the September 1913 collapse of 66-67 Church Street tenements, offers further context on the poor housing conditions and exorbitant rents experienced by many Dubliners.

MATERIALS

A tape measure and a roll of masking/painter's tape. Painter's tape is recommended because it comes up easily and its bright color reinforces the special constraints the activity imposes on students.

Nuts and Bolts

1 The activity begins with the students and instructor selecting a page or two from the play to read aloud, with three or so student volunteers reading from their desks. You might have a brief discussion of the scene and how you imagined it to be performed.

2 Next, take out the tape measure and roll of bright blue painter's tape. Instead of discussing that a tenement's dimension was 225 square feet, move desks back and demonstrate exactly what living quarters of 15' by 15' would look and feel like.

3 After clearing the area and quickly taping it off, begin to repopulate the area according to the stage directions using desks, backpacks, handbags, and other items at hand. O'Casey's stage directions call for the following items to be placed on the floor: a dresser, a box of coal, a hob, a small bed, a fireplace, a table and chairs, a long-handled shovel, a frying pan and fender, and a galvanized bath. There is no need to account for items that protrude from the walls, although it's worth mentioning: the mantel shelf, a votive, a photo of the Virgin Mary, and a teapot dangling from the hob.

4 The student volunteers stand in the area and do their best to move about in accordance with the opening moments of the play. They do not need to read the lines or act out the scene at this point but simply to replicate the movements.

5 Once they have a sense of the space, ask them to read the lines aloud again, this time while replicating the movements.

As students replicate the movements described in the text, you may touch on the three points below:

1 There is so much coming and going in *Juno,* yet very little room to actually come and go. Does every movement thus become a "power move" of some sort or is there a pecking order where each character more or less knows his or her own place? How much of the tension in the play stems from characters challenging this pecking order and/or negotiating in a different, more strategic manner?

2 Given the larger size of modern stages—even small black box stages— what is gained, lost, or simply altered when *Juno* is staged in a more expansive manner or on a larger stage? What aspects of the text are reshaped by such a staging and to what end?

3 Tenement life was devoid of privacy; if the revolving door and other farcical aspects of *Juno* do not make that clear, the very stage directions do: a bed, bath, table, and food preparation area all exist side-by-side. Given this lack of privacy, how do the characters in *Juno* value or discuss privacy and how does that align with our own expectations of privacy in a digital age? If you follow teaching *Juno* with Casey's other play *Shadow of a Gunman*, a discussion on the relationship between hearsay and privacy can also prove productive.

Reflection

By having the students move about in a very confined space—within what is usually an already tight space, the classroom—the role that space and privacy have in *Juno* becomes not only visible but profoundly felt. Students develop a better understanding of the temperament of the characters, the effect that constant interruptions might have on said characters, and their continual desire for either a pleasant, distracting conversation or a brief moment of peaceful silence. Beyond that, though, what I most value about this activity is how it deepens students' performative imaginations by getting them to think about the staging choices that revival productions make. Why do many productions not hold to the 225 square-foot dimensions of a tenement? What do productions gain from a more expansive staging? What do productions lose? How do stage dimensions affect an audience's perceptions of the events onstage and how do said perceptions reframe certain thematic elements of the play? All of these questions become more resonant after this activity.

This activity works particularly well if you are teaching the other plays in O'Casey's Dublin Trilogy, *Shadow of a Gunman* and *The Plough and the Stars*, as these plays are also largely set in the tenement world. Additionally, this activity helps students better grasp what the political resonance that a continual invasion of space/loss of privacy would have to an Irish audience first watching *Juno* in 1923, an audience still experiencing the last stages of the civil war and whose memories of the Anglo-Irish War would still be very fresh.

MACHINAL BY SOPHIE TREADWELL

Kerri Ann Considine, University of Tennessee, Knoxville

IN BRIEF

Use a metronome to create a mechanical soundscape.

PURPOSE

This exercise will allow students to get a feel for the sound, timing, and atmosphere created by the play's language; see expressionistic techniques in action; and illustrate the mechanistic qualities of the dialogue and its impact on performance. Above all, it emphasizes how the mechanized environment shapes the quality of human relations and creates anxiety in the central character.

PREPARATION

Students should read the play in its entirety before class. If students do not have the text, make copies of the first scene of the play for all the readers (I usually have them read from the beginning of the play to the Young Woman's first line—the emphatic "No!").

Before the day of the exercise, I discuss expressionism and show clips from some expressionist films, including Fritz Lang's *Metropolis* (1927), F.W. Murnau's *The Last Laugh* (1924), and the clip from Charlie Chaplin's *Modern Times* (1936–*post-Machinal*), where he becomes stuck in the cogs of the machine (see Resources on Companion Website).

MATERIALS

A metronome or metronome app on a smartphone.

Nuts and Bolts

1 Distribute copies of the scene to those who will be reading.

2 Assign parts. Have the students read through the scene once with little to no direction. Moving the actors to adjoining seats can help them play off one another's energy (even if they are reading while seated). In smaller classes, having the students sit in a circle works well, as everyone can see everyone else and they are all close together. In larger classes, bringing the actors to the front of the room (or together somewhere in the room) helps the reading keep its momentum.

3 Discuss the quality of the language (i.e., truncated, staccato speech or "telegraphese") and how this type of dialogue is typical of expressionism, which focuses on the effect or sound of language over textual meaning.

4 Discuss the mechanisms of the office (e.g., the environment, the roles, the tone, the atmosphere) and how this is reflected in the characters, their "props," and the dialogue.

5 Have the students read through the scene again, this time accompanied by the metronome. Partway through the scene, slightly increase the speed of the metronome. If appropriate, you could increase the speed again as the scene gets closer to the end. Two suggested places to increase speed are the entrance of Mr. Jones and the entrance of the Young Woman.

6 After the second reading, ask the actors how the second reading compared to the first. Ask the audience members how they felt watching the scene with the metronome.

7 Use this comparative question to lead a discussion on what the metronome adds to the scene and how and why the soundscape is important. This exercise is a useful starting place for a discussion of the language, timing, and mechanistic qualities that can be traced throughout the play.

Reflection

When I began teaching *Machinal* I found it was difficult for students to move past the episodic structure and expressionistic language and see what larger ideas this play might suggest in production. When I first did this exercise, I did it by simply having the students tap on their desks together instead of using a metronome. While the tapping worked, the metronome had a far more compelling effect on the action and added a sense of the mechanical soundscape. In the discussion, I find that both the actors and the audience members report feeling anxious, tense, and constantly poised to jump into action. It is, therefore, easier for them to relate to the Young Woman's mind-set at the start of the play and to understand her distress. I ask students about how this could be staged, and the experience of working with the metronome leads them to some interesting ideas about incorporating the office equipment and other machines into movement, costume, set, and lights. A play that used to seem inaccessible now sparks all manner of creative thoughts about staging and design.

THE HOUSE OF BERNARDA ALBA BY FEDERICO GARCÍA LORCA

José I. Badenes, S.J., Loyola Marymount University

IN BRIEF

Masking and unmasking invisible power in the play.

PURPOSE

Federico García Lorca's play *The House of Bernarda Alba* is ultimately a commentary about the invisible performance of power through gender. I want students to become aware of the artificial connections between sex and gender created by society. The construction of gender based on people's sex and the lack of visibility behind this contrived gender/sex system are worth pointing out to the students. Moreover, the way that one's culture constructs gendered behaviors and norms through essentialist models and discourse of naturalness masks the coercive power behind such definition of gender roles. This exercise, based on the use of masks, helps students to understand that gender is constructed, performative, and artificial.

By performing a scene of the play that emphasizes the dissonance between sex and gender in the character of Bernarda, I have been able to get students to better understand (1) the constructed artificiality of gender, (2) the dissociation between sex and gender, and (3) the invisible power dynamics behind the patriarchy. As the scene also stresses Pepe el Romano's invisibility, students appreciate Lorca's innovative method of illustrating how the patriarchy can maintain its power through oppression and symbolic violence.

PREPARATION

Students should read the play in its entirety having analyzed the play's context, characters, themes, and symbols beforehand. To utilize the maximum amount of class time, it is also recommended to select the participating students in advance, and ask them to meet on their own and rehearse the scene discussed below. Alternatively, the instructor may share links to the videos in advance.

MATERIALS

YouTube links to the play in either English or Spanish. A female mask to be worn by the male student playing Bernarda. It is up to the students to come up with any additional props or costumes for the performance.

Nuts and Bolts

1 Begin by showing a clip of the last scene of the play (see Resources on Companion Website). If the play is taught in Spanish, I show them Mario Camus' 1987 adaptation of the play with Irene Gutiérrez Caba as Bernarda. If the play is taught in English translation, I show them Stuart Burget's and Nuria Espert's 1991 English made-for-TV adaptation with Glenda Jackson as the matriarch.

2 Ask the students to discuss the invisibility of the male element in the play, particularly Pepe el Romano's, and how it is connected to the character of Bernarda Alba. For example: (a) Why are there no men to be seen on stage though they are constantly referenced throughout the play? (b) Though he is not seen, how is Pepe's power experienced in the play? (c) What is the clash between Pepe and Bernarda about?

3 Select eight students (seven women and one man) to act out the very last scene of the play when Adela's affair with Pepe is revealed to others by her jealous sister Martirio, leading to Adela's suicide.

   a Again, depending on time constraints, the instructor may assign these roles in advance or even meet with the students separately. Work should be done in advance with the male student playing Bernarda by suggesting he wear a grotesque female mask and some feminine elements on his clothes (not full drag). The students do not need to memorize the lines, but may either read them verbatim from their texts or improvise dialogue as they see fit. I also leave it up to them to come up with the setting, the props, etc., based on their analysis/understanding of the play.

4 The assigned students perform the skit after the clip. At the very end, after Adela's suicide has been discovered and Bernarda commands that her daughter be buried a virgin, I have instructed the student playing Bernarda beforehand to come in front of the class and pronounce Bernarda's last word "Silence" as he rips off his mask.

5 I then ask students to comment on the following:

   a Bernarda performed by a woman versus Bernarda performed by a man in half-drag wearing a female mask: What insights do you get about Bernarda by having her played by a man and not a woman? What would be the significance of the male actor wearing a female mask and that he not be in full drag?

b Pepe el Romano's invisibility: Why is the male element absent? Why is it essential that the male element, in particular Pepe, not be seen? What would Pepe represent?

c Pepe versus Bernarda: How are Pepe's invisibility and Bernarda's performance by a male connected? What is the significance of the male actor ripping off his female mask at the end for the audience to see?

d Gender and patriarchy: Are masculinity and femininity something natural, having to do with our being male and female or are they culturally conditioned and constructed by the patriarchal mind-set? If artificially constructed, how does patriarchy exercise its power to make us think it is all natural and unquestionable? How does the play teach us this, in particular the student skit? Does the power of patriarchy prevail or not at the end of the play? How so? Is there any hope for change?

Reflection

Success of the exercise depends on the following: (1) students' thorough familiarity with the play beforehand, (2) coaching the students who will perform the skit, particularly the male student who will play Bernarda, though giving them plenty of free rein in coming up with the skit, (3) providing the male student with the female mask, (4) procuring either the English or Spanish DVD version of the play for contrast, (5) having students reflect on and write about the theme beforehand, and (6) asking specific questions having to do with the performativity of gender at the end of the skit.

I base the exercise on Angel Facio's 1976 Madrid production of the play where the actor Ismael Merlo played Bernarda, whose face was heavily made up so that it looked like a mask. Doing so locates the feminine on the male performing body, thus emphasizing dissonance between "the body of the performer, the sex of the character and the gender role enacted by the character."[1] The play's strict separation of gendered spaces, the invisibility of the male element, and the performed discontinuity between body, sex, and gender put into question such binary categories as well as the presumed "naturalness" of gendered behavior.

---

[1] Paul McDermid, *Love, Desire and Identity in the Theatre of Federico García Lorca* (Norfolk: Tamesis, 2007), 182.

In the character of Bernarda, the play evidences a "masculine construction of femininity"[2] away from the male body, what Judith/Jack Halberstam calls "female masculinity." However, Bernarda's version of masculinity sadly replicates rather than challenges the oppressive masculinity associated with the patriarchy. Pepe el Romano, through his very invisibility, symbolizes this patriarchy whose power lies in its ability to replicate itself among female figures in authority. Despite Adela's attempt at freedom, entrapment into culturally constructed sex and gender roles continues at the end of the play. However, there is hope that by at least unmasking and exposing patriarchy's invisible power in Bernarda's words to the fleeing womanizer—"One of these days you will fall"—the wish may come true.

---

[2]McDermid, *Love, Desire and Identity*, 172.

OUR TOWN BY THORTON WILDER

Timothy Johnson, Marymount Manhattan College

IN BRIEF

Using an improvised ritual to create community.

PURPOSE

Thornton Wilder's play provides a timeless message about life, love, and death, set within a small New Hampshire town. The themes of connection and loss depend on the students' understanding of the deep connections that can be created within a community. This exercise performs a ritual that establishes a sense of community, helping the students to understand the play and develop a sense of comfort and connection among one another.

PREPARATION

Type up 10–20 lines of text from anywhere in the play, from a range of characters. Cut the lines of text into strips, fold them, and place them inside of a bag or hat. Instructors will need to teach students, particularly students in literature courses who do not have experience acting, the following terms before doing the exercise:

1 The fourth wall—To specifically imagine the existence of something facing the audience that is related to the scene's setting/environment.

2 Gesture—A brief motion pattern that has a clear beginning, middle, and end.

3 Side coaching—To give instructions to students while they are doing an exercise. The students should remain primarily focused on staying in the action of the exercise when the instructor speaks, not looking at them, yet using their suggestions as best they can.

MATERIALS

Strips of paper with lines on them.

Nuts and Bolts

1 Place chairs in a straight line upon a designated Performance Area in the classroom; the chairs will face the Stage. The instructor should sit in the center chair and the students will join her or him on either side.

2 Each student will pull out a line of text. Ideally, the students can memorize their pulled line of text before doing the exercise.

3 The instructor then reads aloud the following instructions:

a "Setting: The imaginary playing area is the top of a hill. From up here about two miles away one can see Main Street in Grover's Corners, NH on the 4th Side (4th Wall). Looking from one's left to right is the Congregational Church, the Town Hall, the Grocery Store and Mr. Morgan's Drug Store, followed by the Public School. The date is May 7, 1901. It's a mild day of 70 degrees in the late afternoon, 3:54 pm. Above you is a clear blue sky, without a cloud in sight. At times you can hear the song of a bird as it flies by."

b After I say "Places/Lights Up," one at a time, when the impulse hits you, enter the Performance and recite your line.

c Each student's goal is to connect with each person using the following Tactics: To Interact; To Listen; To Engage with one another using only the line you pulled as the extent of your vocabulary and spoken language.

d As you speak with one another, you may share as few or as many words from your line of text as you are instinctively led to. Using subtext, i.e., underscoring your meaning underneath the actual words you say, will enable you to clearly communicate with your seemingly limited vocabulary.

e Each person you encounter has, like yourself, chosen to come to this hill to connect. You must really see one another and choose to welcome every single person with your line of text or any portion of it.

f At times I will Side Coach. If and when I do, do not look at me … Stay in the moment! Think of my side-coaching as supportive thoughts to further assist you in achieving the goal of the exercise.

g At some point, after everyone has been introduced to one another, I will instruct you, one at a time, to teach the group an improvised gesture combined with some or all of your text. So you demonstrate it, followed by the rest of the group repeating together your gesture and spoken text.

h Next I will instruct you all to join hands and form a circle to have a conversation. Only one person may talk at a time, as you each listen and take a turn spontaneously responding with a word or two from your line of text that you sense will add to the conversation.

i Finally, I will say "It is time to leave," indicating that one student at a time spontaneously says goodbye to the group and leaves the hill by returning to their seat. After the final student has exited I will say "Blackout."

Reflection

The beauty of this exercise is twofold. During the activity, students soar within Wilder's imagined world of Grover's Corners, realizing how the ordinary dialogue points to the abstractions. Secondly, during a discussion afterwards, they are filled with having been transformed from students in a classroom into participants in a community. Wilder clearly wants the actors and audience to summon the invisible, for he instructs that props be imaginary. This directive incites the audience to conjure up the world and to hear the play from their own experiences.

Wilder's play creates a small-town community on the stage. But communities are not just geographical; a community of people can be recognized for the ways in which its members coexist and support one another. The source of this support comes from a willing decision to connect with the very folks within one's surroundings. The tactics listed under letter *c* (To Interact; To Listen; To Engage) should be explained to the students as things they need to do to achieve their goal to connect with each person. This exercise illustrates the core need of humans to be validated by others, simply by choosing to take the time "to look at one another." It is a priceless occurrence to have one's students experience a deep sense of comfort with one another. In any classroom experience, but particularly drama classes, this connection will support any upcoming process work and encourage students to play and take risks, with the assurance of their classmates' support.

Sample lines that have worked for this exercise are:

1 "Do any human beings ever realize life while they live it—every, every minute?"

2 "So I guess this is an important talk we've been having."

3 "The important thing is to be happy."

Sample gestures that students have used for are:

1 Waving one's hand.

2 Extending both arms up to the sky and then down to the side of one's body.

3 Bending at both elbows to circle one's lower arms.

This exercise touches upon "something way down deep that's eternal about every human being," as Wilder himself suggests, which is the effect that our thoughts and actions have upon one another that transcend even death, living on in hearts and minds through written and oral history, along with those of "the saints and the poets."

MOTHER COURAGE AND HER CHILDREN BY BERTOLT BRECHT

Robert J. Vrtis, Luther College

IN BRIEF

A "guess the gestus" game to understand character as an expression of a social attitude and class status rather than as a psychological entity.

PURPOSE

This exercise involves students in an active analysis of *Mother Courage and Her Children* by having them "try on" the characters from the play. In particular, students experience Brecht's intention behind "gestus" to encourage the audience to engage in broad social critique while watching the performance.

PREPARATION

Provide students with Brecht's definition of *gestus*. See the Appendix on Companion Website.

MATERIALS

Simple props can be useful in creating images. Some play-specific examples might include a small bag of coins, a pair of cups for "wine," a headscarf, helmets, a bundle of linens, a small drum, a hat.

Nuts and Bolts

1 Begin by having the students make note of the various characters both named (Mother Courage, Swiss Cheese, Yvette, etc.) and identified only as their occupation (Cook, Commander, Chaplain, etc.), and ask the students to list them in a top to bottom social hierarchy.

a Ask "Who has power over whom?" Then brainstorm a few ideas about where it was difficult to stratify people and how they ultimately made choices. Clarify the source of their power: Is it because of money, religion, or military control?

b Remember that Brecht is very concerned about the interactions and influences of militarism, capitalism, and religion in this play. Each may constitute a different source of power and they may all interact to reinforce one another. A general's power, for example, is increased if he is engaged in what is perceived to be a religiously justified war for the soul of a country.

2 The students should also note particularly strong images from the play: moments that they feel convey some important theme of the play even if they cannot yet fully articulate it.

3 Lead the students in a discussion about the term "gestus," the characters' attitude as expressed through the body and/or the voice. Begin by looking at gestus as physicality, i.e., physical movement and comportment, as well as vocal modification. Then explain that gestus conveys simple information about character type as well as emphasizes how human behavior is socially constructed, i.e., a product especially of class circumstances, cultural beliefs, and attitudes toward those around you. Helpful examples could be drawn from the service industry, such as the deferential behavior shown by cab drivers and hotel porters.

4 Remember that for Brecht, a gest does not necessarily contain a social dimension. He is, however, primarily concerned with gests that do, as those are the ones that can open up a space for social critique. After the discussion on gestus, encourage the students to brainstorm their preconceived notions of a few character types from their immediate lives (school) and cultural contexts (work, religious, or social affiliations). I find students can offer up the character types of their campus well when prompted (e.g., certain majors, clubs, organizations, teams have types associated with them). See if the students can describe the physicality or vocal signals that they believe mark someone as being in this group. They may also have ideas about elites, the working class, or other social types from a broader cultural context. Acknowledge the difficulties and inaccuracies of working with stereotype and encourage the class to be generous and productive as they describe the traits of these types.

5 Next, turn back to *Mother Courage and Her Children* and assign each group pairs of characters from the play for whom they will create a specific gestus and perform it for the entire class.

a The students will design a gestus for both characters—a way of moving, gesturing, vocalizing, and expressing an overall attitude toward the world. This will be a "guess the gestus" game of sorts, so have the groups keep their characters to themselves.

b I recommend these pairings: Mother Courage and Yvette, Swiss Cheese and Recruiting Officer, Commander and Eilif, Cook and Chaplin, Peasant and Lieutenant.

c Consider the physicality of the characters first. Here it is helpful to contrast the groups' expectations of one character against their expectations of the other. Ask, how do these characters move through space? Do they take up a large amount of the space around them or try to take up very little? Do they lead from the head? Chest? Belly? Pelvis? When they sit do they seem to own all things around them? How do they view others? How do they view the other character in this pairing? What attitude do they take toward people? Be sure to watch each other and generate ideas together.

d Once the physicality of each character is established, try vocalizations. There's no need to use lines from the text. Instead, based on your knowledge of the play so far, speak in the words you think they might use. How does this character greet people generally? How does this character greet the other character in this pairing? Which character speaks more boisterously? Quietly? Crisply? Do they use a range of pitches or stay fairly monotone?

e Finally, try as a group to create a snapshot image of these two characters. This should be a final pose that expresses the gestus of each character, taking advantage of the presence of the other character in order to more fully express their attitude to the world.

f Once the characters are established among the small groups, have each group select two people from their group to perform the gestus they have devised for each character. For each group, have both characters enter (one after the other), walk to a central place, briefly greet the audience, and then assume a final position that would be a snapshot of these characters.

6 Invite the class to guess the characters based on this performance. Then, encourage other groups to make changes or additions and have the character(s) perform again. Discuss the gestus of each character and why students make the associations they do about who the character is.

7 Finally, transition to exploring gestus as social commentary. Here you'll combine characters to make a snapshot that conveys some sociopolitical commentary brought about in the action of *Mother Courage and Her Children*.

8 You may use whatever scene you feel most benefits your class, but below I have provided an example:

a In the first scene the recruiting officer and the lieutenant size up Eilif and Swiss Cheese hoping to recruit them for the army. Create a picture in which the recruiting officer simply walks around the two, looking them up and down. If you'd like a line from the text, the officer can comment, as he does, that "these lads of yours are straight as birch trees, strong limbs, massive chests ... What are such fine specimens doing out of the army?" Now try it again, with the recruiting officer acting as if he is investigating livestock, feeling the muscles without asking permission and closely scrutinizing the sons (as you can see him doing in images from the Berliner Ensemble's 1949 production).

b Briefly discuss the issue the image is meant to address, especially what changes with the added physicality. What does it mean, for example, to treat humans as a commodity?

9 From here, you can allow the class to transition into a discussion of the images that have stuck with them since reading the play. Can they identify a gest written into the text? Do they think that a particular scene could contain a social gest? What is the social gest or political commentary being made with a given gest? What do they think the audience might perceive and can small alterations change the message. If students are having trouble describing the image, encourage them to stage it!

Reflection

This exercise provides a chance for students to address stereotypes and assumptions they hold. Such discussions necessarily have to be limited but do not avoid them. Explore how Brecht thought stereotypes were useful in communicating ideas in his work. It is also helpful to encourage an atmosphere of fun, which was so important to Brecht no matter how fraught the material he was handling. Students do not often see that side of Brecht on the page. Here is the time to show that exploring complex sociopolitical issues can still be enjoyable in its own way.

With respect to *Mother Courage and Her Children*, there are particular things to nudge the class toward in order to explore the themes of the play itself. First, it is important to remember that in Brecht's view the characters do not behave in a way that is natural (or inevitable) and, therefore, their behavior is not impossible to change. In fact, their behaviors result from their social and economic conditions, and they are fully capable of changing their behaviors.

Secondly, Mother Courage herself is a preeminent capitalist, so be sure to view this as a critique on the capitalist system. Through this character Brecht seems to ask: Is there room for compassion, kindness, love, or any of the attitudes we expect from parent to child in a capitalist system? What about between strangers, as with Mother Courage's unwillingness to sacrifice her supplies to save lives in Scene 5? Here, the instructor might find help from Brecht's own words on the play. In "From the *Mother Courage* Model," he says that the play is meant to express "that war is a continuation of Business by other means, making the human virtues fatal even to those who exercise them."[1]

Finally, Brecht is interested in the nexus of capitalism, militarism, and religion in this play. Explore the connections between these systems and how they are physicalized on stage. The students should ask how each feeds into the other, how they strain against each other, and especially how people use them for their own ends.

---

[1] John Willett, ed., *Brecht on Theatre: The Development of an Aesthetic* (Hill and Wang, 1964), 220.

LONG DAY'S JOURNEY INTO NIGHT BY EUGENE O'NEILL

Janet Roberts, Eugene O'Neill Society

IN BRIEF

Create a soundscape and visual landscape to highlight atmosphere and mood.

PURPOSE

In *Long Day's Journey into Night*, two types of substance addictions plague the characters: drugs (morphine) and alcohol (specifically, whiskey). James Tyrone and the sons, Jamie and Edmund, abuse liquor, and the mother, due to a doctor's ill-thought prescription, repeatedly leaves the room to take her morphine dosage. Her behavior throughout the course of the play becomes more dissociative as she is lost both in a drug-induced mental fog and in a hazy sense of her past. This exercise demonstrates to the students, through both sound and movement, the characterization of the mother as both a phantom to other family members and her own sense of unreality as she walks back into the ghostly past of her own memories.

PREPARATION

Arrange sound clips of a fog horn, of snoring, ship's bells ringing, a concert piano being played. Also video clips or images of the following: fog drifting, a sea's waves moving, a convent with nuns. This will create the soundscape of the play as well as a visual projection of Mary Tyrone's memories.

If interested in making topical connections, the instructor could also prepare some background information about the current opioid crisis and how it affects families. Alternatively, one might provide research about morphine prescriptions during the first part of the century (see Resources on Companion Website).

MATERIALS

Cue up the sound clips and images.

Nuts and Bolts

The exercise works with both sound and movement to create the aural soundscape and visual landscape of the play. Instruct students that the exercise will focus on Act 3 and will involve close attention to setting and stage directions that O'Neill provides.

1 Soundscape, Aural Activity: Listen to the following sounds one by one. Ask the students to express the sounds in their own words, as well as how the sounds make them feel. Draw attention to the language used in the play to describe the sounds:

  a fog horn: "mourning like a mournful whale in labor" and Cathleen's words: "it's like a banshee"

  b ship bells: "warning ringing of bells on yachts at anchor"

  c James Tyrone's snores: keep Mary awake

  d sound of concert piano being played

2 Visual Images, Characterization: Provide a characterization of Mary Tyrone. Point out the lines from O'Neill's stage directions as well as the comments others make that present a visual portrait of Mary.

  a "The strong detachment in her manner has intensified. She has hidden deeper within herself and found refuge and release in a dream where present reality is but an appearance to be accepted and dismissed unfeelingly—even with a hard cynicism—or entirely ignored."

  b "[Mary is] terribly lonely ..."

  c "She is uncertain in her walk and grinning woozily"

  d "[She] starts to walk blankly"

  e "She moves off through the front parlor."

  f Tyrone says to Mary: "(Harshly) Up to take more of that God-damned poison, is that it? You'll be like a mad ghost before the night's over."

3 Motion and Dance Enactment:

  a Sleepwalk with a partner (easy): Students close their eyes or are blindfolded and receive assistance walking around the classroom with this visual impairment in order to dramatize a person walking in a psychosis or in a dream state.

b Dancing in a trance (moderately difficult): Create a dance like motion, representing this illusion of a fantasy world of memory into which Mary has entered, enacting two scenes: (a) a young girl with the convent nuns (solo with accompaniment); (b) (solo) being a concert pianist "playing the air." Students can mime the husband and sons standing nearby, watching Mary escape into a memory, deep within herself and the contrast between the two kinds of physicality can be noted.

Reflection

Sounds are evocative and elicit memories that warn us about risks and endings. In doing this exercise, students will see how sounds and movement both contribute to the play's foreboding atmosphere and create a shadowy or confused environment, particularly around the character of Mary. A larger part of the play relies upon the family's denial: of past events or of the present reality. The characters refuse to address their failures head-on and prefer a vague or indistinct view of their problems. Mary goes one step further and chooses to dull her consciousness with morphine and inhabit a dream-like world in a drug stupor.

It is important that the students experience how this theme looks and sounds upon the stage. O'Neill creates a sound- and vision-scape replete with opaque references to fog as a way of underscoring the family members' flaws and Mary's withdrawing inward to her own memories. Ask the students to consider O'Neill's vocabulary: What could words such as "refuge," "cynicism," "dismiss unfeelingly," or "entirely ignore" imply? Other connections could and should be made; O'Neill is concerned with fog because he spent considerable time on ships before becoming a playwright. What does the shroud of a "white cloth" add to the risk in "fog" or lack of clarity in "seeing"?

In order to understand the play's tension, students need to see addiction and depression physicalized. Addiction is one reason characters cannot cope or find solutions, as is the emotional pull from the past, and the movement of walking around in a dream state or in a trance visually demonstrates how helpless these characters are. All day long the four members rehash old arguments and blame each other for past wrongs, but nothing is ever resolved because of their physical or metaphorical somnambulance. O'Neill has created descriptions of sounds and movement to suggest the quagmire of the family's dysfunction. Sounds such as the fog horn or the whale in labor should not be ignored, but can be used to illuminate for the students the intractability of the family's situation.

THE GLASS MENAGERIE BY TENNESSEE WILLIAMS

Jessie Mills, Pomona College

IN BRIEF

Students perform a monologue with music to underscore the nostalgia and burden of memory.

PURPOSE

In his opening monologue, Tom muses that "[this] play is a memory ... In memory everything seems to happen to music. That explains the fiddle in the wings." Tennessee Williams, indeed, writes a small treatise regarding the music as a character in the text. Williams elucidates, "[an] extra-literary accent in this play is provided by the use of music ... it is the lightest, most delicate music in the world and perhaps the saddest ... It serves as a thread of connection and allusion between the narrator with his separate point in time and space and the subject of his story." To better understand this idea, students will pair a section of Tom's opening monologue in *The Glass Menagerie* with music to underscore theme, character, and the performative connection between emotion and text.

PREPARATION

Students should read the play in its entirety before class, unless the instructor wishes to use this exercise as a precursor to pique students' interest in the text. In either scenario, I recommend the instructor distribute a one-page handout of the opening monologue. Instructors may also wish to indicate a small excerpt of the text that will be performed or have students choose 5–10 lines of performance within the monologue.

MATERIALS

1   A speaker system with wireless or cable connection (but if unavailable, students can use the speaker function on their devices).

2   Students' smartphones, computers, or tablets.

Nuts and Bolts

1 First, split the class into groups (as small as two and as large as ten depending upon class size).

2 Next, briefly review (or introduce) Williams' discussion of the music as a character in the text.

3 Building on Williams' discussion, ask students to find a single piece of music that delivers on Williams' directive. This should be subject to students' opinions; while the song need not match perfectly—it does not have to be the lightest or the most delicate—it should evoke the feelings for which Williams strives. Students may choose from their own music library, a streaming service, or an online recording.

4 Once a piece of music has been selected, have the students collectively stage their monologue excerpt as paired with their soundscape as a proof-of-concept. Bolstered by Williams' note that "*The Glass Menagerie* can be presented with unusual freedom of convention," I encourage students to stage their work as free from any particular restraints. It need not be grounded in realism, nor does it need to be staged as one performer. Rather, students should allow the music and text to guide their staging.

5 Next, have each group perform their monologue excerpt with their song selection. Depending on class size and the number of groups, the instructor may ask for a few volunteers but, ideally, each group should have time to present.

6 Finally, after all groups have performed, lead the students in a wrap-up discussion:

   a How did the different song selections affect the same monologue?

   b How did each selection of music either evoke or subvert Williams' direction that it is "the lightest, most delicate music in the world and perhaps the saddest." How did this affect the performance or text?

   c In what genres or conventions were the performances staged? How did that affect our understanding of the text?

d Did the music help you understand the text? Did the text help you better hear the music?

e What did each music choice tell us about Tom's character? The play?

f What did you take away from this exercise?

Reflection

In my experience, the act of testing Williams' directive in physical form is invariably rewarding. In selecting music, students are given the opportunity to develop a personal stake in the synesthetic connection between emotion (nostalgia and Tom's ever-present guilt over his mother and sister) and the text. Moreover, students often select contemporary pieces of music (or, at the very least, music that is compelling to them), affording *The Glass Menagerie* and Tom's journey immediacy and relevance.

This exercise also capitalizes on theme and character as it draws out Tom's complex and often contradictory internal struggle. Reading the text alone, students can often form simplistic judgments about Tom's character: as an unreliable narrator, as a selfish young man, a tragic hero in need of escape, etc. In performing and viewing performances of this character's experience through an embodied, emotional lens, students are faced with the complexities of his relationships, journey, and inner demons.

Not to be overlooked—the staging or "proof-of-concept" of this exercise also affords students the opportunity to briefly experience the collaborative artistic process.

DEATH OF A SALESMAN BY ARTHUR MILLER

Suzanne Maynard Miller, New York City College of Technology (CUNY)

IN BRIEF

Students write social media posts and private diary entries in the voices of the characters from *Death of a Salesman* and then perform them by reading them aloud.

PURPOSE

Arthur Miller originally considered calling this famous play *The Inside of His Head.* Miller's initial title illuminates the central struggle Willy Loman faces: the conflict between his public persona and his private self (or, what's really going on inside his head). Throughout the play, Willy is driven by the obsession to be "well-liked" and to be seen as a champion. Equally haunting to him, however, is the fear that people loathe and laugh at him behind his back. To help students understand how the Loman family members cope with Willy's unstable personality and fluctuating reality, students write social media posts (public) and diary entries (private) from the characters' points of view.

In addition to exploring the dynamics within the Loman family, students examine how each Loman enables, resists, defends, and/or dismantles the dreams and delusions that float about the household. This exercise helps students understand character development and tone and connect these dramatic elements to the play's themes. By creating and then performing the characters' social media posts, as well as their private diary entries, students have the opportunity to experience the range in each character's "voice." The exercise also illustrates how the type of medium we use for our self-expression often influences what we choose to express.

PREPARATION

Students should read the entire play before doing this exercise. That said, the exercise works well either as an entrée to class discussion about the play or to enhance a discussion already in progress.

MATERIALS

Writing materials.

Nuts and Bolts

1 Begin with a warm-up (either through writing or discussion). Share the original title of the play, *The Inside of His Head*, with students and ask them to do a 5–10-minute writing exercise arguing which title (*Death of a Salesman* or *The Inside of His Head*) is the better one and why.

   a To adapt this writing exercise to a discussion, ask half the class to argue that Miller's original title better represents the play. The other half must argue that *Death of a Salesman* is the better choice. Each side should back up its argument with ideas, scenes, and direct quotes from the play. Give each side some time in class to gather evidence from the text and to build an argument before the debate begins.

2 After the warm-up exercise, have the students choose a member of the Loman family to "be." Put together groups (as much as possible) that represent the family, and have the groups choose a scene or part of a scene (depending on how much time you have, how many groups you have, etc.) to perform.

3 The students then perform the scenes for the class. Lead a class discussion that explores the following questions:

   a Based on the dialogue (and stage directions), what do you think each character wants or needs?

   b Why does the character want or need this and from whom or from where does he or she hope to obtain it?

4 Next, discuss various attributes of social media platforms and have the class consider which platform each member of the Loman family would use if social media were available during the time in which the play is set. This is a good moment to explain the term "anachronism."

5 Students then write at least one social media post and one diary entry that corresponds with whichever character they were performing (in step 3).

a The posts and entries should be written in the first person and in the "voice" of the character: for example, Willy's social media posts might brag excessively about Biff, whereas his private journal entries will be more sorrowful and desperate; Linda's social media posts might have the bright and cheerful tone of a "perfect" postwar housewife (sharing a recipe she's made with the newfangled whipped cheese or tips for pinching pennies), while her journal entries may reveal extreme worry about Willy and disappointment in her boys.

b Remind students to think of the social media posts as something that will be viewed by others, whereas the diary entries represent the character's private thoughts, even though both will be shared as part of the class exercise.

c When writing the social media posts, the students should keep in mind that everything else about the Loman family remains the same; they are still a struggling lower-middle-class family in the 1950s. It's important that their diary entries and social media posts reflect what is happening in the play; in other words, entries and posts should stay close to the play's plot and themes.

d After completing the writing, students read the diary entries and social media posts aloud, and the instructor facilitates a conversation about private versus public selves as this distinction relates to the Loman family. Possible topics for discussion include the following: Willy's inner turmoil versus how he presents himself, Linda's "real" talks with her sons versus the facade she keeps up for Willy, the conflict that tears at Biff's heart and reaches a boiling point during the restaurant scene, and Happy's superficiality (does his consistent inauthenticity, ironically, make him the only authentic character?). The conversation can also be connected to the relationship between private and public selves in modern-day society.

e To end this section of the exercise, students come up with hashtags for their social media posts. Ultimately, this may lead to a discussion about how hashtags can be seen as a need for community and validation.

6 Return to the text itself and have students perform their scenes (from step #3) again. This time, ask students to pay close attention to the presence of each character's private and public persona. Suggest that students adjust their performance (emphasizing certain words and/ or inserting pauses in the dialogue) to highlight whether a character is exposing his or her public or private self at any given moment. After this second performance, the following questions may be included in a group discussion:

a What new choices did the actors make when performing the scene?

b What differences in performance and interpretation did members of the audience notice?

c Where, specifically, do the students notice the delineation between the public and private self?

d How is the text of what characters say in conflict with the subtext of what they mean?

7 To bring the exercise full circle, return to the initial question: Which title—*Death of a Salesman* or *The Inside of His Head*—is the stronger one and why?

Reflection

The nature of the two different media will help shed light on the different layers the characters inhabit (i.e., the private diaries expose the characters' demons and doubts, while social media posts make evident how the characters want the world to see them).

Writing from the characters' points of view encourages the students to make insightful and informed choices when performing the scene. Likewise, having the students share their characters' posts and diary entries before the repeat performance allows students to see where the characters overlap in terms of what they want to achieve—and where their desires are in conflict. Through the written exercises and class conversation, students explore how the playwright designs the characters' personalities and motivations to both build the play's plot and give life to its themes.

WAITING FOR GODOT
BY SAMUEL BECKETT

Ian Andrew MacDonald, Bowdoin College

IN BRIEF

Perform a hat trick to underscore how actions can fill the time for Vladimir and Estragon.

PURPOSE

Waiting for Godot can be approached from many different angles. On a surface level, it is a play about waiting and about being together and being alone while waiting. As they wait, people find actions to perform and words to say, and thus pass the time. Waiting is, in a sense, a performance. It is a performance of relationships, of emotions, of ideas, and, very concretely, of actions.

Estragon and Vladimir find many things to do to pass the time while waiting for Godot. Stage directions help us picture, then bring to life the actions Beckett imagines to fill the stage, the time, and the space while waiting. At the barest level, stage directions provide the characters with things to do to pass the time. How do these actions influence how readers and spectators understand and appreciate the characters, their situation, their relationships, and the larger sense of the play? Beckett composes very specific actions for his characters, and following them precisely creates clear choreography on the stage. What the meaning of that choreography is in the context of the play is up for discussion. Initially, though, this exercise, with the chosen passage of the text, will help students see how stage directions, particularly with a Beckett play, are as important as dialogue, and that performing the directions can help make sense of them in a way simply reading them with your eyes cannot.

Nuts and Bolts

This activity is focused on the stage directions of the hat exchange in Act 2 of *Waiting for Godot*.

1 Divide the class into small groups of three, with two actors and one stage direction reader. Each group will need three texts of the play and three hats. Go through the sequence with the three hats four or five times at least, then show the scene to the rest of the class. See what sorts of emotions and reactions can arise from or be added to the choreography while keeping up the timing of the sequence.

2 Start the reading of the scene (including stage directions, read by the designated stage direction reader) with:

    a Vladimir (*seeing Lucky's hat*) Well! [...]

3 And end—after the hat exchange stage directions—with:

    a Vladimir Then I can keep it. Mine irked me. (*Pause.*) How shall I say? (*Pause.*) It itched me. (*He takes off Lucky's hat, peers into it, shakes it, knocks it on the crown, puts it on again.*)

        Estragon I'm going.
        (*Silence.*)

4 It is helpful, when first doing this scene, for the actors playing Estragon and Vladimir to put down their texts and focus on the hats once they come to the long set of stage directions. The actors should be very clear as to which hat belongs to Lucky, which belongs to Vladimir, and which belongs to Estragon. It may be helpful to have three hats of different shapes or colors for practicing this scene (though in the play, it seems that the three hats are very similar).

a Distinguishing between the three will make following the stage directions much easier.

5 For a first pass through the directions, the reader of the directions should stand facing the actors and read the directions very slowly, giving Estragon and Vladimir enough room to carry out the directions with the hats and get a feeling for the actions they are performing. After one reading through the directions, the reader and the actors should repeat the routine again, more quickly.

6 With each pass through the directions both the reader and the actors should pick up the pace, seeking the rhythm of the hat exchange, so that it becomes like a kind of juggling game.

7 When it comes time to show the sequence to other students, the reader of the directions can stand to one side of the actors so Estragon and Vladimir can be seen clearly.

8 Ideally, there should be enough time left for several, or perhaps even all the groups of, students to show their versions of the sequence to the rest of the class.

9 After watching students present this sequence, ask the whole class what they noticed about the scene and the relationship between stage directions, action, and dialogue, particularly Beckett's relationship to stage directions.

Reflection

Students sometimes express frustration and confusion facing *Waiting for Godot*. They say that nothing happens in the play, that nobody does anything, and that the actions that do occur in the play are confusing. This exercise takes a sequence of potentially confusing directions from the play and clarifies it to illustrate how humans entertain or distract themselves from challenging problems of existence. With his stage directions, Beckett routinely specifies the actions that the characters undertake. Beckett's vision for characters is quite complete, with stage directions offering very precise movements, actions, and timings for actors and readers to consider for the characters. Performing a Beckett play often dictates a certain degree of physical constraint for the actors involved. The stage directions force actors into particular physical states and conditions that may generate emotions and give keys as to how the characters relate to one another.

Important lesson: Don't give up on a play or a scene upon first reading. Often it takes repeating and rehearsing before it starts to make sense and really live up to its full potential. In this sense a play on paper can be seen to be like sheet music: it's there, on the page, but bringing it to life and finding its rhythm and its possibilities take work and practice.

The hat sequence demonstrates several things that are very worthy of students' attention:

1 Stage directions are important, and this exercise will help students see just how precise Samuel Beckett's stage directions are. In Beckett especially, you will be rewarded for following them carefully. They lead to a very careful choreography of actions that place part of *Waiting for Godot* squarely in the tradition of clown and vaudeville performance, with the emphasis on comic timing. Are there other places in *Waiting for Godot* where the stage directions seem to convey particular meanings, where they provide insight into the lives of the characters and what they do on the stage?

2 What *Waiting for Godot* is "about" can be debated, discussed, and theorized. What the play is is a performance of waiting. With the pauses in the play in particular, the audience is made to wait too, just like Estragon and Vladimir, waiting for what comes next. The stage directions fill out the action of waiting, giving our characters things to do that may or may not mean much, but which can sometimes entertain, touch, and distract while waiting. *Waiting for Godot* includes "gags" or "bits" from vaudeville, stock games, and routines that seem to suggest some possible ways to spend time while waiting. What else do we do while waiting?

WAITING FOR GODOT BY SAMUEL BECKETT

Graley Herren, Xavier University

IN BRIEF

Performing the politics of adaptation.

PURPOSE

This exercise shows how political contexts impact the performance and reception of *Waiting for Godot*. Students examine two case studies: 1993 Sarajevo and 2007 New Orleans. Both productions used *Godot* to comment upon tensions in their communities at the time of performance. Students consider how the play both invites and resists such appropriations.

PREPARATION

This exercise can be more or less labor-intensive, depending on whether or not the instructor wants to use it as an exercise for teaching research and oral presentation. At the very least, preparation involves reading *Godot*. On the heavier end, students may research the two productions and report their findings to the class. On the lighter end, the instructor may prepare a lecture on this background information or deliver that information as a reading assignment.

MATERIALS

None.

Nuts and Bolts

1 Either through advance readings, instructor lecture, or student research/report, provide background on the Bosnian War as context for appreciating the 1993 Sarajevo production and on Hurricane Katrina as context for appreciating the 2007 New Orleans production.

2 Identify and discuss specific creative decisions made by director Susan Sontag designed to accommodate the special needs of her war-ravaged performers and audience. Consider why Sontag selected this play for performance and how she accentuated certain moments and passages as commentary on the Bosnian War and the international response (or lack thereof). Analyze the motives and impact of Sontag's substantial cuts and significant departures from *Godot* as written by Beckett.

3 Identify and discuss specific creative decisions made by producer Paul Chan and director Christopher McElroen designed to contribute to the rebuilding efforts in New Orleans after Hurricane Katrina. Consider the impact of these environmental performances of *Godot* at a crossroads in the decimated Lower Ninth Ward and on the porch of a destroyed house in Gentilly. Look at specific moments and passages that take on new meaning in this environment. Examine the production's implied commentary on the Bush administration's response (or lack thereof) to the post-Katrina crisis. Survey various audience responses to these shows.

4 Highlight the historical conditions from which Beckett wrote *Waiting for Godot*, emphasizing his role in the French Resistance and his time on the run from the Gestapo during the Second World War.

5 Guide students to look for moments in *Godot* that potentially reveal the author's or characters' political principles. Look for moments that could be read as delivering political critiques. Look for moments that resist appropriation for specific political causes. Try to figure out why this play has such enduring appeal in times and places of political strife.

Reflection

I like this exercise because it introduces students to the historically and politically specific contexts in which performances take place. As teachers of dramatic literature, we often look for ways of emphasizing the performative dimensions of texts we teach. But what often gets overlooked in those discussions is the fact that there are reasons why certain plays are selected for productions at certain places and times. Beckett's *Waiting for Godot* has frequently been staged with turmoil raging outside the theater. This exercise attempts to figure out why that is. This exercise also reminds students that producers, directors, performers, and audiences don't always check their preoccupations in the lobby along with their coats. They bring their lives into the auditorium with them, and they take the play they've just seen back out into the world as they leave. As bizarre and otherworldly as *Godot* can seem to undergraduates encountering it for the first time, I hope that this exercise helps convince them that this play is very much a by-product of and a comment upon life as it is really lived outside the theater.

THE CRUCIBLE BY ARTHUR MILLER

Deric McNish, Michigan State University

IN BRIEF

Play the game "witches and villagers" to perform the power of hysteria.

PURPOSE

This short performance activity gives the experience of mass hysteria and prompts a discussion about contemporary parallels to the Salem witch trials of 1692 and 1693. As is well known, Arthur Miller dramatized the Salem witch trials in response to McCarthyism and the "Red Scare" of the 1950s. This exercise, an adaption of the game "Werewolf," demonstrates the contagious quality of such fearmongering.

PREPARATION

The exercise is an adaptation of the party game "Werewolf" that has many variations. The instructor must prepare cards for the number of students in class. Traditionally, 90 percent of the cards would say "villager" and would designate the cardholder as the villager. The remaining 10 percent would assign the players to be "werewolves." For this version of the game, however, we will instead use "witches and villagers" and 100 percent of the cards will be marked with a "V" for "villager." There are two sets of instructions: the rules you tell the students and the real rules.

Students read the play. The instructor may also wish to assign research or give an introductory lecture on McCarthyism.

MATERIALS

Index cards or slips of paper all marked with a "V" for villager.

Nuts and Bolts

1 Prepare an index card or slip of paper for each student in the class.

   a Mark all of them with a "V" for "villager."

2 Tell the students that everyone is either a villager (with a "V") or a witch (with a "W").

3 Have the students look at their card to learn their identity, then they should conceal it and make sure nobody knows which they are.

4 There are two phases of the game: night and day. We begin at night. Tell everyone to close their eyes and put their heads down.

5 Announce that all the witches should quietly open their eyes and make themselves known to each other. Of course, nobody will open their eyes.

6 Instruct the witches to agree quietly upon someone to eat, then point to that person.

7 Wait a moment, then tell everyone (make a point of saying "including the witches") to close their eyes and put their heads down.

8 Announce that it is now daytime and tell everyone to open their eyes.

9 Choose a student at random and announce, "You've been eaten by the witches!"

   a That student reveals their card (which will be a "V") and can no longer speak for the rest of the game.

10 The class then must discuss and decide who they think is a witch (and remember: the instructor has to keep up the ruse for the class that witches are present).

   a When they agree, they point to that person and say, "Burn the witch!"

   b The accused student turns over their card (also revealing a "V"), then joins the student who has been eaten.

11 Then we return to nighttime and repeat the charade (steps 4–8).

12 Continue for about 10 minutes, until all students have been eliminated or until they realize that you haven't been playing fair, i.e., once they catch on that everyone is a villager.

13 The next step (after apologizing for the subterfuge) is to lead a discussion that connects the exercise to *The Crucible*.

   a What made you decide to accuse someone?

   b Why did you go along with those accusations?

   c Who were the leaders and how did that dynamic arise?

   d Did they notice anyone performing a certain way, either taking on an accusatory stance or exhibiting behavior that misled others to accuse them?

e Did this game feel like hysteria?

f How does *The Crucible* connect to McCarthyism?

g What's going on in the world today that connects to witch hunts and mass hysteria?

h What contemporary examples of "court of public opinion" help shape their understanding of the text?

Reflection

Understanding mass hysteria in a personal and meaningful way is essential to understanding *The Crucible*. I do this fun exercise as a way to begin discussion after the students have read the play. As with all plays, *The Crucible* was meant to be seen, not just read. Anyone who has had the privilege of watching a good production of this play understands the almost unbearable tension that the audience endures as they watch the innocent be accused. Reading the play doesn't provide what Ben Brantley calls "raw terror," but this game cultivates a feeling of unease in a safe and playful way. It works well in a traditional classroom because it can be done without movement, although freedom of movement can help. I've seen quiet groups get very animated during this exercise. I also empathize with the students once they realize the game was "fixed," but they understand it serves a purpose. If time allows, you may decide to play "for real" at the end of the class.

CAT ON A HOT TIN ROOF
BY TENNESSEE WILLIAMS

Cameron Watson, Antaeus Theatre Company, Los Angeles

IN BRIEF

Turn up the heat on the characters to understand their dramatic suffering.

PURPOSE

At the core of *Cat on a Hot Tin Roof* is a family's balancing act between the family members communicating truthfully and protecting their deepest desires. They "walk around" certain taboo subjects as both a defense mechanism and a manipulation device. Like a "cat on a hot tin roof," each character is doing something that is hurtful to them both physically and emotionally, and yet each is desperate to remain in this painful place for as long as they can. In a performance of this play, it is crucial for the actors to understand how each line has a certain "heat" beneath its feet, a certain pain, discomfort, sense of suffering. And yet, each character has the resilience of a cat, that is, a sense—be it true or false—of having nine lives. Ultimately, this exercise is about understanding the footing of each character—be it firm or teetering—and how to bring that sense of instability into the performance.

PREPARATION

Students should read the play in its entirety before class.

MATERIALS

None.

Nuts and Bolts

1 Assign each student a specific character.

a Depending upon the size of the class, you may group them all by the same name (e.g., a group of all Maggies, a group of all Bricks, etc.) or you may place the students in groups of eight and assign each one a character.

2 Ask the students to make a list of adjectives describing their character's physical appearance as they imagine it. Look for clues in the text.

3 Ask the students to make a list of adjectives describing their character's emotional life as they imagine it. Look for clues in the text.

4 Have the students pick one line from their character's dialogue. The shorter the better. For example, "I've got the guts to die," or "Why is it so damn hard for people to talk?" or "I'm not good," or "I'm a rich man." The line should be easy to memorize.

5 Have the students share their findings either with each other or the class as a whole.

6 Create a space in the classroom for the students to walk about safely. Move the desks to the sides or, if not possible, consider using them as obstacles.

7 Encourage the students to move about the space without any idea of where they are going or why they are moving. Tell them to be very free. Clear their head of any expectations or results they might want to reach for. Move their whole body—arms, hands, legs, torso, head. Travel to all corners of the space, aware of others, but not worried about what they are going to do.

8 Now, based on the adjectives they came up with, have the students begin to walk around the classroom imagining that they are the character.

a How might they walk in a way that reflects some of those adjectives? Fast or slow? Straight or meandering? Broadly, delicately, lightly? Have the students try several different styles until they arrive at one that most feels like the character to them.

9 Once the students are walking around as their character, tell them to stop when they encounter another student. Approach this other student and say their line directly to them.

a Both students should stop, and each should say his or her one line to the other, then resume walking. At first, there will be a little laughter and playfulness, and that is fine. But after a few exchanges, the students start to fall into a rhythm.

10 After several of these exchanges, tell the students that the ground beneath them is heating up. It's getting warmer.

a How might this influence their walk? Do they move faster? Do they pick up the feet a little higher?

b As they continue to walk and speak their lines when they encounter another student, inform them that the ground is getting warmer and warmer, until it is painfully hot.

11 Once the ground is as hot as possible, have everyone stop. Tell them to plant both feet firmly on the ground.

a Feel the excruciating heat rising slowly through their shoes, their feet, their ankles, their legs. Imagine it is painful and agonizing, and yet, they must stand still.

12 Inform them the ground is so hot, they must actually balance on one foot.

13 Give them a moment to focus on what they are feeling both physically and emotionally in this moment.

14 Now, feeling all this heat beneath them, have each student say their line a final time, one at a time, while balancing on one foot on an incredibly hot roof.

Reflection

Students often have fun with the silliness of this exercise, but also come to realize the seriousness of it. By imagining the ground beneath them as hot, they begin to understand the pain each character constantly feels. By balancing on one foot, they also begin to empathize with the instability each character faces. By doing both, they begin to connect with the characters in both a physical and emotional way.

In working on deeply emotional and complicated pieces like *Cat on a Hot Tin Roof*, it is very important for students to clear a space for their own performative imaginations. Through working on this play in class and in production, I have discovered that we all tend to reach for what is expected or what it "should be like." For example, a student might think, "Oh, this is the famous scene in Act 1 between Maggie and Brick and it is supposed to go like this …" Since Williams' play is iconic and comes with iconic images from past productions and film versions, it is very important that the students connect with the truth of what these characters feel.

Creativity is born from freedom. I know that to be true. This exercise is a good way to "let go of expectations" and to get out of your own head and out of your own way. Once you have cleared that path, your emotional well is much more available because it is coming from you and your own truth, and not some "idea" of what Maggie and Brick must feel like. By walking around "on a hot tin roof," the students can imaginatively walk in their character's shoes and begin to understand their pain, instability, and longing.

ENDGAME BY SAMUEL BECKETT

Lindsay Adams, The Catholic University of America

IN BRIEF

Perform the stage directions to experience the theme of constraint.

PURPOSE

This exercise will help students to understand the integral way Samuel Beckett uses stage directions in his work, particularly in this play where the sense of events and even life itself coming to an end is paramount. It encourages students to explore how stage directions relate to authorial intent within a script.

PREPARATION

Students should read the play in its entirety before class.

MATERIALS

Writing implements and paper. Collect "found objects" in the classroom to designate specific props as indicated in the script. The more absurd the better—for example, using a stapler as the telescope, an empty chair as the ladder, or a jacket as the handkerchief. Or, if the instructor prefers, he or she may bring in the actual items referenced in the script.

Nuts and Bolts

1 Set the room up for small groups with a cleared performance space at the front of the classroom where students will present.

2 Start the exercise by separating students into small groups (three to six in each) and assigning them the character Clov or Hamm.

a An easy, quick, and impactful way to do the exercise is to assign different scenes and characters to different groups. For example, one Clov group could look at the character's stage directions on the first seven pages, while another Clov group looks at the next seven pages, etc. The same for multiple Hamm groups.

b Another option, which takes a little longer, would be to assign each group both of the characters of Clov and Hamm for specific pages and then vary the page assignments by group.

c If you are not able to have students cover every page of the play, that is all right. However, it is essential for them to see the actions Clov and Hamm take at the beginning and end of the play, so prioritize the first and last pages of the script.

3 Task the students with finding every piece of stage direction that refers to their character in those pages. They may highlight them in their text or write them out (in order) on a piece of paper.

a Ask them to pay special attention to any specific character movements.

b Ask them to identify and discuss any change in emotional state indicated in the stage directions.

c Ask them what they think the stage direction is saying about the character.

4 Once they are finished, get two volunteers from each group to enter the performance space at the front of the classroom. One will read the stage directions out loud and the other will act out the stage directions without the dialogue.

a Start with Clov or Hamm from the first pages and then continue that character's physical journey through the stage directions to the end of the play. Follow with the remaining character and repeat the process.

5 Ideally, the instructor should highlight the power shift that has occurred throughout the play, noted chiefly in the difference between the beginning and the ending tableaux.

a Ask if students recognize the power shift that occurs throughout the play. Point out to them the difference between the image of Clov standing and waiting by the door at the beginning of the play while Hamm is seemingly asleep, covered by a sheet, and the image at the end of the play: "Clov, dressed for the road. Panama hat, tweed coat, raincoat over his arm, umbrella, bag. He halts by the door and stands there, impassive and motionless, his eyes fixed on Hamm, till the end … [Hamm] covers his face with handkerchief, lowers his arms to armrests, remains motionless. Brief tableau."

6 After the performance part of the exercise, do a reflection with the students about what that experience was like. What conclusions did students draw from watching the actions? Ask whether these conclusions differed from the ones they held from just reading and analyzing the text?

7 Optionally, you can finish the exercise with another 10-minute discussion about how we view stage directions. Hand out an article on the American Repertory Theater production of *Endgame* directed by JoAnne Akalaitis in 1984 and have a brief discussion on authorial intent and why the production sparked controversy (see Resources on Companion Website).

Reflection

This exercise is about identifying and performing the constraints placed upon the characters who methodically repeat the same movements, from Hamm's insistence on being in the exact center of the room and opening then folding his handkerchief to how many steps Clov takes. Just as the term "endgame" refers to the concluding stage of a chess game when only a few pieces remain, there is a specific type of "chess piece" movement each of the characters can make. This movement limitation exhibits itself not only in the macro—where characters are unable to make definitive choices or change their circumstances (e.g., Nell and Nagg being stuck in their trash cans) but also in the micro—where character gestures are exactly described in minute detail and seem endlessly to repeat themselves.

While intensely specific in its stage directions, *Endgame*'s theme of mankind's limitations is remarkably expansive. The play speaks to all the different ways humans can be confined: whether it be a physical or mental limitation, such as imprisonment, disability, or infirmity, or the kind of personal limitations we face in our day-to-day lives, such as suffocating relationships or dead-end jobs. The repeated actions the characters take that seem to lead nowhere are not so different from the kind of routines that we all follow in one way or another.

Understanding this play requires the reader/audience to experience these physical limitations for themselves. In watching a performance, they experience this physical limitation as audience members. They are placed in one chair, they must stay seated, and they are not allowed to move. If they are reading the play, to fully understand it, they need to experience the constraints of movement (and performance) that these characters face. That personal experience of the confining world where the characters live allows students to recognize the different ways in which we are confined in our own lives.

THE BIRTHDAY PARTY
BY HAROLD PINTER

Christopher Wixson, Eastern Illinois University

IN BRIEF

Create an atmosphere of menace with an uninvited guest.

PURPOSE

The biggest challenge to teaching Pinter's "comedies of menace" is communicating to students how the plays "feel" in performance. This exercise provides students with an experiential introduction to hallmarks of Pinter's dramaturgy—silence, menace, and what Pinter referred to as the atmosphere of the "weasel under the cocktail cabinet."

PREPARATION

Before the session, I arrange for an adult "Guest" with whom the students are not familiar to do a little acting. The instructor can stage this exercise at the end of the session before the students read the play or at the beginning of the first session on the first two acts of the play.

MATERIALS

None.

Nuts and Bolts

1 The instructor begins by conducting general business (e.g., lecturing about the syllabus, schedule, upcoming/current assignments, or even providing background about the playwright). There will need to be enough "ordinary class talk" to sustain 5 or 6 minutes.

2 After 2 or 3 minutes, the Guest enters the classroom and stands still by the door. Silently, she or he may look at the students or the floor or the clock but not the instructor. She or he should not seem agitated or visibly upset; nonetheless, she or he is there with a purpose and appears serious, perhaps concerned.

3 The instructor, speaking throughout, never acknowledges the Guest's presence, and the Guest never looks at the instructor. After a minute or so, the Guest walks to the chalkboard/whiteboard and calmly, methodically, and slowly writes the word "PLEASE."

4 Then, the Guest walks out of the classroom. Again, the instructor never acknowledges him or her and merely continues to deliver whatever the content is just as on any regular class day. Throughout, the instructor continues talking as if nothing is happening/has happened.

5 Once the Guest has departed, the instructor may then begin the discussion of the play. Again, act as if nothing out of the ordinary has happened. The instructor should see how long they all can maintain normalcy until a student interrupts and questions what just happened.

6 If students do not interject, then the instructor may finally ask, in the context of discussing the play, "Have any of you ever experienced a sense of menace?"

7 Of course, the instructor eventually admits to staging this exercise and then leads the students in a discussion of their experience.

Reflection

The first signs of student discomfort usually express themselves as giggles and whispering, and it is imperative for the instructor not to "break character" and to continue speaking. The noise level steadily increases often drowning out the instructor (although it often comes in waves). When the instructor deems the exercise to have made its point, she or he can then ask the students to describe how they felt and identify specific elements of the "performance" that engender those feelings.

If students have read some or all of *The Birthday Party* already, the instructor can ask them to make connections to choices the playwright makes to engender a similar reaction in his audience and discuss why he makes those choices. Obviously, the appearance of the Guest in class correlates directly to the arrival of Goldberg and McCann, immediately transforming the dynamics and energy of the boarding house into something sinister.

I ask students to identify moments in Act 1 (particularly in Stanley's lines) that indicate something more deeply disturbing is about to happen, and students often cite Stanley's drum solo at the end of the act as a moment of interpretive doubt and apprehension similar to the Guest's classroom visit.

Of course, the experience of the class exercise works well with Act 2 in which the banal ritual of the party turns into a sustained sequence of fear and aggression and culminates in violence. While students usually are still unsure intellectually what to make of the play at this point, their experience with the classroom Guest makes them self-aware that their anxious confusion is a deliberate choice by Pinter and thus provides a pathway from audience experience toward thematic discussions. For instance, students will note how the competing kinds of authority between instructor and classroom Guest as well as the ambiguity of the Guest and her or his situation resonate with uncertainty about identities and motives among the characters in the play.

Students often describe "shifting" views on the Guest's visit as it happens and the discomfort attendant on not knowing the true story—exactly the state in which Pinter keeps his audience and precisely the distinctiveness of his dramaturgy. Doing a close reading of the party scene as a class enables students to mark those shifts in the play and their effect on their relationship to the characters and what is happening in front of them.

If students have not started the play before the classroom activity, the instructor can ask students to read for the choices Pinter makes to create that unique atmosphere in Acts 1 and 2 and be prepared to discuss why he does so. Besides communicating the "menace," this exercise leads into other areas pertinent to Pinter plays, as student comments have led me to see, including gender issues depending upon the gender identification of the Guest and instructor. Oddly enough, though, only one student in more than twenty years of doing this exercise has actually left the classroom to tend to the guest.

RHINOCEROS BY EUGENE IONESCO

Rebecca Cameron, DePaul University

IN BRIEF

Use of sound effects to disrupt rational thought and establish thematic background.

PURPOSE

This exercise helps students understand the role of sound effects in creating the combination of humor, danger, and existential angst that often characterizes absurdist drama. In the play *Rhinoceros*, with its emphasis on what Ionesco called "collective hysteria and the epidemics that lurk beneath the surface of reason,"[1] the trumpeting sounds of the animals reinforce the growing power of the rhinoceroses as well as their fundamental irrationality. The exercise helps students recognize how the rhinoceros' sound effects modulate from frightening "noise" to "melodious" over the course of the play, suggesting the disturbing appeal of the collective movement as it gains momentum.

Ionesco's *Rhinoceros* includes a variety of sound effects that convey the presence of rhinoceroses in town. Early in the play, characters respond to the sound of a rhinoceros "galloping" and "trumpeting" across the stage, a sound that becomes "deafening" by the middle of Act 1. This sound effect is intriguing, in part, because it seems to be an imagined sound: rhinoceroses snort, growl, and even squeak and cry, but they typically do not "trumpet." It seems likely that Ionesco had in mind the sound of elephants trumpeting; the French term he uses, *barrissement*, is commonly associated with elephants.

---

[1] Eugene Ionesco, *Notes and Counter Notes: Writings on the Theatre*, trans. Donald Watson (New York: Grove Press, 1964), 199.

PREPARATION

Students should read the play in its entirety before class. It is also recommended that the instructor give a brief introduction to absurdist drama and/or assign short excerpts from Martin Esslin's *Theatre of the Absurd*.

MATERIALS

This exercise as written requires a computer on which to play a sound effect that can be heard by the entire class, but it could be modified to require no technology if students are instructed to design and produce their own sound effects orally. Smartphones are also an option.

Nuts and Bolts

1 Set up classroom technology so the instructor can play a sound effect that will convey the sound of a rhinoceros galloping and trumpeting. A possible modification of this exercise might be to ask students to design and produce their own sound effects rather than using existing recordings. Either way, have the sound effect cued up before the exercise begins.

2 Ask seven student volunteers to read the parts of Berenger, Jean, Logician, Old Gentleman, Waitress, Proprietor, and Grocer's Wife. Ask some of them to sit in pairs (Berenger and Jean together, and the Logician and Old Gentleman together).

3 Begin the reading with Jean's line near the middle of Act 1, "So you're giving up, just like that?," all the way through to where the cat is crushed by the rhinoceros. Do *not* play the sound effect during this first reading.

4 Have the same students repeat the scene as above, only this time, when they get to the appropriate place in the dialogue ("You're already making progress in logic"), play the rhinoceros sound effect at a loud volume, and continue to play it over and over, potentially louder and louder.

5 Follow the reading with a group discussion of the significance and placement of the sound effect, and how the two performances differed.

Reflection

This exercise made me more aware of how prominently sound figures are in creating the impression of a rhinoceros' invasion or epidemic on stage.

Ionesco calls for a wide variety of rhinoceros-related sound effects in his script, ranging from chaotic and destructive to melodious. These sound effects contribute to the common reading of the play linking the rhinoceros' invasion to the Nazi occupation of Europe, but they also lead students to consider the broader existential possibilities of the play—particularly that the idea of an irrational world that cannot be explained by reason, logic, or conventional clichés.

Students can see immediately the failure of logic through the Logician's ridiculous arguments about cats, which is further enhanced through the ironic timing of the sound effect immediately following his remark that "You're already making progress in logic." I have found, however, that my students have more difficulty seeing the problems in Jean's advice to Berenger when reading the play, since his advice to cut down on his drinking and expand his cultural experiences seems like sound insight. Reading the scene aloud helps them hear the echoes taking place between the two conversations on stage, and hearing the bizarre and intrusive sound effect helps them recognize that neither form of instruction is particularly helpful in the face of the baffling strangeness of the conflict. Of course, the students also find the sound effects humorous, which helps them experience the unsettling humor of absurdist drama in a legitimate context.

A RAISIN IN THE SUN BY LORRAINE HANSBERRY

Carrie Klewin Lawrence, 3rd Space Theatre Collective

IN BRIEF

The use of props to reveal subtext as well as character tension.

PURPOSE

Props influence performance, especially the performance of subtext, and *A Raisin in the Sun* is rife with issues simmering below the surface. The family members have unrealized dreams that they hide from each other, but their dreams manifest themselves in seemingly petty arguments and daily struggles among the characters. By distilling a scene to a main objective, one prop, and a phrase, students will explore the basic subtext of the play in preparation for performance. They will begin to understand the allusion to Langston Hughes' question "What happens to a dream deferred?"

PREPARATION

Students should read the play completely before starting the exercise. It is necessary to identify the dreams/objectives of each of the characters, especially those of Ruth and Walter, and to recognize how the playwright has communicated those ideas.

MATERIALS

Copies of the scene. Table, chairs, plate. Fork, napkin, cup, optional.

Nuts and Bolts

1 After the students have read the play, ask them to identify the dreams and aspirations of each of the characters. Ask students to identify one clear objective for each character. What do they want from the other character? Where are the characters succeeding, and where are they failing in the pursuit of these dreams? Ask the students to write three or four simple "dream" (super-objective) sentences for each character specifically identifying these dreams. For example, Ruth might say "I want happiness for our family," or "I want another baby" while Walter might say "I want my own business" or "I want to be my own boss."

2 After a general discussion, choose scenes for the students to study involving a prop that is significant for the subtext it represents. The following exercise specifically focuses on the struggles of Ruth and Walter, but other scenes involving symbolic use of props to reflect character aspirations are:

a the dress/fabric Asagai gives Beneatha to encourage her to marry him and go to Africa; he wants marriage, but Beneatha wants self-actualization;

b the contract Lindner leaves with the family to request they not move into the neighborhood; he wants racial segregation, but the family wants a home;

c the plant Mama has that needs some light; she wants her family to grow—to be the "harvest" of her hard work.

3 Ask for two volunteers to play out loud the scene in Act 1, Scene 1, between Ruth and Walter. Take it from Walter's line "That's my Boy" to Walter's line "We one group of men tied to a race of women with small minds." Discuss the large focus on eating (or not eating) eggs.

4 Ask the students to select one "dream" statement/objective from step 1 to focus on while exploring the scene.

5 Using the plate as a prop, and only the phrase "eat your eggs," ask the actors to play the scene. How can they use the phrase "eat your eggs" and the plate to get what they want? What observations can be made about the behavior of the characters, the use of the prop, and their objectives? Do they push, pull, play tug-of-war, dump, or slam the plate? Students should be encouraged to stay seated at first and focus only on using the phrase from the text and the prop to communicate. Curiously, as much as this is a text-based exercise, large silences may emerge and should be allowed and investigated.

The exercise can be expanded to create additional staging by using additional props, standing or moving about the stage. In addition, other lines can be explored and should be taken directly from the text. Lines can also be changed slightly for a more personal/realistic interaction. For example, Ruth might say "eat your eggs," while Walter might respond "eat my eggs," or he might respond instead with another of his actual lines of text. At this stage it is important that the line of text for each character is applicable to the character and easily repeatable.

6 Next, repeat the scene with each character using just one of the "dream" statements, such as Ruth's sentence "I want to have a baby" and Walter replying, "I want to be my own boss." Repeat as needed to explore each objective. In both steps 5 and 6, encourage the students to make and maintain eye contact. How does the subtext and use of the prop change with each phrase used?

7 After the actors explore the scene with only simple phrases and a prop, ask them to run the scene again using all of the actual text and the prop(s) as desired/indicated in the scene. How did the exercise affect the actors? What did they discover about the underlying struggles of the characters? Is the subtext obvious? Are the objectives of the characters clear? Is the prop being handled in an effective manner? To enrich the scene, repeat the exercise as needed alternating between a phrase from the text and "dream" statements until the relationships, objectives, and movements become clear.

Reflection

Hansberry originated the title for her play from Langston Hughes' poem "Harlem (A Dream Deferred)." Each of the characters in this play speaks about specific dreams: Mama wants her son to reflect the values of his parents, Beneatha aspires to be a doctor, etc.

Discuss the specific conflicts in each of the scenes—what is said and what is not said by the characters in reference to their dreams and goals? It is important to point out to the students the real subject of the argument may not be the topic of "eggs" or a piece of paper but may be something simmering below the surface. It's a good time to ask, "Why don't people really say what they mean?" Can we truly articulate our own dreams clearly, and what happens when they come in conflict with another person's dreams?

In the above example, the prop of the eggs serves as a metaphor for the conflict between the characters. Having characters struggle over a prop while announcing their dreams aloud gives the prop additional meaning. As the students either force the prop onto another character or try to take it away, they will exhibit instinctive human behavior and simultaneously illuminate the basic objectives and subtext of the scene.

Alternatively, this exercise can also be used to create blocking early in a rehearsal process by momentarily freeing the actors from the text, allowing them to focus on creating a physical score that will serve as a base from which to build upon. By removing the pressure to remember and use all of the words, this exercise encourages students to create their own staging and movement based on impulse, which they will remember since they created it and which the instructor or director can adjust as needed. By allowing the actors to focus solely on the manipulation of a prop, while pursuing a simple objective and repeating one phrase from the text, the actors will intuitively discover the underlying messages of those words and actions, leading to believable actor interpretations.

Finally, all props have meaning and the way that characters use them carry strong messages. Every prop required and used in *A Raisin in the Sun* has a story to tell. Encourage the students to look for the symbolism and metaphors contained within each prop and to explore the subtext of how each of the props is used by the characters.

THE ZOO STORY BY EDWARD ALBEE

Peggy Stafford, Purchase College, SUNY

IN BRIEF

Create and perform a zoo story to explore the themes of loneliness, social status, and alienation.

PURPOSE

I have often found when teaching *The Zoo Story* that students are perplexed and disappointed when they get to the end of the play, and Jerry fails to tell his zoo story. This exercise allows students to imagine what might have happened at the zoo and then, through performance, experience new dynamics in the play when the story is included.

PREPARATION

Students should read the play in its entirety before class. Ask them to note specific references to animals within the play, and to jot down thoughts and associations related to these references.

MATERIALS

Two chairs to serve as a bench.

Nuts and Bolts

1 Organize the students into partners (Partner A and Partner B).

2 Ask partners to tell each other a story about animals—maybe a favorite pet or a story about a wild animal (a squirrel, deer, mouse, etc.). Maybe their first trip to the zoo. As Partner A tells a story to Partner B, ask

Partner B to be totally distracted, not listening (on their phone, looking around the room, avoiding eye contact). Now have Partner B tell a story to Partner A, but this time Partner A is listening intently. Be sure to instruct students to commit to their storytelling and listening/or not listening.

3 Open up a classroom discussion:

   a What was the difference in the experience? Performance?

   b What does it feel like when we're telling a personal story and nobody is listening?

   c Why do we tell stories? Why do we want people to listen?

4 Ask students to return to their partners and share moments in the play where animals or stories about animals were referenced. Ask them to reflect:

   a What do these references tell us about the characters?

   b How do they connect to the play's themes of loneliness and alienation?

   c Have partners share the connections they made with the class.

5 Read aloud together a section of Jerry's dog story, starting with "And it came to pass that the beast was deathly ill ... " and ending with the line "... I hoped that the dog would understand."

6 Lead a class discussion that explores the following questions:

   a What does the story tell us about Jerry's life?

   b How do the story of the dog and other stories in the play draw these two characters, who wouldn't normally interact, into close contact?

   c How does Jerry's promise of a zoo story keep Peter engaged?

7 Read aloud together a section of the final scene of the play, starting with Jerry's line, "Very well, Peter, we'll battle for the bench, but we're not evenly matched." Stop at Jerry's line, "Oh, Peter, I was so afraid I'd drive you away. You don't know how afraid I was you'd go away and leave me. And now I'll tell you what happened at the zoo."

8 Have students return to their partners and imagine together what happened to Jerry at the zoo.

   a They can either create bullet points to describe the events as they unfold or work individually to write the zoo story as a short monologue (long paragraph).

   b For students who do not have a lot of experience improvising or telling stories in front of an audience, I would recommend you have them write their zoo story down and read it. Also, limit the length of the story. Jerry's just been impaled by a knife, and when the story goes on for too long the action becomes implausible. You only need to read the stage directions aloud the first time through the scene. After that you can skip them, letting the students perform the action.

9 Create a space in the classroom for the setting: a bench in Central Park.

10 Ask for a volunteer partner team to perform the final scene of the play, incorporating the zoo story they just created into the scene.

    a If the students wrote a short monologue they will read what they wrote. If the students wrote bullet points they can use these to improvise the story.

    b They should insert the story after Jerry says, "And now I'll tell you what happened at the zoo."

    c After inserting their own zoo story/monologue, the team should resume the scene as Albee wrote it, picking up with Jerry's line, "I think … I think this is what happened at the zoo … I think," and continuing through to the end of the play.

11 After at least four performances of the scene with the student-generated story inserted, stop and discuss what effect hearing Jerry's zoo story has on the play.

    a Does it tell you anything new about Jerry?

    b Does it add to the story in any way?

    c Do you think that the absence of the story tells us more about Jerry's desperate need to connect with another human being?

    d In what ways does the play itself become Jerry's zoo story?

Reflection

This exercise is meant to open up a conversation about the power of storytelling. I find that students discover, through performance, that the play doesn't really need a "zoo story"; that, in fact, the absence of the story more pointedly drives home the play's themes of loneliness and alienation. Of course, there are some students who believe that a zoo story would make the play more complete. They feel cheated at the end when the story is not delivered. In fact, Albee is quoted as saying that he initially wrote "a half page of rather good stuff" for Jerry's zoo story, but that he had to "trim back an aria-like moment" because he felt it was implausible that Jerry would deliver this story "with a knife buried deep in his belly, probably slicing the aorta." He said, "I took a knife of my own to it and brought it down to a proper two sentences."

At the core of this play is Jerry's need to tell his story. Two strangers, from different socioeconomic backgrounds, meet in a park and talk. They live in a society that doesn't value community or a shared sense of belonging. In his desire to be seen and heard, Jerry breaks a social barrier and strikes up a conversation with Peter. This is his attempt to survive in a world that feels absurd and void of meaning or purpose, like that of an animal in a zoo. And he does so through storytelling.

The ability to tell stories distinguishes us from animals. Stories allow us to contextualize and better understand our lives, the world, and those around us. Jerry draws Peter to him by telling him stories about his life and also by the promise of his zoo story. It is this promise of a story that creates a bond between the two men and what keeps Peter in the conversation. Which is why Jerry never tells the story or fulfills his promise. If he were to do this, there would no longer be a reason for Peter to stay engaged. And the real story that Jerry actually wants to tell Peter is the story of his life, that is, how he feels alone, caged-in, and alienated in a society that doesn't value him. Once that story is told, Jerry is left depleted and spent. He has given Peter everything that he has left: the story of his life. When Peter can't quite comprehend or chooses not to hear this story, Jerry authors the end of his own narrative and demise.

In my experience with this exercise, I find that by looking closely at the references to animals in the play, students make connections about their own humanity and what separates them from animals. They ask questions about the barriers they put up in their lives that separate them from others. You can draw a further analogy to the theater as a kind of zoo: How do we as an audience look in on those caged characters? Peter as the tamed animal? Jerry as the feral one? And in what ways, as spectators, do we connect or keep our distance?

WHO'S AFRAID OF VIRGINIA WOOLF? BY EDWARD ALBEE

Michael Y. Bennett, University of Wisconsin-Whitewater

IN BRIEF

Illustrate how differences in intonation influence interpretation of characters' relationships.

PURPOSE

This exercise asks students to consider an alternative reading of dialogue in *Who's Afraid of Virginia Woolf?* that emphasizes the teasing, game-playing nature of George and Martha's relationship. By punctuating the dialogue with laughter, a deeper interpretation of the play and its characters opens up, particularly the complex relationship between George and Martha.

PREPARATION

Students need to have read the play in its entirety before class and bring their copy of the play to class.

MATERIALS

Copies of performance reviews of the play from *The New York Times*, etc. (see Resources on Companion Website). Copies of the beginning of the play (end point of reading is your choice).

Nuts and Bolts

1 It is easy to think of George and Martha as having a dysfunctional marriage because they are constantly yelling at and insulting the other. For this class, begin by asking the students to imagine a dysfunctional marriage, and ask them to describe it. Then, ask whether or not George and Martha's marriage is dysfunctional, and why or why not? Tease out what a dysfunctional marriage is and is not.

2 Now assign two (of your most talented) students to read the parts of George and Martha. You will read this same scene twice, but do not let them know this ahead of time, from the beginning of the play to whenever you want to stop it (e.g., from the very beginning of the play to the all-caps "FUCK YOU" is a good stopping place).

3 For the first time through, tell the student assigned to read George to read it as if George were tired and frustrated and speaks his lines slowly, and tell the student assigned to read Martha to read it as if Martha were shrill and berating and speaks in starts and stops.

4 For the second time through, tell both students to be playful, and to pause at times to laugh and chuckle (e.g., when discussing Martha's "rubbing alcohol") but to maintain a fast back-and-forth pace.

5 Ask the class to assess and comment upon these two differing relationships (i.e., the relationship between George and Martha as read the first time through versus the same relationship read the second time through). Then, ask the students to discuss which of the two readings is more in line with the play as a whole (i.e., the first being a sign of a dysfunctional relationship and the second being a sign of a complex wedded life). Guide the students into understanding that the latter reading makes for a more interesting play: instead of the fighting that results from a childless woman and her husband who doesn't live up to his potential, the second reading allows for more complex, multifaceted characters, who both love and hate, self-love and self-loath, and whose interconnectedness results in such codependent behavior as displays of jealousy and desiring to be desired.

6 After this discussion, pass out a few different performance reviews of this play from *Theatre Journal* and/or *The New York Times*/*Village Voice* over the years. In the small groups, have the students read and discuss the different performance reviews (e.g., Brantley and Isherwood's reviews in *The New York Times*). Have them, as a group, write out the differences in interpretation from each of the reviews.

Reflection

This play comes out of the long American dramatic tradition of family tensions exploding in the living room. The only difference with this play versus plays by Eugene O'Neill, Lillian Hellman, Thornton Wilder, Tennessee Williams, and Arthur Miller is that Albee's play is cast not in the mold of tragedy but in the mold of tragicomedy. That is, this is a play that provokes us to laugh at the dark, rarely admitted aspects of married life. As with most tragicomedies, we are encouraged to see the humor of uncomfortable situations; George and Martha are essentially "stuck" with one another and their disappointing lives, and there is something wryly comic about the way they attempt to alleviate their personal pain by hurting another.

Too often this play is seen as vicious and mean and dark. But much of that has to do with (mis)understanding and thinking that George and Martha simply have a dysfunctional relationship. Or, another (mis)conception is that Martha is simply a bitter, old woman because she never had a child. These assumptions can play into understanding the play as a whole, but neither of these interpretations capture the complexity of the characters nor their relationship. Instead, what if we think of their relationship as a microcosm of the ups and downs of a long wedded life? This is a couple who hurts because of the loss of not being able to have children, and instead, they seek to fill that void with feelings, whether good or bad. They lash out as a way to make a strong connection in order to replace the loss of the potential bonds and connectedness of parenthood.

DUTCHMAN BY AMIRI BARAKA

Michael Y. Bennett, University of Wisconsin-Whitewater

IN BRIEF

Using lighting and sound techniques to underscore the disorienting aspects of racist language.

PURPOSE

The exercise helps students imagine a more nuanced version of the character of Lulu in *Dutchman*. With the tendency to read the play only as a racial allegory, instructors should press the analysis further and demonstrate the disorienting techniques Baraka incorporates into the play's design. By watching a well-known cinematic piece that uses flashing lights and sounds as code for madness, students see how employing erratic sound and lighting design can impact and illuminate both performance and interpretation.

PREPARATION

Students need to read the play in its entirety before class.

MATERIALS

Copies of a monologue of your choosing by Lulu. Smartphones with flashlight or blinking light feature enabled.

Nuts and Bolts

1 Begin by asking the students to imagine a rhythmic and steady pulse or beat and a similar pace of flickering light. Now, ask them to imagine that light and sound gradually and slowly increase throughout the play. This will set them up for the movie clip, in some ways to surprise and jar them by, then, showing them the following film clip.

2 Show a film clip of the tunnel boat scene from *Willy Wonka and Chocolate Factory* (1971), and discuss how the light and sound accelerate in speed, producing an entropic type of madness. Draw attention to the difference between Willy Wonka's (Gene Wilder's) impassive face versus the passengers' growing fear; What in the clip suggests Willy Wonka is crazy? What in the clip indicates the ride itself is harrowing?

3 Now ask a volunteer or assign a student to read Lulu's speech from the handout and turn off or dim the classroom lights.

4 For the first time through the reading, ask one additional student to drum with a pen a rhythmic beat that gradually increases in speed on their desk table, and ask another student to flash their smartphone flashlight at regular but increasingly fast intervals.

5 Then have a second read-through, but this time, ask about a quarter of the class to drum with their pens on their desk as they feel fit, but in increasing intensity while not maintaining a regular beat until it is loud and violent and chaotic sounding. Ask another quarter of the class to flash their flashlights, increasing the frequency and the length of the flash, and also moving the light in more directions as the intensity increases.

6 After these two readings of the same monologue, in order to start a discussion, ask, or ask a version of, the following: Don't these two sound and lighting designs produce not only very different emotional and/or visceral responses, but don't they suggest very different interpretations of the play? What are these different interpretations?

Reflection

Given Lulu's seductress qualities and the presence of her "apple" in the play, it is easy and tangible to understand Lulu's character as an Eve/Temptress figure, who is enticing the malleable Clay with her overt sexuality. This creates a symbolic and allegorical reading of the way that white Americans manipulated integrationist discourse during the Civil Rights Movement, to the detriment of African Americans. This overall understanding is helpful for students puzzled by the play, but the reading becomes reductive, as it is, essentially, an allegory that merely displays a one-to-one correspondence with the biblical figure(s).

Instead, the two different lighting choices in the exercise offer two different, and much more nuanced, readings of the play. (1) In the first design, the steady and rhythmic beat suggests that it is Lulu's steady and persistent overt and implicit racism that is the cause of Clay's death; Clay's inability to mount an effective response to Lulu (the individual), further, is to blame, which paints a psychological portrait of the effects of racism on individuals. (2) In the second design, Clay becomes more of a generic black man responding the best he can to the demands of a racist world, because the world is random, heartless, and irrational, and Clay is stuck in this mad, mad world ... a world off its tracks, so to speak.

THE HOMECOMING BY HAROLD PINTER

William Hutchings, University of Alabama at Birmingham

IN BRIEF

Emphasize the personal pronoun "you" to reveal Pinter's menacing subtext.

PURPOSE

This exercise will help students understand the oblique and innovative style of Harold Pinter's early plays, particularly *The Homecoming*, by drawing attention to the voice—especially vocal inflection, tone, and silence—in order to perceive Pinter's subtext.

PREPARATION

None by the students. The instructor will need to make photocopies and highlights. See below.

MATERIALS

Duplicate photocopies of the opening 1–2 pages of the play, enough for each actor. One set will be a clean copy with no markings. The other set will have the second-person pronoun "you" highlighted with a marker each time it appears.

Nuts and Bolts

1 Ask for two student volunteers.

2 Give them the "clean" copy of the opening scene.

3 Ask them to read the lines in the style of Noel Coward (i.e., affluently glib—"Mahtini, Dahling?"—upper middle class; this will serve as an example of how *not* to do it).

4 After the first performance of the scene, I allow students to express their general bafflement at (a) why these characters talk to each other the way they do, (b) what happens in the scene, (c) why there are so many pauses and silences in the text, and (d) what it is all "meant to mean." I then emphasize that they may not be reading it with an appropriately Pinterian "tone" and that his characters are from the English working class, which had become newly prominent on stage following John Osborne's *Look Back in Anger* (1956) as well as the works of other playwrights nicknamed the "Angry Young Men." Coming from socioeconomic backgrounds that were seldom taken seriously in modern drama heretofore, these playwrights were quite different from—and often derisive toward—such then popular playwrights as Noel Coward.

5 Give the same actors the "highlighted" copy of the same opening scene.

6 Have the actors repeat the same lines with a much more menacing tone, observing the pauses and silences as if they were rests in music (tell the students count to 5 before speaking) and using a more working-class dialect. Most importantly, direct them to emphasize ("punch") the word YOU at every highlighted occurrence—making it in effect a "second person accusatory" pronoun. Thus: MAX: WHAT [pronounced "WOT"] have YOU done with the scissors? [Pause.] I SAID I'm looking for the scissors. WHAT have YOU done with them? [Pause.] Did YOU hear me? I want to cut something out of the paper. LENNY: [with utter indifference] I'm reading the paper.

7 For the following class day, students are assigned to continue reading (or reread) *The Homecoming*, underlining the word "you" every time it is used—and counting how often each character uses it. Though they are encouraged to "find a different voice" for each character, they are told to "punch" the word "you" every time it occurs. By the second day of discussion, they find the play utterly, astonishingly transformed. Like it or not, they have entered Pinter's world.

Reflection

The students are typically stunned at the difference in tone—the overt if unexplained aggression of Max, the utterly passive disregard (which they also recognize as disrespect) of his son Lenny, and the ever-so-distinctive "menace" that prevails in this household. A discussion of Pinter's subtext ensues, emphasizing (a) that Pinter's characters are likely to sound far less verbose and far more voluble than their counterparts in the other dramas they may be reading, that (b) traditional exposition of characters and context has been drastically reduced, and that (c) the characters' backstories and motives may be—and may remain—ambiguous or even entirely unclear.

Decades before the twenty-first-century coinage of the word "micro-aggression," Harold Pinter made such sharply nuanced, subtly menacing acts of verbal self-assertion a trademark-worthy innovation on the modern stage. Though students rarely if ever recognize the fact before our first day's discussion, they already live in Pinter's world, which they discover as soon as they are asked about sharing a dorm room with other students or a household with a "significant other." Especially when moving in but also later, the dorm room or apartment is a space of endless contestation: dishes will or will not stack up unwashed in the sink; socks will or will not be left on the floor; pantyhose will or will not hang over the shower rod. Ensuing arguments are never really about what they're supposedly about; the dishes, the socks, the pantyhose, etc., are mere triggers. The subtext is always dominance, i.e., who defines and hence "owns" or "controls" the rules of the shared space and thus controls the space itself. Sartre was indeed right in *No Exit* (which I teach a couple of weeks before *The Homecoming*): Hell is indeed "other people." Yet, as students also know well, a cohabitant's "silent treatment" can be no less aggressive than a shouting-match. All of these examples are, I contend, "Pinter moves": assertions of autonomy in defining the shared space, ceaseless reappraisals of dominance versus submission, your way versus theirs. Roommates (except when assigned by the university, as first-year students often are) and "significant others" are at least chosen; family members, like those in *The Homecoming*, are permanent, hence even worse. When such conflicts are explained in those terms, students "get it" far faster and more permanently than they would ever have expected before coming to class.

On a personal note, in a receiving line on the occasion of Harold Pinter's 70th birthday (the only time that I met him), I said to him: "There is no other author who as quickly and as permanently transforms the way my students think about relationships, about language, and about power. Even years later, alumni have come up to me saying 'I just have to tell you about the Pinter move that my [husband/wife/boyfriend/girlfriend/roommate] tried on me!'" "They actually call them Pinter moves?," he asked. "Yes indeed," I assured him. He seemed very pleased indeed.

THE HOUSE OF BLUE LEAVES
BY JOHN GUARE

AJ Knox, Platt College

IN BRIEF

Using status to understand humiliation and laughter in John Guare's black comedy.

PURPOSE

John Guare writes that his play *The House of Blue Leaves* is explicitly about humiliation "more than anything else," and this exercise places students in the shoes of the characters to understand the driving force of the play and of the growing mania of the piece in performance. Guare's characters are fascinated with celebrity and becoming famous, although it is clear that Artie lacks talent and his songwriting is in vain. This exercise invites students to get a sense of how humiliation functions within the play, both as a motivating factor for the characters and as a source of laughter.

PREPARATION

Ideally, this activity is done after students have read the first act, but before the second. However, it can be completed at any point during the discussion of the play—it is a useful introduction to the characters, and it is likewise a unique way to engage with students' sympathies after having read the play. It is beneficial if students have viewed at least the prologue of the 1987 film adaptation starring John Mahoney (see Companion Website).

MATERIALS

Red and blue stickers, red for half of the class, blue for the other half. Slips of folded paper, enough for each student, all of which have a star on them, and a container for the slips.

Nuts and Bolts

It is helpful to explain the steps of this activity beforehand, without spoiling the "twist."

1 Introduce the game: everyone is going to partner up and perform an incredible, 10-second one-person show for their partner. There are three kinds of people: ridiculous people, talented people, and one "hidden genius." The goal of the game is to discover the hidden genius and invite them to Australia.

2 Each student should pick a red or blue sticker at random and affix it to their shirt. After they have done that, explain the colors: blue stickers mean that students are ridiculous, and red stickers mean that students are talented (remind them that this is a role-playing exercise and does not reflect judgment on their actual person).

3 Next, explain the slips of paper: only one has a star on it, and whoever draws the star is the secret "hidden genius." Ask students to draw slips of paper, but tell them not to show their slips to anyone else and not to announce what is on their paper. The hidden genius cannot declare their genius—they must be "discovered." Tell students the game is over when somebody discovers the hidden genius and invites them to Australia.

4 Students will find a partner and take turns performing their incredible one-person show. The show can be anything and should only be about 10 seconds long (e.g., sing "Row Row Row Your Boat," Rub your belly and pat your head, etc.). Note: In my experience, students can freeze up at the prospect of a one-person show. I emphasize that each person should approach their own one-person show believing it is the greatest show ever conceived, even if they're just singing "Happy Birthday."

5 When watching a show, students usually have one of three responses:

a If the performer is talented (red): praise them with applause or flattery.

b If the performer is ridiculous (blue): laugh at their show, but don't praise it.

c If you believe that your partner might be the hidden genius, you can invite them to come to Australia with you—only if you think they're the genius.

6 After each pair has had a chance to perform their shows and get a response, they find new partners and repeat, about five times. For larger groups, you may split into small groups instead of partners. Allow each person to perform for their small group; repeat with new groups three times or so.

7 Some reminders for students:

a Stick to the script. Perform a show, give a response. Partners can redo their show if desired or asked, but do not stray from the show-response format.

b The hidden genius cannot announce that they are the genius—they have to be "discovered" and invited to Australia.

8 Once the game is over (the instructor will end it and announce that the genius should not reveal themselves just yet), ask the students to break off individually and write a song or poem about their experience—it only needs to be about four lines or so, but it should be evocative of Artie's songs: simple, playful, and rhyming. Take 5–10 minutes.

9 Ask the hidden genius to step forward and speak/sing their song. Multiple students will step forward at this point, revealing the "twist," at which point I allow anyone who would like to share their song to do so.

10 After all willing students have performed their songs, discuss the process as a group.

Reflection

With each student believing that he or she is the unique "hidden genius," no one will offer an invitation to Australia, because each student will be anticipating an invitation himself or herself. In my experience, students grow increasingly frustrated that nobody is recognizing their genius. Some students invariably figure out the twist, but rarely is it anything more than a nagging doubt in the back of their mind; some express feelings of betrayal from the instructor at having been lied to—this is also an important theme throughout the play and can lead to a rewarding discussion on the role of deception in the play.

In the discussion, connect the exercise to characters: Artie believes himself to be a genius, Bananas is belittled and ridiculed despite her talent and love, Ronnie has carried his humiliation with him, and Billy is a character who feels superior to others. This exercise asks students to empathize with the characters. How did it feel to be laughed at, thinking you were performing your masterpiece? How did it feel to get praise, but never true success? Further prompts: Did you ever doubt that you were the hidden genius? What did it feel like to realize you were not "unique" at the end? What was the difference performing for a red or a blue person? Did your sticker color ultimately matter?

The laughter elicited throughout Guare's play almost always comes at someone's expense. This exercise should also inform students about the relationship between humiliation and laughter therein; for Guare, laughter is rarely joyous and often cruel. Likewise, in using the color system, students are forced to make assumptions about people's status and this can lead to fruitful discussions of the prejudices within the play.

DEATH AND THE KING'S HORSEMAN BY WOLE SOYINKA

Önder Çakırtaş, Bingol University, and Miriam M. Chirico, Eastern Connecticut State University

IN BRIEF

Learning about the sacred nature behind African masks as a means to understanding the ritual dimension of the play.

PURPOSE

As it is expressed by Soyinka in the preface to this play, music is essential for evoking the links between the worlds of the living, dead, and the unborn. Other nonverbal elements such as the dance, dress, and masks intrinsic to Yoruban culture also play a role in understanding the mythopoeic dimension of *Death and the King's Horseman*. Music, dance, and costumes represent the spiritual beliefs of an ethnic tribe in the play. Only by understanding the religious significance of these arts can students begin to comprehend the simultaneous existence between the divine and the human that underlies the central confrontation of the play: the rituals necessary for maintaining social order. While students cannot be expected in a short period to learn sufficiently about the Yoruban cosmology, understanding the considerable functional gap between religious masks and masquerade masks will at least point to the communal spiritual beliefs underlying Elesin's tragedy and Olunde's suicide.

PREPARATION

Due to the play's setting in Nigeria, among the Yoruban people, instructors should provide students with some historical context regarding British colonialization of West Africa and the Yoruban deities and cosmology. The

Norton Critical Edition offers many valuable essays for such instruction, such as Tanure Ojaide's "Death and the King's Horseman in the Classroom." Many online sites provide information about Yoruban culture, particularly the Egungun masquerades connected to ancestral worship. Video clips of music, dance, and costumes can be shared with the students as part of the introductory lecture material. Students should be instructed to read the full text of the play.

MATERIALS

African mask(s) and Halloween or Carnival mask. Oftentimes, African-American Studies, Art, or Theater departments have these masks on display and students could be directed to these areas to take notes. If masks are not available website images could be used.

Nuts and Bolts

1 Present the African or Yoruban mask to the students and ask them specific questions about the mask. If the viewing has been done outside of class, ask for volunteers to share their notes while projecting an image of an African mask as well as the Halloween mask.

2 Consider playing Egungun music while the students study and brainstorm about the African mask.

3 Questions should require students to not only describe the masks but consider the use of the two different kinds of masks:

    a What colors or designs are on the mask?

    b How might the mask be made? What are the materials?

    c What parts of the mask look realistic (i.e., human)? What parts of the mask look nonhuman (animal) or spiritual?

    d How does the mask reflect the identity of the person wearing it? How does the mask represent many people?

    e How might other people react toward the mask?

4 Students do not need to come up with the correct answers as they are not expected to be experts in African masking. But these side-by-side comparisons should lead to consideration of how masking within a religious community has greater significance than the use of masks for Halloween parties or masquerades.

5 Instructors might emphasize how in traditional African practices, ritual masks transform the wearer into the spirit or deity represented by the mask. The transformation relies upon other art forms such as dance and music, and is usually incorporated as part of a greater ritual.

6 Turn to the stage directions at the beginning of Acts 2 and 4 and point out how Pilkings and his wife Jane wear these Egungun costumes and masks. Read aloud the conversation where Amusa is disturbed by the British disregard for these ceremonial costumes and ask the students to explain why Amusa is bothered, and why Olunde, later on, asks "And is [the Royal Highness's visit] good cause for which you desecrate an ancestral mask?" Ask the students to consider the notes they took in their response.

Reflection

Every nation has its own music and various religious rituals. In a country that is colonized, there is a strong tension between those who want to preserve their traditional way of life and culture and the governing people. In this play, music, dance, and costumes are the non-dialogic elements that represent the existence of an ethnic group's identity.

Students should perceive, even without fully understanding, the ritualistic dimension to this play that is important. They will recognize how masks, costumes, music, and dance are important nonverbal elements that constitute religious ceremonies at the foundation of the Yoruban's social order. If they remain ignorant of these cultural practices, they are in the same position as the Pilkings and other British colonizers: indifferent outsiders.

In a world theater class, instructors could discuss the similarity between classical Greek theater and African theater, as Soyinka himself has done. Within the Greek theatrical practice, an actor, *hypokrites*, would study the mask beforehand in order to be absorbed into or become one with his role. Also, the use of the masks in the chorus unified the choral members into one body. However, the African use of masks within the context of religious ceremonies goes further in permitting the wearer to lose himself and be possessed by the god or spirit and become a medium for the community to converse with the otherworld.

A similar exercise might be created by comparing musical selections, such as between the Yoruban drumming and Western music, but this is more challenging. Soyinka pointedly contrasts the vibrant, onstage Yoruban music to the Argentinian music that emanates from a hand-cranked gramophone as Pilkings and Jane dance the tango, to indicate the symbolic relevance of music that comes from and is celebrated by one's own people versus a mechanized, cultural import without significance. Playing and contrasting two well-recorded pieces of music would not create the same disparity.

FEFU AND HER FRIENDS BY MARÍA IRENE FORNÉS

Ann M. Shanahan, Purdue University

IN BRIEF

Performing the play's multiple perspectives in order to reinforce a feminist critique of realism

PURPOSE

This exercise illuminates central features of the dramaturgy of *Fefu and Her Friends*, María Irene Fornés' meditation on the complex relationships between bodies and spaces in theatrical representation, especially the bodies of actors and audience members who identify as women, by challenging the limitations typical to fourth-wall realism. By diminishing the space between audience and actors and encouraging the audience's fluid movement from scene to scene, the play engages a way of knowing through the senses and through the body. This embodied method acts in contradistinction to traditional theatrical means of knowing exclusively through an individual's visual sense and/or by relying upon the mental capacities of logic and thought. Instead, audience members as well as actors are invited to arrive at meaning collectively, collaboratively, and through the whole body.

Secondarily, but related to this, the exercise highlights how the nonlinear treatment of time in the play can encourage audiences to understand the layered quality of patriarchal oppression, not as a one-time, cause-and-effect injury to women but as a type of traumatic experience that possesses multiple origins and can be triggered across time. Parallel to the play's content is Fornés' chosen dramaturgy, which exposes how traditional realistic modes of theatrical representation contain biases and perpetuate oppression. Simultaneous to exposing the oppressions of that style, the play proposes more liberating alternatives that reflect the feminist aesthetics of the 1970s when the play was written.

The play's critique of the biases inherent in the style of theatrical realism can be meaningfully illuminated by considering it in counterpoint to Ibsen's *Hedda Gabler*. Therefore, this exercise works best in classes where students have also read and studied *Hedda Gabler* and traditional realism, and especially where there is some coverage of feminist critiques of realism.[1]

Fefu and Her Friends is a dramaturgically sophisticated exploration of the relationship between content, form, and style in the traditional realistic performances of women-identifying characters in the theater.

PREPARATION

Ideally, the students should read the whole play ahead of time, along with *Hedda Gabler*, if possible. Students should have some understanding of the dynamics of fourth-wall realism and ideally some understanding of women's history in the United States in the 1930s (when the play is set) and 1970s (when the play was written), as well as some knowledge of feminist critiques of realism (e.g., Dolan, Case).

If students have read *Hedda Gabler*, it is useful to propose the relationship between the two plays before beginning the exercise, and ask where students see parallels in content. Likely answers include a titular woman character shooting a gun at men offstage; the setting in a domestic interior—with French doors; reference to autumn leaves; presence of judges (Judge Brack and Julia's "judges"); Fefu and Hedda both feeling trapped indoors and envious of men's freedom; the shooting of a central woman character at the end of the play and the reaction following.

MATERIALS

Eight copies of the play text. This exercise requires a classroom space(s) large enough to designate four discrete rooms or enough space to place students in four different corners of a large room.

---

[1] Sue Ellen Case, *Feminism and Theatre* (New York: Routledge, 1988); Jill Dolan, *The Feminist Spectator as Critic* (Ann Arbor: University of Michigan, 1988).

Nuts and Bolts

The focus of the exercise is to compare the content and form of part two, where the four scenes are enacted simultaneously in multiple locations, to parts one and three of the play, in addition to the plotting of other realistic plays.

1 Cast the eight roles (see note below).

2 Establish four separate spaces in the classroom for actors to read part two and divide the audience into four groups to watch the four scenes. Establish a direction for audience movement, clockwise or counterclockwise.

3 Read aloud with limited movement (or make minor suggestions) pages 7–11 if time permits; 24–40; 55–61 if time permits (pages are taken from the 1978 PAJ Publications version of the script).

4 Audience groups watch the reading of part one in a stationary position (proscenium, arena, or other seating); for part two (repeated four times) they move from space to space. Reading part two takes about 22–25 minutes. Audience returns to watch the end of part three together as they did part one.

5 An abbreviated version involves reading only the scenes in part two once and moving the audience at three shared intervals during the single simultaneous reading of the scenes. The instructor might call out "freeze" to direct the actors to hold their lines and positions while the audience moves. This is not preferred as the experience of important content is missed, but does allow the key points to be demonstrated.

Reflection

I have found that undergraduate students, particularly in their first and second year, do not understand this play unless they experience it through an engaged exercise such as this. Typical first responses to reading the play initially are "I didn't get it"; "I was confused"—interspersed with "I was scared by Julia's monologue," and the like. Audiences are provided little explanation regarding who the characters are and what they are doing, when the play is set, etc. By engaging the material bodies of the students as readers/performers and audience in material space, the combined impact of the play's content, form, and style begins to "make sense." The performed presentation of the content in the classroom invites students to know by trusting all of their senses and embodied meaning-making capacities. To quote the character Emma's quotation of educator Emma Sheridan Frye in the play: "Environment knocks at the gateway of the senses."

In my experience, students after the exercise comment on feeling more "involved and engaged" than in traditional theater. They appreciate the relationship between the nonlinear structure and space, and connect it to their feeling of increased involvement. As opposed to a linear story featuring a single protagonist, the play asks the audience to make sense of the information they are provided as we do in life, experiencing several characters at once, without structured exposition serving up information in a linear fashion. The significance of this experimental dramaturgy can be synthesized meaningfully through a discussion following the reading/performance of the cryptic ending of the play when Julia appears wounded (perhaps mortally) from an offstage gunshot, and her friends encircle her silently. How do we understand the cause and effect of the gun firing offstage and the blood we see on Julia? Is she alive or dead? The connection between the shooting of a rabbit offstage and Julia's wound can be made through the audience's trust of their senses, empowered through their increasing embodied experiences of the play.

Furthermore, teaching the play *Hedda Gabler* alongside *Fefu and Her Friends* and comparing the two pieces prove illuminating with respect to both Fornés' feminist themes and her experimental dramaturgy. For example, the unresolved ending of *Fefu* allows for an openness of interpretations particularly when compared to the finality of Judge Brack's closing line "people don't do such things" in *Hedda Gabler*. The closing of the play with a male voice, reifying norms and re-containing Hedda's transgressive acts in a patriarchal frame, corresponds to the multiple forms enclosing Hedda, both social and theatrical: the proscenium frame around the domestic interior at the fourth wall, the frame within the frame of the upstage inner room where Hedda kills herself, along with the framed image of her father. By contrast, by the time we get to the end of *Fefu*, the frames around the domestic spaces have been broken down; point of view has been diversified by the movement of part two, and the multiple friends replace the singular male voice in *Hedda*. Diversifying the frame and the perspectives empowers each audience member to determine if Julia is dead, or not.

One important note on assigning or "casting" roles: I ask for the class to consider and come to informal consensus on how to handle identifications of race, gender, sexuality, ethnicity, ability, and other categories of identity when casting the roles. I draw the students' attention to the fact that all of the characters are women-identifying, which is crucial to the play's large dramaturgical project as laid out above; sexual identity is suggested in some cases, race and ethnicity are suggested as white by the social and economic histories of the characters but is not prescribed, and ability is complexly rendered in the character of Julia. I have found it practical and fruitful for the uses of this exercise to cast students who volunteer openly, independent of the ways they identify in gender, race, sexuality, or otherwise.

AND THE SOUL SHALL DANCE BY WAKAKO YAMAUCHI

Jennifer Lale, Indiana University

IN BRIEF

Understanding how characters' connection to music reminds them of their identity and past.

PURPOSE

Wakako Yamauchi's stories and plays give voice to the often overlooked Japanese experience in America: the relocation camps during the Second World War and the difficult lives of immigrant farmers and itinerant workers. Her early play, *And the Soul Shall Dance*, depicts both the harsh reality of the Japanese immigrants as well as an ephemeral longing for their homeland, which is best captured in song. The character of Emiko, for example, whose tough nature manifests itself by her smoking and drinking, weeps openly when she hears Japanese songs played on the Victrola. Although she appears eccentric to the other characters, including the husband who abuses her, her deep inner life is valued by Masako, the young girl who witnesses her drunken singing. Her singing, considered by others a mark of her insanity, provides a model of imaginative freedom in contrast to the hard-working community striving to get ahead. Songs in Yamauchi's stories and plays add to the script by conveying traditions and values of Japanese culture.

Students, in reading the play, may understand the political harm created by the internment camps, but they may miss the role the aesthetic consciousness plays in this text. The exercise asks students to consider how music and songs could illuminate some of the more ephemeral themes that go beyond the script, such as the ambivalent desire to return to Japan, or the feeling of isolation as an immigrant, or even the nature of the soul. Although most students will not be familiar with Japanese music, using their own knowledge of songs from musical theater as a connection will expand their experience of the text.

PREPARATION

The students should have already read the play prior to the class period.

MATERIALS

It is useful to have the example songs of each style cued up for students to hear. Do not feel the need to play the entire song but rather give them a taste of it.

Nuts and Bolts

1 Introduce the students to sample musical theater songs and types. For example:

   a Duet (e.g., "All I Ask of You" from *Phantom of the Opera*; "We Make a Beautiful Pair" from *Shenandoah*; "The Confrontation" from *Les Misérables*)

   b Patter song (e.g., "Getting Married Today" from *Company*; "You Got Trouble" from *The Music Man*)

   c Ballad (e.g., "Maria" from *West Side Story*; "Johanna" from *Sweeney Todd*; "Edelweiss" from *The Sound of Music*)

   d Ensemble piece (e.g., "Magic to Do" from *Pippin*; "Seasons of Love" from *Rent*; "The Song of Purple Summer" from *Spring Awakening*)

2 Divide the class into groups of 4–5 students per group.

3 Working together, each group will make the play's text, already rich in musical content, into a piece of musical theater by deciding on four places where more songs could be inserted. Each song needs to fall into a different category that exists in American musical theater. Students may be unfamiliar with musical theater, so the instructor should consider playing an example or two to illustrate each type of song.

4 Turning to *And the Soul Shall Dance* and working in groups, determine four places where songs could be inserted. Students must provide a rationale for their decisions, answering the following questions:

   a Where the song occurs? Does it occur at the inciting incident, the climax, or the denouement? Why is there a song there?

   b Who sings the song? What type of song is it? What title should it have?

c What is the song's function? Does it further the story, detail emotion, establish atmosphere? Does it reinforce plot, character, thought, language, music, or spectacle?

5 Have each group share their choices in turn. Find commonalities—did everyone decide on the same ballad location or character? What does this indicate about the play's own music? Where are the differences between groups? What might that say about the way the play is received by individuals as audience/readers?

Reflection

And the Soul Shall Dance includes moments of music and dance performance that connect the characters to their Japanese heritage in a place where their culture is not respected or is unacknowledged. The music in the play indicates the rich inner life of the Nisei characters. This legacy of culture gives the characters freedom by knowing and feeling connected to their own roots, despite being socialized as Americans.

The students may or may not be familiar with the music used in the play to express Japanese culture nor with many of the performance conventions addressed by the drama. Many students, however, are familiar with music and musical theater and can connect how moments of exposition, conflict, and emotion can be conveyed through characters moving into song.

By drawing upon their experience of musical theater, the importance of the music in the play as well as the emotional arc of each character can be more fully realized. I have done this activity with classes and found that they understand how the relationships between the characters build—like a patter song between Masako and Kiyoko, teaching her about living in America, or a ballad by Oka mourning his dead wife. It is always a fun activity and the students get creative and engage with the text in a way that begs them to think of it as performance, rather than as pure text.

ZOOT SUIT BY LUIS VALDEZ

Ellen C. Mareneck, Bronx Community College (CUNY)

IN BRIEF

Students "try on" dialect and dress to perform identity.

PURPOSE

This exercise guides students to look at cultural pride through the lens of dress (the zoot suit) and dialect (Caló, or Mexican American slang) and explore how these two performative elements were used by the media and white society against young Mexican Americans as they became the targets of racism in 1940s Los Angeles.

PREPARATION

Prior to the class, students should learn about the Zoot Suit Riots (see Resources on Companion Website). They should read the play in its entirety before class as well. The instructor should provide the students with a glossary for Caló (see Resources on Companion Website).

MATERIALS

There is an open-source website called "Zoot Suit Dramaturgy" from the University of California at Santa Clara, which the Theater Arts Department put together for their 2014 production of Zoot Suit. This is where teachers will find not only a detailed history of the setting and the play but also a complete glossary of Caló slang as well as scene-by-scene translations of the slang as it is used in the play. Showing pictures of the Pachucos in their zoot suits from the time, as well as playing some Big Band music of the time period (Duke Ellington, Harry James, Benny Goodman, etc.), helps give students a visual and aural sense of the time period.

Nuts and Bolts

Start with Discussion Questions available in the Appendix on the Companion Website.

1 Divide the students into groups and assign each one of the following five scenes:

a The Interrogation (1.4): This is a long scene that can be broken up; it includes the interrogation at the police station when Henry is first arrested, as well as a memory scene of Henry and his mother and brother and sister before going out dancing on that fateful night.

b The scenes between Pachuco and Henry (1.3, between Pachuco and Henry when he is first arrested, and 2.5, when Henry is in solitary confinement).

c The scenes between Annie and Henry (1.8, the part after George introduces them to the point when George comes back into the scene, and 2.3, when Alice visits Henry in jail).

2 Ask the students to underline each word or phrase that is in Caló—and look them up in the "Glossary" (see Companion Website).

3 Have them translate the dialogue into standard English.

4 Once the "translated" scripts are ready, and the students have had a chance to rehearse briefly and informally, invite each group to the front of the class to perform their scene.

a First, have them perform the translated version.

b Second, have them perform the original version.

5 After each group performs their scene in this way, discuss with the class and the actors the differences in language and dialect:

a Altered how they played the character

b Heightened, lessened, or changed the message of the scene:

i For the actors

ii For the audience

6 After all the groups have performed and discussed their scenes, return to your discussion from the Discussion Questions in the online Appendix regarding youth culture performances of identity through dress and dialect.

Reflection

When *Zoot Suit* premiered on Broadway in 1979, it was the first Broadway production of a play by a Mexican-American playwright that featured an all Hispanic-American cast. Since then there have been others, including *In the Heights, On Your Feet, Hamilton,* and John Leguizamo's *Latin History for Morons. Zoot Suit* needs to be recognized in the American canon as a play whose polemics of racism and violence disguised as patriotism versus the struggle for equity and racial justice continue to play out on our national stage today. As Latinx people become the largest ethnic minority in the United States, making up 18 percent of the U.S. population,[1] they are still a tiny minority in terms of representation both onstage and in the audiences of American theaters. Teaching this play and helping students step into the "calcos" (shoes) of these Pachucos and Pachucas engendered a sense of empathy and self-awareness in my students. It gives students a glimpse of how theater can be a voice for the marginalized and a force for change.

---

[1]Antonio Flores, "How the Hispanic Population Is Changing." Pew Research Center, September 18, 2017.

TRUE WEST BY SAM SHEPARD

Suzanne Maynard Miller, New York City College of Technology (CUNY)

IN BRIEF

This exercise demonstrates how performing with material objects reveals the themes of affluence and jealousy.

PURPOSE

This exercise helps students to understand how the characters' use and destruction of material objects in the play illustrate their own privilege or financial insecurity, as well as their sibling rivalry. A simple object that is not inherently powerful or valuable (the way a gun or a stack of money is) can still generate tension between characters, cause shifts in power, and advance the plot. In this exercise, the car key represents a valuable object (the car), but, even more so, it represents access to power—the means to travel to a job interview.

PREPARATION

Students must read through at least Scene 1 of *True West*. Scene 2, on which the improv exercise is based, may be read either before or after doing the exercise. Reading Scene 2 before doing the exercise may inform how the improvised scene unfolds, while reading Scene 2 after doing the exercise will likely help students consider more closely the reasons for the power struggle between Austin and Lee.

MATERIALS

A key. The information sheets (see the Appendix on Companion Website).

Nuts and Bolts

1 Put the students into pairs.

a Character A is "The Key Holder" and Character B is "The Challenger."

b Distribute the information sheets from Appendix on Companion Website.

2 Begin the exercise by explaining that the characters are sitting in Character A's kitchen in a remote area of the country that does not have public transportation, cabs, ride-sharing service, or even cell service. The two characters may not leave.

3 The pair improvises a scene in which The Challenger attempts to get the key from The Key Holder, while The Key Holder tries to resist this request. This is done only through dialogue; at no point during the exercise should there be any physical confrontation.

4 Give each student his or her respective information sheets (see Companion Website) and give The Key Holder a physical key (or equivalent). Allow each student time to process the material. Throughout the scene, the students may refer to their information sheets and reveal any details necessary to help them achieve their goals.

5 Set a timer for 4 minutes. During this time, the students use the information on their sheets to improvise dialogue. After 4 minutes, inform the students that they have 1 additional minute. When this final minute is up, the scene ends, regardless of who has the key.

Reflection

By immersing themselves in a scene that mimics the power struggle between Austin and Lee, students gain a deeper understanding of the dynamic that exists between the brothers. More broadly, the exercise exhibits how backstory and character traits can affect a character's action and helps students to understand the subtexts of sibling rivalry, societal respect, and acquisition as a mark of success. Additionally, by using a physical object in their scene (a prop), students gain an appreciation for tools other than dialogue that are available to the playwright. Students experience how such tools can set a scene into motion and raise the stakes.

TOP GIRLS BY CARYL CHURCHILL

Verna A. Foster, Loyola University Chicago

IN BRIEF

Perform overlapping dialogue to highlight the competitive nature of women's achievement.

PURPOSE

This exercise will help students understand the function and effect of the overlapping dialogue in Scene 1, i.e., how the dialogue establishes realism or hyperrealism, how the women's experiences are similar despite cultural differences, and how the women are self-centered. Students will also appreciate the significance of the silent Waitress in relation to gender and social class.

PREPARATION

All students should read the play in its entirety before class, but I assign a segment of Scene 1, Marlene's dinner party, to seven students (the six speaking characters plus the silent Waitress) and ask them to rehearse the scene by themselves in advance. I usually select the lines from Marlene's recognition of Griselda's arrival to Nijo's "Nobody gave me back my children." I also provide brief instruction asking the students to work especially on the overlapping dialogue.

MATERIALS

Students bring to class simple items of clothing to distinguish characters from one another and props such as paper plates and plastic glasses. They use classroom furniture to form the restaurant table and chairs.

Nuts and Bolts

1 Read the scene aloud. Discuss the scene's context with the class (the historical/fictional background of each character, or that the scene is in "mythic time," etc.)

2 Figure out exactly what the lines mean and to whom each character is speaking at any given moment. Practice overlapping dialogue again in the classroom.

3 Ask the students to pay attention to stage directions, explicit and implicit. (Encourage the students to figure out the Waitress's movements for themselves.)

4 Ask the student actors what their characters' motives are and how each of them feels in this scene. Discuss their choices for appropriate tone of voice and gestures.

5 Discuss what items of costume and props they brought to class.

6 Finally, discuss the Waitress. Who is she? What are her movements? What is her significance? What role does she play?

Reflection

I am always impressed by how well my students (mostly non-theater majors) perform and handle the overlapping dialogue in this scene. After the performance, all of the students, who are often confused in reading *Top Girls*, understand how Churchill's overlapping dialogue works to create a realistic experience of women coming together at a dinner party. More importantly, they see how the overlapping draws attention both to the women's shared experiences in patriarchal societies across different times and cultures and to the ways in which almost all of the women try to focus the conversation on themselves.

After an extensive discussion of the experiences of Marlene and her diverse guests, I typically ask: What is the Waitress's story? The importance of the Waitress (a woman who is not a "top girl" and whose story is thus uninteresting to Marlene and her guests) is often an eye-opener for the students as it is difficult for them to read her silence and its significance in the text or to think about her at all. The lack of connection between the silent Waitress and the other women who speak to her only to give orders becomes palpable in performance.

Witnessing the scene helps the students to problematize any simple interpretation of the play as depicting women as victims of patriarchy or valorizing "top girls." Furthermore, it enables them to understand Churchill's socialist feminism. This deep analysis of the opening scene allows the students to better understand Churchill's critique in the following scenes of the ways in which successful women get ahead while ignoring the needs of women of a lower social class and indeed benefiting from their labor.

CLOUD NINE BY CARYL CHURCHILL

Suzanne Delle, York College of Pennsylvania

IN BRIEF

Use costume design to illuminate and create character.

PURPOSE

This exercise shows how design elements, specifically costumes, support character development, as well as encourage creativity and participation. In *Cloud Nine*, male actors literally play female characters and vice versa. These casting specifications give us the opportunity to explore how clothes create a persona and how we can explore ideas of gender through costume design. Churchill asks the actors to think about what it means to be a man or a woman—which characteristics are associated with which genders—as designated by the clothing one wears.

PREPARATION

Students should read at least Act 1 of the play before class.

MATERIALS

Paper and colored pencils for each group. Random but simple costume pieces so that there is more than the number of students in the class. Examples of multiuse costume pieces might be scarves, skirts, capes, hats, etc. Internet access.

Nuts and Bolts

1 Provide a list of characters for Act 1 (or a complete dramatis personae for the entire play if students have completed the reading).

2 Ask each group to make a list of casting needs and restrictions they would have as casting directors if *Cloud Nine* was chosen for a professional theater season. Have them identify what qualities they would need for the actors as they play multiple characters, genders, and races.

    a If it is a larger class, the instructor may assign different acts to different groups.

3 Depending upon the makeup, see if it is possible to cast a few roles from within the group.

    a Having students who identify as the specific gender or race of the character read some lines aloud helps students physically see how the characters are perceived in performance.

    b Have the students make note of how and why these traditional casting choices could lead to a particular performance.

4 Lead the students in a Michael Chekhov acting exercise where random costume pieces are placed in the center of the room and each student picks one. They can wear the costume piece in any way they'd like—traditionally or nontraditionally.

5 Each student should find a place in the classroom where they can be alone to discover how wearing this costume piece makes them feel. They should try to move and explore physicality while wearing this.

6 Chekhov asked that the actor repeat over and over "My name is ____" until they discover what this character's name is. Then repeat "I am a _____." The answer could be father, nurse, astronaut, mobster, etc.

7 After side coaching this for a bit, the instructor should encourage the students to walk around the room as their character and interact with each other by saying hello or introducing themselves.

    a The instructor could also line the students up facing each other so that they have to meet in the middle and have a conversation in character.

8 Have the students turn their costume pieces back in and discuss how the exercise made them feel. Were they able to create a character just from a costume piece? Was anyone's character a different gender than the one they identify with?

9 With this new understanding of how costume affects actors' choices, have the students return to their groups and reconsider their conclusions from 2 and 3 above. How have their casting choices changed?

10 As an added element, have the students costume design Act 1 or Act 2 by drawing and coloring using colored pencils or finding photos on the internet. Allow time for each group to report their designs back to the full class.

    a This option may be assigned between classes for presentation at a later date.

11 The instructor may also wish to show clips or stills from professional theatere and see how close students came to the choices made in those fully realized productions.

Reflection

Students often have a difficult time imagining this play when reading it because of all the cross-gender casting. Adding to their confusion is their lack of historical familiarity with the behavioral and clothing restrictions during the British Victorian era. Moreover, when reading the play aloud, or discussing the gender dynamics for actors, students will often rely on gender stereotypes. All of these conditions prevent full understanding of the performative nature of this play.

Starting with the corset and landing at a stiletto heel, we could catalogue the many ways that clothes keep us constricted; Churchill gives her designers the freedom to use their imaginations to highlight issues of identity. When a male actor plays the role of subservient wife Betty in Act 1, how can a costume designer highlight the truth of that historical relationship in the context of the world of this play? What are our associations with certain items of clothing? Would we consider a pair of jeans masculine today? What about seventy years ago? How is color seen in terms of gender? Would we dress a little boy in pink, for example? In Act 2 of *Cloud Nine*, Clive wants the audience to stop seeing the humor in the gender confusion and return to strict gender norms. What colors and patterns might he be dressed in opposed to, say, Harry in Act 1? While these characters are British, in Act 1 they live in Africa and Joshua (while played by a white actor) is indigenous. How might their nationality affect their wardrobe? Do Americans like to show patriotism through certain types of outfits? This exercise allows students to explore their own creativity while also encouraging them to explore what their own outfit choices say about who they are.

Michael Chekhov believed in creating a character from the "outside," meaning that actors could use a costume piece as a way to explore their character rather than using the traditional American Method acting training of objectives and sense memory. I suggest the instructor side-coach the entire exercise and allow students the time to discover who their character is. Not every acting exercise works for every student, but if they can carve out their own small area in the classroom to explore and play with the costume piece, so they are not self-conscious, you may find that some students really respond to this type of character development.

The second part of this exercise—the design creation—should bring any more literal-minded students back to committing to the day's work and understanding of the play through costume design. Drawing or finding ideas on the internet awakens creativity in different ways. Adding this part of the exercise to the day shows that there are many different ways to work in theater and be a part of a production (not just acting). I have found students love to argue about what colors and textures certain characters will wear.

"MASTER HAROLD" ... AND THE BOYS BY ATHOL FUGARD

Paula Fourie, Stellenbosch University

IN BRIEF

The use of music and dance as physicalized metaphors for social harmony and the expression of individual freedom.

PURPOSE

The exercise leads students to understand the symbolic meanings that both music and dance convey in *"Master Harold" ... and the Boys.* Though it operates very subtly in the written script, music plays an important role in the performance of the play, as a suggestion of harmony that is lacking in an apartheid-dominated society. Frequently referred to by the characters, and often approximated by them, music is clearly something longed for as both a salve for their current problems and a vague but promising hope for the future. When the sound recording finally is heard in the concluding moments of the play, we witness how music plays a transformative and even magical role that goes beyond the scripted words. Similarly, dance functions as a physical response to the music. As embodied creativity, the ballroom dancing is in stark contrast to the enforced bodily labor that ordinarily constitutes Sam and Willie's daily physicality. Students engage in dance-like movement in this exercise to perceive the differences between movement in service to someone versus movement in collaboration with another.

PREPARATION

Students should read the play in its entirety before class.

MATERIALS

1   Copies of the relevant lyrics of "You're the Cream in My Coffee" (by B. G. De Sylva, Lew Brown, and Ray Henderson) as well as a sound recording from the 1928 musical *Hold Everything*. Several recordings are available, so feel free to choose whichever one appeals to you. I have found Jack Hylton's recording most useful due to its brisk tempo.

2   Sarah Vaughan's recording of "Little Man You've Had a Busy Day" by Al Hoffman, Maurice Sigler, and Mabel Wayne.

3   A metronome or digital metronome, readily available on streaming services and the internet (optional).

Nuts and Bolts

1 Create a dance floor in the classroom by pushing desks and chairs to the wall. In a venue with fixed furniture, clear the aisles to create as much space as possible.

2 Start off by playing the class a recording of the song "You're the Cream in My Coffee."

3 Next, keeping a steady tempo at approximately 100 beats per minute, guide the class in rhythmically reciting/singing the text of the first two verses. It might be necessary to go through this line by line before putting it all together, i.e., "You're the cream in my coffee/You're the salt in my stew …"

4 Now, divide the class in half. One half starts as the "band," the other half as the "dancers." If working with student groups with restricted mobility, ask a few volunteers to do the dancing. The dancers begin by adopting what they regard as the typical postures of Sam and Willie in the tea room. Some may go down on hand and knee to mimic scrubbing the floor, others may stand at attention.

5 After a minute or so of this, and keeping strict tempo at about 100 beats per minute, the "band" rhythmically recites (or, optionally, sings) the text of "You're the Cream in My Coffee." In response, the dancers each take an imaginary partner in their arms and dance to the rhythm, in whichever fashion they choose. It is not necessary for students to dance a complicated step, nor move in any particular way, merely to imagine themselves as ballroom dancers moving to the rhythm.

6 After this, the two groups swap around, the "band" now doing the dancing, the "dancers" providing the rhythm. If you wish to extend the exercise, repeat the verses given above.

7 Next, each student chooses a dance partner. Have the students (not just the "dancers") begin this part of the exercise by again adopting Sam and Willie's working postures. Play the recording of "You're the Cream in My Coffee" once more, instructing students to begin dancing when they feel ready. If not all students feel comfortable choosing a partner, perhaps ask for a few volunteers instead.

8 After the dance, invite students to discuss their different bodily experiences of firstly dancing with an imaginary partner versus dancing with a fellow student, and secondly, dancing to approximated music versus dancing to the recording. Discuss the last part of the exercise within the context of Sam and Willie's last dance, reminding students of the terrible exchanges between Hally and Sam that preceded it, as well as Willie's final injunction, "Let's dream."

9 Finally, in connection with Willie's "Let's dream" statement, dim the lights. Play Sarah Vaughan's recording of the song "Little Man, You've Had a Busy Day." If students are comfortable doing so, invite them to choose a dance partner and let them enjoy the dance. Alternatively, ask students what might Willie and Sam be dreaming of.

Reflection

Approaching theater as a musicologist interested in the function and symbolic weight of music, I have become acutely aware of the importance of music and its deliberate absence in this play. As Fugard's associate director during the 2016 off-Broadway revival, I also experienced the challenges facing the actors when providing or dancing to approximated dancehall music, and the significant contrast between these imitations and the orchestrated music heard in the final moment as the jukebox comes alive with those descending arpeggios. This contrast offers an entry-point into a discussion of why that lush sound is reserved for the final moments of the play, why Willie makes the sacrifice of forfeiting his bus money for the sake of providing music instead, and what it adds to that last dance. Could students, for example, imagine Willie and Sam dancing in silence? How would it change that moment? Watching the two men listen and dance to the recorded music offers a compelling counterargument to Hally's wordless departure; the performance ends on a different note than reading only the scripted dialogue suggests.

This exercise is designed to help students gain an embodied understanding of dance as a form of creative self-expression in contrast to the bodily labor that otherwise constitutes Sam and Willie's daily physical movements. In my experience, students are very alive to the difference in their bodies when dancing with an actual partner, as opposed to an imaginary one. There is much scope for discussion here about the metaphor of a "world without collisions" and that such a world in fact demands teamwork and cooperation. Furthermore, feeling their bodies react differently to dancing to the sing-chanting of their fellow students and then dancing to orchestrated recorded music, students are also in a better position to grasp the symbolic power of music in the play, the tension between self-generated approximations of the jukebox's sound, on the one hand, and the lushness of a jazz ensemble, on the other.

"Master Harold" … and the Boys is widely considered one of Fugard's most nakedly autobiographical plays. Looking at the playwright's own life, it is significant that music has played a very important role in it. Before his disability took its toll, Fugard's father was a jazz pianist and leader of the Port Elizabeth-based Orchestral Jazzonians, and for a significant period of his own youth, Fugard struggled (and failed) to master the piano himself. In my own research, I have suggested that Fugard's early musical experiences created in him the unfulfilled desire to make music, and with it, the privileging of music as a superior form of creative expression, regarded as even more transformative than words. Foregrounding music in a discussion of *"Master Harold" … and the Boys* may therefore generate interesting and fresh discussions not only about the play but also about the role of personal memory in Fugard's oeuvre.

GLENGARRY GLEN ROSS
BY DAVID MAMET

Michael Schwartz, Indiana University of Pennsylvania

IN BRIEF

Demonstrating to students the power of tone, diction, and dialect in creating character and tension.

PURPOSE

Rhythm, tempo, and often foul language constitute a major part of David Mamet's craft and impact. Bowdlerizing the script and removing the offensive language can illustrate for the students how language—specifically profanity—is key to who the characters are and the decisions they make.

PREPARATION

Students should ideally have the play read before the exercise. Some background regarding Mamet and some of the actors who have performed a great deal of Mamet (Joe Mantegna, William H. Macy, etc.) can probably be helpful as well (see below). Some explanation of the practice of "bowdlerizing texts" may help to provide context for this exercise.

MATERIALS

None.

Nuts and Bolts

1 Choose a scene from *Glengarry Glen Ross* and ask the students to read it out loud. One good example is the Act 2 exchange between Roma, Levene, and Moss, beginning with Moss' line, "Those fucking deadbeats," but there are many possible choices.

2 After the initial reading of the scene, students in groups look at the scene and find non-vulgar ways for the characters to express themselves. You could tell the students to pretend they are movie executives dubbing over the script's profanity with substitute words, a process called "bowdlerizing" the script, so that the movie can be suitable for broadcast (not premium cable) TV. Students can also choose to simply delete the swear words or rewrite the lines without the profanity. Provide an example for the students, e.g., the line "Those fucking deadbeats" becomes "Those unpleasant people who don't want to work."

3 The students present their rewritten and edited ("cleaned up") versions of the scene for the class. These subsequent presentations can lead to a discussion of how and why the profanity works as dialogue, and what is missing or what changes when the profanity is removed.

4 The exercise can further include changes in tempo and delivery for students who have more experience in performing. For example, what if the characters spoke without interrupting each other? What if the characters spoke with refined accents? After such experimenting (with opportunities to play around), the instructor might ask the students how the dialogue as it is presented on the page determines the "who" and the "where" of these characters.

Reflection

The students are invited to question their own perceptions of profanity—how and why characters (and playwrights) use it in dialogue and how "appropriate" the language is in performance. In the same way other kinds of dialogue are explored for their rhythmic score, such as poetic dialogue, students also are encouraged to explore the rhythm and tempo of profanity. Instructors may need to guide the discussion in order to suggest how profanity is a form of verbal violence and has the potential to shock or establish power over another. These ideas are important in order for the students to understand the kind of intentional impact Mamet's dialogue has.

It might also be worth mentioning that many actors who have performed Mamet's plays (and this one in particular) note that the dialogue often seems problematic to them on a first, silent read, but starts to "work" for them when they start to say it out loud. In one example, noted actor Alan Alda found the key to performing Levene in *Glengarry Glen Ross* came to him while watching an Abbott and Costello movie; he connected the rhythms of the two veteran vaudeville performers with the back-and-forth rapid rhythms of Mamet's dialogue.

FENCES BY AUGUST WILSON

Baron Kelly, University of Louisville

IN BRIEF

Create "fenced off" performance spaces for characters.

PURPOSE

This exercise will help students explore "fences" as a metaphor for the characters' lives. For example, how Troy is fenced out (from baseball), fenced off (prison time), and fenced in (by family, the church, or the military). It may also be used for any of the characters in the play.

PREPARATION

Students should read the play in its entirety before performing this exercise. Ideally, students could be given an introduction to the significant legal actions concerning black/white relationships and racial segregation in the 1950s at the beginning of the Civil Rights Movement.

MATERIALS

Masking tape, as well as a handful of props that are specific to the play: e.g., a baseball, baseball bat, empty gin bottle, trumpet, a rose, key, lunch bucket, football, a cake plate, a basket with laundry in it, a pile of wood, a bowl of discarded fruit. Not all are needed, but at least one per character is required.

Nuts and Bolts

1 In an open space, section off the room into squares with masking tape.

2 Ask students to select a character (or the instructor may assign them).

3 Allow the students to select one prop from those available. For this first part, have them choose one they feel is the most relevant to that character and give them an opportunity to explain why.

4 Ask the students to choose a line or lines that speaks to the importance of that prop.

5 Place the students in their own squares to give them the sense of being "fenced off" from the others.

6 Within their square, allow them to perform their lines in four different ways:

    a First, holding the prop in their hands;

    b Second, with the prop placed outside their fence but within reach;

    c Third, with the prop placed outside their fence and far out of reach;

    d Fourth, with their prop placed within someone else's fence.

7 Repeat step 6 with as many different characters as time allows and have a conversation about the experience. What did the students notice about how their performances differed depending upon the proximity or availability of the prop?

8 Break the students into groups without duplicating characters and ask them to select a larger scene from the play.

9 Repeat the steps above, this time having students perform the scene from within their own fences yet engaging with one another.

10 Allow them to perform the scene several times with their props in different locations. The instructor may have them all perform with the same proximity (e.g., everyone performs the scene with their prop in hand) or with variation (one with the prop in hand, another with the prop nearby, another with their prop in someone else's fence, etc.).

11 If the instructor chooses to let students play with multiple props, the students can take turns using the objects as each person speaks his or her lines. For example, if the scene is where Troy confesses his infidelity, the student reading Rose might pick up one object on "I done everything a wife should be" and another on "After all these years to come dragging this into me now." Then, having put these objects down, she may pick up another on "Why Troy?" and another on "Well, you can't wish us away." The student reading Troy might pick up a prop on "We can talk this out" and another on "firmed up my backbone." Whether or not the student picks up an object for each line or each key phrase depends on what seems right to them in the moment. The students do not need to choose a relevant object, but rather pick up whatever comes to mind/hand.

Reflection

When actors come to a piece of text, there is no internal reference in their heads unless it is created. Actors may refer to a place, and they may even decide with the fellow actors where that place is in relation to the stage, but the concrete reality has to be imaginatively created. Actors need to create a specific internal landscape so that the dialogue can live within the immediate exchange of one character with another. The way to that internal landscape is to create an external landscape in which they can perform, and establishing lines of fencing in the classroom is one way this landscape can be achieved.

This exercise is valuable because it physically recreates a sense of prohibition and restriction connected to the play's theme of "fences." As an acting exercise, it emphasizes the act of choosing a prop and using it to communicate to another person, to show the person you are talking to what you mean. By giving them props but changing their proximity and relationship to it, the exercise emphasizes how the characters perform their proximity and relationship to one another as well as to the larger society. In other words, the props represent the longing, desire, restriction, and limitations we put on ourselves and each other.

The more playful the instructor is with this exercise, the more the students use the props to represent their words and communicate their meanings. After the exercise is concluded, the students should have a deeper sense of the words in relationship to each other, but also a deeper sense of the restrictions and limits placed upon Troy, Rose, Cory, and other characters by society.

THE OTHER SHORE BY GAO XINGJIAN

Oscar King IV, Loyola Marymount University

IN BRIEF

Perform the "tension" that pulls between an individual and a larger collective.

PURPOSE

Gao Xingjian's *The Other Shore* seems at first not to have a clear through-line. While Western narratives are often characterized by setting, theme, plot, and resolution, Eastern ones are often comprised of action/reaction in a continuing somersault. *The Other Shore* is a strong example of this tension: rather than following a well-defined narrative pathway, Gao Xingjian's *The Other Shore* circles around tensions between individualism and collectivism, and the search for salvation and personal agency that often results when the two forces collide. Using pieces of yarn, the students physically "feel" these tensions working in the play, specifically in a classroom-adaptation of the opening scene between the Actors and the Lead Actor with Rope.

PREPARATION

Students read the play. Move desks so students can move around the room. Introduce students to Mao's cultural revolution and the rise of Chinese Communism (see Companion Website).

MATERIALS

1 Two different colored skeins of yarn.

   a Cut one color into 10 ft segments; cut the other into 20 ft segments, with one of each for every student.
   b For this example, we will use "Red" and "Blue" yarn. Each student should receive one length of Red yarn (20 ft long) and one length of Blue string (10 ft long).

Nuts and Bolts

1 Separate the participants (10–15 students) from spectators (remaining students).

    a The participants are the Crowd (center of room), and the spectators are the Audience (outskirts of room, leaving space for an "out" corner)

    b Hand the two lengths of yarn to each member of the Crowd.

        i One student reads the opening to the play:

            1 ACTOR PLAYING WITH ROPES: Here's a rope. Let's play a game, but we've got to be serious, as if we're children playing their game. Our play starts with a game.

2 Write instructions on board:

    a <u>Move</u> clockwise or counterclockwise _____ number of steps

    b <u>Wave</u> yarn in right (or left) hand up and down

    c <u>Tug</u> on string in right (or left) hand

    d <u>Spin</u> slowly clockwise (or counterclockwise)

3 Ask a volunteer from Crowd to be the "Lead Actor," then have the remaining members of the Crowd form a circle around the Lead Actor.

4 Have Crowd members (*not* the Lead Actor) give one end of their Red yarn (20 ft string) to another member of the Crowd (connecting everyone in Crowd together).

    a Someone in Audience reads the next lines from the play's opening:

        i ACTOR PLAYING WITH ROPES: Okay, I want you to take hold of this end of the rope. You see, this way a relationship is established between us. Before that you were you and I was I, but with this rope between us, we're tied to each other and it becomes you and I.

5 Instruct Crowd to give the end of their Blue yarn (10 ft string) to the Lead Actor at the "hub" of the Crowd/within the tangle of yarn.

    a Another person from Audience read these lines from the play's opening:

        i ACTOR PLAYING WITH ROPES: Let's make this game bigger and more complex. Now I want all of you to hold on to one end of your rope and give me the other end. This way you'll be able to establish all kinds of relationships with me, some tense, some lax, some distant, and some close, and soon your individual attitudes will have a strong impact on me.

6 Crowd's goal is to hang on to the ends of their yarn as long as they can.

    a If they drop their blue string, the Crowd member must announce their separation, then leave the tangle to stand in the "out" corner.

b   All students in the Audience must boo at any students in the "out" corner.

7 Lead Actor calls out commands from the board at random. The members of the Crowd can choose to obey the Lead Actor or to disobey him or her.

a That is, if the Lead Actor were to call out "Move three steps clockwise," the students can choose instead to "move five steps counterclockwise" or to stand still and to wave his or her strings, tug on his or her yarn, etc.

b The more people who obey the Lead Actor, the more organized the group will be. The more people who disobey the Lead Actor, the more chaotic the jumble of yarn will become.

8 As the game progresses, encourage the class to act against the Lead Actor more frequently. Challenge someone to try to cross the entire room, or to spin around until he or she is wrapped up in the yarn, or to tug harder on the yarn.

9 Continue the exercise until two or three students have been broken from the Crowd to stand in the "out" corner.

a If students are not becoming so tangled that they break from the group, the instructor can call people out who look like they're getting tangled or can have the Lead Actor increase the pacing.

10 Choose a new Crowd from the Audience, a new Lead Actor, and repeat as desired.

11 When you are finished, ask the students to reflect on their experiences as Lead Actors, as parts of the Crowd, and as members of the Audience.

a In the interaction between Card Player and Man, who is PULLING whom? How do we see individual goals impacting the collective? Where are they in conflict? Where do they coincide?

b What did students think of their experience in the tangle? What would have made following the Lead Actor's directions easier, or harder?

c How did the Leader feel at the center of it all? Powerful, or entrapped? Could he or she tell when people broke loose?

d In the play, how do we see Crowd's interaction with Man/Woman either echoing or differing from their own experiences as Crowd and Lead Actor?

e Can a work of art (i.e., a play) be separate from politics or is there no "apolitical" work of art, as Gao Xianjian himself proposes?[1]

---

[1]Quoted in Gilbert C. F. Fong, "Introduction," in *The Other Shore: Plays by Gao Xingjian*, trans. Gilbert C. F. Fong (The Chinese University Press, 1999), ix–xlii, xxvii.

Reflection

At its heart, the play is about individuals searching for salvation and doing so amid the pressures to conform to the whims of a larger collective unit. The point of the exercise is to represent the impact that a collective has on an individual and the impact that individuals have on a larger collective. As members of the Crowd, students must choose conformity (obeying the Lead Actor, a stand-in for any figure in a leadership role) or individuality (finding their own way and thus breaking from the group). As an individual, you are separate from the chaos of the yarn, but that doesn't mean that you are free, nor that you are safe (as the Audience's attention turns to you with booing). This is similar to the manner that the Crowd learns from Woman, then turns on her and kills her. The same is true of the Crowd's relationship with Man: they follow him for a time, then turn on him during his interaction with Card Player.

In this exercise, acting as an individual means that while you get some small agency from choosing your own way, you also affect the rest of your peers. Furthermore, this perspective critical of individualism connects to conversations about the rise and reign of the People's Republic of China and Chinese Communism, in which the good of individuals is sacrificed for the good of the collective. According to the rulers in Communist China, the "leader" of the group feels every action from the collective and likewise the collective feels commands and actions of the leader.

This exercise, by highlighting the theme, unifies the narrative of *The Other Shore* throughout seemingly insoluble events. Gao Xingjian has even stated, "*The Other Shore* is different from conventional drama. One of the differences it that the play does not attempt to put together a coherent plot. I only intend it to be a revelation, to portray some of life's experiences and feelings in a pure dramatic form, i.e., in the same way that music is pure."[2] While the play has far more to it than merely these themes of control and of individuals versus the collective (e.g., "poor theater," improvisation, the search for Nirvana, and conformity in Communist China), this exercise offers students an introduction into the "action/reaction" story grammar that shapes much of Eastern writing and is distinct from the Western attributes of "setting, theme, plot, and resolution" and one of the play's central topics.

---

[2]Quoted in Fong, "Introduction," xxvii.

THE PIANO LESSON BY AUGUST WILSON

Miriam M. Chirico, Eastern Connecticut State University

IN BRIEF

Understanding how an onstage property can designate the spiritual world.

PURPOSE

The Piano Lesson's plot mimics the debate in classical Greek theater between two equally valid points of view: whether to sell the family piano or to keep it. Boy Willie's position to sell the piano for money in order to purchase the land upon which his family was enslaved is valid, particularly because his economic argument is not simply acquisitive greed but represents his goal to obtain equality with White America. Berniece's position to preserve the piano, however, ultimately wins out as the last scene shows, but her "sentimental" reasons for doing so (i.e., intuitive or emotional reasons) seem empty and without rationale. Due to Boy Willie's loquacious nature, his argument for selling the piano dominates the play, and his economic logic alludes to future prosperity. Only by explaining the spiritual argument behind the piano as a place of ancestral identification and connection does Berniece's argument seem on par with Boy Willie's.

This exercise illustrates the legacy behind the piano. The piano is more than simply an onstage property, but rather serves as both an ancestral shrine and point of contact with the spiritual world. In this play where two siblings hold convincing views over whether to cash in on the past to ensure a family's future or to honor the suffering and resilience of one's ancestors, it is important to perceive the piano as a musical instrument and a work of art, but above all, as a spiritual totem.

PREPARATION

None. This exercise provides an introduction to the play, so it is not necessary that the students read the play before class.

Nuts and Bolts

1 Positioning the totemic object in front of the class, ask the students to offer their own understanding of totems. A totem is usually an animal or animal part that serves as a badge or emblem of a tribe, and when several are grouped together on a totem pole or banner they reflect the narrative history of the tribe or serve as a site of ancestral worship. The instructor should point out that these are objects of spiritual significance, most typically associated with Native Americans, although many African people, such as the Yoruban or Shona tribes, also have totemic figures to represent their tribal identity. The totem poles serve many functions, but can be a focus of worship, acting as a connection between the earthly and spiritual worlds. Alternatively, if students are using legacy objects, they can bring them one-by-one to the front of the classroom or place them in the center of a discussion circle, describing the object, to whom it belonged, and how it holds special value in the family.

a After students have provided their objects, ask questions probing why we hold onto objects passed down from family members. If the answer is "for sentimental reasons," as Boy Willie says about Berniece, ask students to dig deeper: What does "sentimental reasons" mean? How might a legacy object be an indication that someone once lived? How does a legacy object provide us with a connection to that person or suggest a connection between generations? For example, can you imagine how the person once held or used the object? Why is this possession of a legacy object important for understanding how we are connected to our families? It may be helpful to remind students that enslaved families were often separated and did not have photographs of one another as mementoes, and so frequently had no sense of familial origins or identity.

b Question student's cultural understanding of ghosts, or more precisely, spirits. In most Western societies, ghosts are imaginary, connected to folklore, or pseudo-scientific and associated with paranormal activity. However, other societies perceive that the spirits of dead people coexist with the living, but on another plane, and Wilson offers this credible presence of ghosts in his play, where several characters see Sutter's ghost. Ask the students to consider the totem or their legacy objects as being impregnated with the spirit of the tribal leaders or their ancestor who once owned them.

2 Read aloud or draw students' attention to the stage directions at the beginning of *The Piano Lesson*. Note in particular the line about how "the legs of the piano, carved in the manner of African sculpture, are mask-like figures resembling totems." Based on the earlier discussion of tribal worship of ancestors and the importance of feeling a connection with those family members who have gone before, ask the students about the onstage property of the piano. What might August Wilson want audiences to see in the piano from assigning it the property of a "totem"?

3 If there is time, ask the students who possess the legacy objects whether they or their family ever would consider selling these objects, particularly if they are quite valuable. What reasons would prompt them to sell the object and why might they decide to keep it instead?

Reflection

The realistic mode of Wilson's play sometimes dissuades students from believing that the ghosts in the play are real; students question whether we should take the spectral visitations seriously, particularly because Wilson does not depict them onstage. Similarly, in reading the play, they fail to see Berniece's playing the piano and chanting a litany to her ancestors as an actual exorcism that rides the house of Sutter's ghosts. In order for the students to understand the play's larger point about ancestral protection and kinship between generations both living and dead, they must see the piano as having spiritual associations—literally possessing ghosts.

The piano serves as a historical document depicting the events of the Charles' ancestors, but it is more than a carved narrative; it binds the generations together, the dead and the living, but it can only do this when Berniece sits down at the keyboard and begins to play. As Michael Morales argues about *The Piano Lesson*,

> Wilson predicated the relationship of the past to the present for black Americans on an active lineage kinship bond between the living and their ancestors. In this sense, the transmission of history becomes a binding ritual through which his character obtain an empowering self-knowledge,

a tangible sense of their own self-worth and identity, that gives them the strength to manage the future on their own terms.[1]

Asking the students to bring in their own legacy objects can add to their understanding of Berniece's mystical experience. Moreover, students who have articulated their own reasons behind selling or keeping the legacy objects will have a better understanding of "sentimental" justification versus economic logic. While Western practice does not necessary believe that the spirits of the dead may coexist with the living, many African cultures do. Wilson asks the audience to believe that the Charles' family ancestors are present in the piano, which would make selling the piano tantamount to selling one's own family. However, although Berniece will not sell the piano, her refusal to acknowledge her ancestors cuts her off from a valuable source of strength. Only when she plays the piano in the final scene does she release the spirits from the piano to do battle with Sutter's ghost. Participating in the exorcism prompts her final epiphany that she must acknowledge her ancestors and, in so doing, claim her cultural identity. Wilson's question is worth sharing with the students: What is the legacy of that past connection to Africa and how is it meant to be used?

---

[1]Quoted in Michael Morales, "Ghosts in the Piano: August Wilson and the Representation of Black American History," in *May All Your Fences Have Gates: Essays on the Drama of August Wilson*, ed. Alan Nadel (Iowa City: University of Iowa Press, 1994), 106.

M. *BUTTERFLY* BY DAVID HENRY HWANG

Miriam M. Chirico, Eastern Connecticut State University

IN BRIEF

Exploring cultural assumptions that condition how we read other people.

PURPOSE

David Henry Hwang's play explores the concept of "Orientalism" or how Westerners have certain stereotypes regarding Asians. One of the overriding questions of this play is how Gallimard could be so confused regarding Song's sexual identity, a confusion that seems attributed more to Gallimard's own cultural bias rather than Song's deception. By tapping into the students' awareness of their own cultural biases, this exercise helps to reinforce the concept of confirmation bias or how "people only see what they want to see."

PREPARATION

Instructor must purchase fortune cookies in advance, enough either for each student or for pairs of students. Bringing in other icons of Chinese food such as the folded take-out containers is also a good idea. Short of this, the instructor can print a series of Confucian expressions, identify them as "fortunes," and hand them to the students to unfold.

MATERIALS

Fortune cookies.

Nuts and Bolts

1 Open up a discussion with students in class about Chinese food, e.g., how many students eat Chinese food, what dishes do they like in particular, and how they would characterize the food.

2 Pass out the fortune cookies and invite them to examine their associations or understandings of the cookie itself: the anticipation at the end of the meal, the element of mystery and surprise involved in opening up the little baked package, as well as the meaning behind a fortune.

  a If cookies are not available, folded up pieces of paper representing fortunes would work, particularly after evoking their memories of Chinese dinners.

3 Open up the fortune cookies and read the fortune; share the message with one another.

4 Fortunes inside the cookie are typically cryptic; ask the students how much weight they place on these fortunes.

  a What does it mean for them to associate fortune-telling with Chinese culture?

  b Answers will vary, but typically Westerners associate the cookies with ancient wisdom of Confucius or prophecy, as the lottery numbers are also printed on the paper.

5 Reveal to them that fortune cookies are an American invention.

6 After the initial surprise, discuss the appeal of the process of opening the cookie as the equivalent of unpacking a mystery, and how we associate this sense of mystery, fortunes, and wisdom with our knowledge of Chinese culture, which, in America and Great Britain, is typically limited to Chinese restaurants.

  a Discussions may vary if Asian students are present who will not have the same stereotypes of Chinese culture. However, their contributions regarding their own experience of racial stereotyping can be valuable after the initial revelation regarding the fortune cookie's origins.

Reflection

The Chinese fortune cookie that typically ends most meals in a Chinese restaurant is an American creation; these are not served in China. Around the time of the Second World War when Chinese food began to gain in popularity, Chinese restaurants began serving these cookies, which they allegedly modeled after ones the Japanese cooks had produced in San Francisco. Telling students this fact after they have opened up their cookies and discussed their long-held beliefs regarding a fake Chinese custom works to illustrate cultural biases using a fairly innocuous example.

In the final scenes of M. *Butterfly*, Song Liling reveals that he's a man and that he's been "fooling" Gallimard in order to steal state secrets. That Gallimard, the French diplomat, could be duped by Song's sexual identity for so long confuses students, who consider the exigencies of sexual intercourse as a reality Gallimard had to face. It is useful to point out to the students how the play depicts the manipulation of one's sexual identity through performance (i.e., Gallimard first encounters Song playing the woman Cio-cio-san or "Butterfly" in the opera) and that the medium of the theater is an ideal place to situate this argument of gender performance. People in the audience would also see Song as Gallimard did. However, we can question the tenuous line between reality and Song's performance of a woman, on and off the stage. Is Song only a man who dressed up as a woman to fool another man? Or is Song a biological man whose fluid performance of gender raises questions about the very system of binary oppositions upon which Gallimard's beliefs are based?

The allusion to Puccini's opera *Madame Butterfly*, with its narrative of a timid Asian woman committing suicide out of love for the dominant Western male, underscores the play and it is worth spending time on this narrative with the students. Even if students insist this racial stereotyping is outdated, the fortune-cookie exercise with its sense of unpacking the exotic mysteries of the Orient can point to the racial bias that is Gallimard's undoing. The relationship between Song and Gallimard could be interpreted as an example of the East's ability to fool the West by using its arrogant stereotypes against it.

If so desired, a brief discussion of Edward Said's concept of Orientalism could help position the racial assumptions in the play, particularly how Western racial construction of "the Orient" depicts Asians as primitive, exotic, mysterious, feminine, obedient, irrational, violent, and inferior, in order to self-define the Occident as the opposite of these traits. Hwang's "Afterword" to the play examines similar binaries, connecting the Western–Eastern racial bias to male sexism and supporting these claims with contemporary examples. In larger part, Gallimard is duped by Song's performance because he has been predisposed from a young age to thinking about men and women's relationships as based on power and domination, and it is helpful to point out these early scenes to the students.

FIRES IN THE MIRROR BY ANNA DEAVERE SMITH

Natka Bianchini, Loyola University Maryland

IN BRIEF

Students learn how word choice can represent character through the creation of monologues.

PURPOSE

This activity introduces students to the genre of documentary drama (or docudrama) and asks them to consider how Anna Deavere Smith makes aesthetic choices to represent the people she interviews through detailed analysis of their vocal patterns and word choice, as well as gestures and the use of properties. In creating in-class monologues based on interviewing their classmates, students will consider the playwright's deliberate construction of monologues, including possible authorial bias, in order to address the larger social and political context of the Crown Heights Riots.

PREPARATION

Students may read the play before doing the exercise, or this exercise may be used to introduce the play. Janelle Reinelt's "The Promise of Documentary" (see Resources on Companion Website) is a great introduction to the ideas presented in this activity.

MATERIALS

Note-taking devices are required, as well as the students' willingness to share.

Nuts and Bolts

1 Place students into pairs for this exercise.

2 Give the pairings 10–15 minutes to work together. Ask each student to think of a personal story about an event that has recently transpired. The student should then spend 3–5 minutes recalling that story to their partner.

3 The student is in control of the content of the story and can share as much or as little as he or she feels comfortable. The partner listens, takes notes, and can ask brief follow-up questions. Once the first student is done sharing their story, the pairings should switch roles.

4 After both students have had a chance to share their stories with their partners, bring the class back together as a group.

5 Ask for volunteers and have a student retell the partner's story (not his or her own) to the whole class. When the story is being retold, the person whose story this is cannot interrupt to correct what is being said or comment in any way.

6 Immediately after a story has been shared, ask the student whose story this is to comment on what the storyteller got right and what he or she got wrong. Ask this student to reflect on what it was like to hear another person telling one's story. These questions address the ethics of representation.

7 Additional questions can be asked about the method of representation. Determine by asking the pair of students which words or expressions, and gestures or props, if warranted, were duplicated from the original story and what expressions were removed. Ask the storyteller if he or she would feel comfortable performing the story again in first-person point of view and discuss what differences emerge from narrating another person's story.

8 From here the class discussion can segue into a large group discussion about the process of creating "documentary" theater and the role of bias, memory, and choice that go into creating a script.

9 This is best done as part of a longer class (75 minutes or more) so that you can have adequate time to discuss Smith's play after the activity, using the students' insights about the creation of docudrama to inform your analysis of *Fires in the Mirror*.

Reflection

This activity primes students to understand the process and approach of creating a piece of documentary theater. Often, it is hard for students to understand that even though Smith's monologues are "verbatim" from her interviews, there is great skill, technique, and even bias involved in the creation of those final monologues that are typically a couple of minutes long, yet based on source interviews many times that length. We discuss the role of the playwright in terms of interpreting her subject's voice and how her word selection shapes both the character and narrative that we experience in the play.

ANGELS IN AMERICA, PART ONE BY TONY KUSHNER

Joseph R. D'Ambrosi, Indiana University

IN BRIEF

Create a community quilt to deepen understanding of performance ritual.

PURPOSE

This exercise inspires students to perceive empathy created through the performative ritual of building a community quilt. It also increases students' awareness to the play's historical significance documenting the AIDS crisis. Using these characters' journeys as a lens, students will dramaturgically dive into the world of the play to better understand how the devastation and politics of the HIV/AIDS epidemic in the United States affected individuals, families, friends, and loved ones in life-altering ways.

PREPARATION

It is helpful to have students watch videos and read articles that provide information about the history of the AIDS Memorial Quilt and the politics surrounding the HIV/AIDS epidemic throughout the 1980s.

MATERIALS

Poster board or large pieces of paper (one for each group). Coloring supplies (markers, crayons, pens, pencils, etc.).

Nuts and Bolts

1 I suggest that the instructor conduct a class discussion about the play before this activity, although this is not necessary for the success of the exercise. It would also be helpful to have students watch videos and read articles that provide information about the history of the AIDS Memorial Quilt and the politics surrounding the HIV/AIDS epidemic throughout the 1980s.[1]

2 Prepare a brief lesson about the HIV/AIDS epidemic, focusing on the attention (both negative and positive) that the epidemic placed on the LGBTQ+ community. Give ample attention to the history of the AIDS Memorial Quilt, presenting photos of the quilt on the National Mall as well as individual panels and the stories behind these panels. Leave these photos up for students to reference as they work on this project. You may elect to assign this information ahead of time for homework and briefly discuss it in the beginning of class.

3 Have a brief conversation that begins to connect the HIV/AIDS epidemic and the stories of those who lost their battle with this disease to specific characters in *Angels in America: Millennium Approaches*. Again, this step can certainly and perhaps should be conducted in an earlier class meeting or as a homework assignment. Break the students into groups of 3–5. Students will work in these groups for the remainder of the exercise. Assign each group one major character in the play. Depending on the size of the class and the number of groups, some characters may be used more than once.

4 Distribute a poster board or a large poster-sized piece of paper and drawing materials to each group. Ask the groups to write the character's name largely somewhere on the poster. They will create their own quilt panels for the character they have been assigned.

5 Instruct groups to choose a quotation from the play delivered by the character that best describes her, him, or them at the beginning of the play and another that describes them at the end of the play. Encourage students to find quotations that highlight their assigned character's journey from beginning to end. What do they fear? Has the character reconciled with their sexuality or with a loved one's sexuality? What is the relationship with others like? With faith? Etc. These quotations should be written clearly on the poster.

6 Students should work together to highlight the character's journey from the first quotation to the second using multiple images or a single image or scene. Creativity is key here. This image does not need to be literal, nor

---

[1]See The AIDS Memorial Quilt: The Names Project Foundation. www.aidsquilt.org

does it need to highlight a specific scene from the play. Like the panels from the AIDS Memorial Quilt, this poster might represent something indicative of the character: hopes, dreams, fears, etc. Students can choose to work together to create a cohesive image, or they may choose to work separately and create an eclectically interpreted piece.

7 Once completed, have students put these posters together in the middle of the room in any order they would like. Together, the class is creating a memorial quilt. Give the students the opportunity to look at each of the panels.

8 Taking turns, each group should read their first quotation, read their second quotation, and discuss their poster choices. The class should be encouraged to see connections between characters.

9 If time remains at the end of class, conduct a brief conversation about what students have learned from this exercise. Ask them if their vision is more clear on the historical information that informs *Angels in America: Millennium Approaches*. How so? How might an exercise like this help actors connect with a character? How might an activity like this connect an audience member to a character? How does bringing together disparate materials to form a substantial piece of bedding provide a metaphor or ritual for community building?

Reflection

This exercise came into fruition during an undergraduate Script Analysis class when one of my students argued that this play is "no longer relevant" and should not be included within the curriculum. After encouraging the student to express his frustrations with the play, I recognized from his responses that as the next generation of theater artists and scholars grows, so does a separation from the history that informs many plays we teach. Even if the plays are relatively recent pieces, such as *Angels in America*, many undergraduates lack the historical memory to understand how the HIV/AIDS epidemic in the United States, affecting the lives of hundreds of thousands of people, informed the creation of this play.

At the core of this exercise is the quilt as a metaphor for conversation and community. Assigning students into groups for the purpose of creating character panels replicates the many friends and families who created panels for victims of the HIV/AIDS epidemic. The reading of the names on these panels on the National Mall in Washington D.C. served as a ritual performance to remember the person and recognize the catastrophic effects of this disease. By creating a quilt panel for each of these characters, a tangible representation of people affected by HIV/AIDS, students begin to understand the impact felt by millions of people just like the characters in the play. To associate these characters with an actual ritual, then, will connect the world of the play to the real world, creating more astute and empathetic audience members and deeper connections for actors.

By putting the students in small groups and assigning them a character to explore using this historical understanding of the world of the play, they are able to better empathize with the characters' emotions, decisions, and growth contextualized within the AIDS epidemic. In other words, understanding history fosters empathy, and performing ritual fosters a deeper understanding of character. The characters' environment and political/social atmospheres, etc., help us understand their way of being. In my experience of using the exercise, students tend to fall in love with these characters. By exploring the history that directly (or indirectly) informs the world of the play, students see through a lens of empathy in their endeavors to understand how the characters within the play live, learn, and develop.

INFORMATION FOR FOREIGNERS BY GRISELDA GAMBARO

J. Ariadne Calvano, University of Louisville

IN BRIEF

To explore how a text designates visceral and physical environments.

PURPOSE

This exercise explores ways of approaching Griselda Gambaro's *Information for Foreigners* through physical dramaturgy. Gambaro unpacks the experience of aspects of the Dirty War in Argentina in the 1970s and 1980s and the practice of *Desaparecidos*—government forced disappearances of dissidents and political rivals across several Latin American countries. Her dramaturgy also explores audience expectations and theatrical conventions, including the audience's complicity in violence. The play is not linear, nor, for the most part, is it literal for the most part. It's a challenging piece and to help the students understand the play they need to try to experience creating viscerally.

My goal here is to get the students to think about creating an environment, rather than telling a story or acting a role. In this exercise, students will consider representations of historical violence and complicity in performance and the complexity added when the performance is rooted in a culture foreign to the original production. Gambaro's work revolves around creating an atmosphere that reflects the experience and themes captured within the play. She grapples with reconciling a past that others have fought to erase. Here, students will perform both the acts of creation and erasure in order to connect more deeply with the play.

PREPARATION

To save time on the day of the exercise, the instructor may ask the students to highlight any language in the text that corresponds to image, space, and time in advance. Otherwise, this part of the exercise may be completed in class. The instructor may also wish to have the students research the Argentinian Dirty War ahead of time (see Resources on Companion Website) or to offer the students an introductory lecture on the topic.

Nuts and Bolts

1 Organize the students into groups of four.

2 If the students have not done so already, have them identify and highlight all language that corresponds to image, space, and time.

    a One option is to have each group focus only on one of the elements.

    b Another option is to assign specific passages/scenes from the play to each group so when it comes time to perform there are a variety of presentations.

3 Once the groups have identified and highlighted specific language pertaining to their particular element (or all three), have them "rehearse" their scene. Ask students to work together to create a physical environment that relays an essence of their chosen text section. They are asked to be imaginative in their creation of a visceral concept from that section that they want their audience to experience. As one of the students reads parts of the scene aloud, they should vocally experiment and attempt to match their vocal quality to the physical shapes, environment, and rhythms created by the other three.

    a In experimenting with the physical body, students may move silently through the classroom while exploring shape in their bodies and the meaning-making that comes from the text, research, and images, and letting these images affect the posture and gesture of their bodies. In this work, they are attempting to translate the words and ideas into their physical form. For example, in exploring violent imagery students might explore a physicality that looks distorted and sharp.

    b Space can be explored in many fashions. Encourage students to employ creative simplicity. Urge them to make their own sounds, as in Foley effects, to achieve an aural environment—for example, dripping water into a metal bucket to create an echo and a sense of time passing as well as the image of a vast, empty space.

    c An exploration of time can include passing of time, speed, rhythm, etc. An image of power can be explored through use of speed with one student remaining still, or moving in slow motion, while others move frantically throughout the space.

4 Once the groups have created a rough performance of their scene (focusing on their elements of image, space, and/or time) invite them to present their scene to the class. They should incorporate their visual, physical, and aural elements into the performance.

a The student reading should again read the scene aloud with the vocal score created during the rehearsal.

5 Once they perform the scene as rehearsed, ask the group to perform the scene again.

a This time, however, the reader should adapt a pleasant and matter of fact tone, or sound happy or excited. In other words, they are now creating a disconnect between the action and the delivery of the story— an often-used tactic during the Dirty War.

b Encourage the students observing to note the contrast between reality and representation.

c The students may find it unsettling and challenging and may revert to nervous laughter as they perform or watch these scenes that result in a disjointed performance that draws dramatic attention to the disconnect between action and message.

Reflection

Physical dramaturgy, as I use the term, begins with historical and artistic research that serves as an actor's imagistic reference point for the historical world of the play, but then gains life in using that work to fuel a physical exploration. This reference work assists them in contextualizing the time, place, and sociopolitical impact in exercises that are then used to explore possibilities of physically representing the characters and violent acts from the text. Employing physical dramaturgy as an approach to represent an experience of violence, disappearance, and complicity creates a bridge for the structure and format of the piece, especially as a site-specific experience.

During the Dirty War, an often-used tactic of the military junta leaders was verbal subterfuge, creating a disjointed sense of language and its employment that persists in Argentina today. This exercise introduces the propagandistic practice to the students and allows them to experience the creation of a physical environment that evokes a palpable reaction, inspired by those historical circumstances crafted into Gambaro's play. Assigning one of the students to read the text enables them all to play with the performance style without requiring memorization and gives them a chance to experiment with the text and images within it. In creating an environment, the activity opens up opportunities to define performance beyond a traditional scope, in acts like creating sound effects or potentially a PowerPoint of background images relating to the imagery from the scene live on stage. Gambaro's text needs to be embodied by the students in order to help them understand the challenges of communicating an aesthetic reality through deep engagement with the text. When attention is paid to the specific words that the students choose to highlight in their preparation for the classwork, the exercise also helps the instructor consider the use of textual imagery in the physical translation of words into action.

OLEANNA BY DAVID MAMET

Elizabeth M. Cizmar, Franklin and Marshall College

IN BRIEF

Use vocal challenges to highlight the power dynamic between aggressor and victim.

PURPOSE

Teaching Mamet's controversial play presents particular challenges with regard to sexual harassment and rape culture. Through his signature ellipses and abrupt character interruptions, Mamet aims for ambiguity and claims the play does not assign blame on John or Carol. Notably, the characters never leave the stage and the audience subsequently does not witness their interactions when the lights fade to black. In performance, it is crucial that both actors advocate for their respective characters and avoid playing the victim or the aggressor. The exercise aims, therefore, to encourage the actors to intently listen to one another while simultaneously establishing the charged dynamic between victim and assailant.

PREPARATION

Students should read the play in its entirety before class.

MATERIALS

None.

Nuts and Bolts

1 Organize the class into pairs. Ideally, one to play John and one to play Carol.

a If the gender balance doesn't allow for traditional casting within each group, have them decide who will play which part. Any nontraditional casting will add to the conversation about the performance of power within the play.

2 Have each pair select an excerpt from the play.

a It should not include long monologues, but rather focus on conversation between the characters.

b Additionally, exclude the end of Act 2 when John "puts his arm around her shoulder" and the end of Act 3 when "John grabs her and begins to beat her." These two charged moments require careful attention to physical content and may potentially alienate students.

3 Once selected, students should familiarize themselves with their excerpts. Have them rehearse only "by rote" so as not to include any predetermined interpretation of the scene. A good example of rote memorization is as if you were to list your phone number, i.e., without emotional attachment.

a If need be, have them run through their lines 2–3 times.

4 Ask for volunteer pairs to perform their "rote" scene before the class.

a Each pair should be seated in a chair about 5 ft apart, angled toward each other but open enough to the class/audience. Have the students run their lines without any inflection of interpretation, punctuation, etc.

5 Next have the same students run the scene, but rather than by rote, have them perform it with intention. They want their scene partner to understand their point of view. In other words, the actors are functioning as advocates for their respective characters, John and Carol.

a Have them remain seated, still 5 ft apart.

6 Next, have them run the scene again, with intention, but after each line, the scene partner repeats back "I don't believe you." For example, in Act 1 when Carol says, "I have to pass this course, I ...," the actor playing John would say, "I don't believe you." Carol then repeats, with more conviction, "I have to pass this course, I," but this time responding off of their scene partner's "I don't believe you" challenge.

7 Discuss with the actors the experience of not being believed and having to repeat the same line to communicate with the actor.

8 Run the scene a final time, this time with the students standing and only integrating "I don't believe you" when their believability is wavering. The student then has to repeat their line with more conviction.

a A line can be repeated over and over if need be.

b The scene progresses when the next line of text is spoken.

9 Ask the actors to examine the performative challenges of "not being believed," how frustration builds, and, at the height of tension, to determine which character surfaces as the aggressor.

10 Ask the entire class to assess if the actors achieved believability and if they appeared to have any "hidden agendas."

11 After repeating this exercise in multiple scenes, from multiple pairs, open up a class discussion about how "I don't believe you" extends beyond an acting exercise and connects with contemporary attitudes on harassment, power dynamics, rape culture, and gender inequality.

Reflection

The "I don't believe you" repetition exercise centers on Mamet's intention of neutrality through ambiguous and incomplete dialogue. With this play in particular, students tend to judge these characters simplistically in order to determine whether they are the villain or the casualty, rather than examine the interplay of power between the two. By doing so, they fail at understanding these characters as equal competitors. Furthermore, by being assigned certain characters for which they must advocate, the students begin to question their initial assumptions about whether or not John is innocent or guilty. Introducing the class to reviews of the play and then engaging in this exercise may reveal that critiques of Mamet's play can possibly be attributed to a director's interpretation and an actor's performance rather than the words on the page. Furthermore, this exercise highlights that Mamet casts the audience as the jury in that their response dictates if Carol is the victim or the assailant.

On the other hand, when a playwright leaves an issue such as physical violence against women open to interpretation, the stated neutrality seems to perpetuate the status quo. Mamet's play is often criticized for perpetuating rape culture and it is therefore essential to create a safe classroom environment when repeating these shaming words. An instructor must be mindful that the male–female power dynamic the play establishes does not overwhelm students who may have suffered from such charged experiences in the past. The play, more than twenty years later, reinforces the contemporary moment where patriarchal power and oppression has visibly saturated media outlets and the entertainment industries. In the Oval Office and in Hollywood, women who come forward to share stories of sexual assault are all too often told "I don't believe you." By addressing how the characters are painted as the aggressor/victim in Mamet's ambiguous text, students can identify how the play's misogyny and lack of neutrality remain as relevant today as it was in 1992.

ROSENCRANTZ AND GUILDENSTERN ARE DEAD BY TOM STOPPARD

Julia Moriarty, Wayne State University

IN BRIEF

Perform a verbal tennis match to highlight pace and tone.

PURPOSE

Tom Stoppard is known for his manipulation of words and acrobatic intellectual debate, and *Rosencrantz and Guildenstern Are Dead* is an example of his dexterity with both language and theme. Inspired by a Michael Chekhov acting exercise, this exercise of tossing a tennis ball back and forth will help students explore the vaudevillian pacing and tone between the two characters. It also connects the Questions Game to the convention of game-playing often found in absurdist theater.

PREPARATION

Students should read the entire play before engaging in this exercise so that they are familiar with the Questions Game section of the play in context. However, the first three steps of this exercise could be introduced before the play is read, as a primer for the text.

MATERIALS

A tennis ball or similar substitute, potentially multiples if class size necessitates working in small groups.

Nuts and Bolts

1 Either with the whole class in a circle or with two volunteers, have students toss a tennis ball back and forth until they are comfortable doing so, saying, "Here" as they pass the ball and "Thanks" as they catch it, or "This is a ball" and "Oh, a ball." Focus should be on tossing the ball easily and continuing the movement of the ball as they catch it, so the ball's movement is smooth and continuous.

2 Breaking into pairs, or asking for two volunteers, retain the same tossing activity while giving students different tactics or qualities to influence their tosses: toss the ball accusingly, toss it demandingly, toss it appeasingly, toss it provocatively. These qualities are the same traits one finds in repartee. Remind students that the ultimate goal is to successfully continue the ball toss without interruption.

3 Using the dialogue from the Questions Game, have students toss the ball on each line of dialogue. If students cannot memorize the sequence, ask pairs of students to memorize pairs of lines that they repeat, and run the pairs and their lines together after they have practiced a few times. A suggested 10-line excerpt (from pages 42–43 of 1967 Grove Press edition):

> **a Guil**   What does it all add up to?
>
> **b Ros**   Can't you guess?
>
> **c Guil**   Were you addressing me?
>
> **d Ros**   Is there anyone else?
>
> **e Guil**   Who?
>
> **f Ros**   How would I know?
>
> **g Guil**   Why do you ask?
>
> **h Ros**   Are you serious?
>
> **i Guil**   Was that rhetoric?
>
> **j Ros**   No.
>
> **k Guil**   Statement! Two-all. Game point.

4 Coach them with varying instructions, changing the directives every 3 to 5 minutes. Invite students to experiment with the tempo by tossing the ball before/during/after the line is spoken. Next, ask them to utilize the qualities from before (accuse, demand, appease, provoke, etc.) with each toss. The exercise can be repeated with one quality for the pair, one for each actor, or with changing qualities throughout the dialogue. Third, challenge the actors to perform the scene without the physical ball while retaining the "tossing" action. In other words, they should instead focus on tossing energy.

5 With a new pair of actors, or changing partners, introduce a new section of dialogue (from page 46 of the 1967 Grove Press edition):

> **a Ros**   Who was that?

b Guil Didn't you know him?

c Ros He didn't know me.

d Guil He didn't see you.

e Ros I didn't see him.

f Guil We shall see. I *hardly* knew him, he's changed.

g Ros You could see that?

h Guil Transformed.

i Ros How do you know?

j Guil Inside and out.

k Ros I see.

l Guil He's not himself.

m Ros He's changed.

n Guil I could see that.

6 Keeping the same groups and scene, invite the actors to make their own choices in terms of qualities and tempo. Once initial choices are made, challenge the actors to perform the scene without the physical ball while retaining the "tossing" action.

7 After the final performance of the scene, discuss what affect the exercise has had on the class's understanding of the text. Is Stoppard's play easy to understand when being read? Does performing it help clarify the text? How do the different qualities affect the interpretation of the scene? How does the game structure of this section affect its meaning?

8 Looking at the text, begin to expand the discussion to other examples of games in the script. What is the difference between those games (coin toss, play-within-a-play, waiting game, etc.) and the Questions Game? What is at stake for the players of these games? What is at stake for the characters in the play? Why do you think Stoppard uses these games throughout this script?

Reflection

Rosencrantz and Guildenstern have one task: to "glean" what afflicts Hamlet. In order to do so, they must interrogate and provoke him; as Guildenstern states: "it's the matter of asking the right questions and giving away as little as we can. It's a game." Asking questions is not an innocuous activity between two people, but a negotiation, one where the interrogator gains the upper hand by demanding that another person reveal information or agree to an action.

The rhetorical tennis match that Rosencrantz and Guildenstern engage in during Act 1 is a verbal display of how people negotiate: for information, for dominance, for leverage. For the two of them, it is a game they engage in frequently as well as a warm-up activity to asking questions of Hamlet. Their Questions Game, performed on the competitive site of a tennis court, demonstrates the targeted, purposeful nature behind asking questions as well as the defensive posture of framing one's response with another question, of literally tossing the ball back to the opponent.

Asking the students to toss a ball back and forth concurrently with Stoppard's dialogue reinforces the contentious yet playful dynamic of the scene. Making the participants aware of how the timing of a toss affects the energy of the scene or how their choices change the tempo allows them to see how asking questions can be teasing, mischievous, or aggressive, and not just innocent curiosity. It is no wonder Hamlet resents Rosencrantz and Guildenstern for playing him "like a pipe."

This exercise addresses many different aspects of performance technique, as well as approaching the specific needs of Stoppard's text. I have had groups take very quickly to this exercise and others take a long time to "get it." Some groups have quickly picked up on the opportunities to customize a performance, while other groups have found greater meaning in the dialogue through the performance of these moments. Questioning initial interpretations of a text and intentionally manipulating potential readings display the flexibility of the script and the importance of informed performance choices. Therefore, I highly encourage keeping a loose grasp on this series, as it is apt to inspire generative conversations.

BLASTED BY SARAH KANE

Angela Sweigart-Gallagher, St. Lawrence University, and Kristin Hunt, Arizona State University

IN BRIEF

Students will explore Sarah Kane's aesthetics of violence through the creation and analysis of short performances.

PURPOSE

The purpose of this exercise is to extend the conversation around the ethics of performing and watching violence on stage through an exploration of the practicalities and effects of staging Sarah Kane's *Blasted*.

PREPARATION

Prior to this class exercise, the class should have read the play along with Christine Woodworth's article "'Summon up the Blood:' The Stylized (or Sticky) Stuff of Violence in Three Plays by Sarah Kane" (see Resources on Companion Website). The class should spend significant time discussing the ethics of staging violence. The class should collaboratively design and discuss a set of ethical parameters for staging violence prior to participating in the staging exercise.

MATERIALS

Flubber, drop cloth, fruit, and other edible items. Instructions handout downloaded from Appendix on Companion Website.

Nuts and Bolts

1 Post a Conversation Starter on the board

   a Why or how is violence used in the play?

   b Give students 5 minutes to write.

   c Share 1–2 responses and collect at the end of class.

2 Mini-lecture/Discussion: *Blasted*'s context

   a Brief mini-lecture on the context of the Bosnian War

   b Violent Acts Review

   c Ask students to create a chart or score of the violence within the play.

   d Ask students to answer the following questions:

      i What is the act of violence and what type of violence is it? Ask students to consider whether the act of violence is something physical, psychological, or sexual.

      ii When does most of the violence happen in the play?

3 Violent Acts Performance Exercise

   a Break students into small groups.

   b Introduce and explain the available props.

   c Distribute the violent acts instructions (available in the Appendix on Companion Website) and give students 15–20 minutes to work in groups (can be extended if time permits).

Reflection

During this lesson students have to consider how realistically or symbolically to stage the violence of the play, and in doing so they consider the effects of that staging on the audience. Some groups struggled with this decision, and it proved to be quite a productive struggle because it forced them to contemplate both the "why" and the "how" of different staging options. By sharing their performances, which took a wide range of approaches to the same moments of violence, they were also able to discuss the impact of these differences on the audience. For example, some students performed entirely in symbolic movement, while others incorporated the props and materials provided or created their own props. For example, in one of Kristin's classes, a group used a piece of paper as a substitute for an eyeball when attempting to stage the moment that the soldier sucks out Ian's eyes. The crunching sound of paper simultaneously removed the action from the realm of realism while adding an element of sonic dissonance that reinforced the discomfiting elements of the violent act being explored onstage. Finally, the students transformed and reused the paper as a more mundane prop, weaving the material of violence into the fabric of the entire world of the play. In Angie's class, one group of four presented a brief movement piece in which one by one they plucked a strawberry from the floor and ate it. Each subsequent performer ate with an increasing amount of disgust, desperation, and mess; the final performer essentially crushed the strawberry against her teeth and smeared it across her face.

In both of our classes, vigorous post-scene discussion emerged, often revolving around the relationship between performers' intentions and audience reaction. For example, students were surprised to find that using a "neutral" prop or nonrealistic material like paper in some ways enabled audience focus on the meaning of the violence itself, but in other ways intensified the sensory impact of the violence, especially through the auditory stimulus of paper crinkling in an actor's mouth.

Ultimately, this staging exercise provides an opportunity for students to work through the difficulties that directors, actors, and technicians face in terms of actually staging the violence in *Blasted*. It also provides an opportunity to expand our discussion, not only about how we interpret these moments as artists or as audience members but also about the ethical dimensions of staging violence.

"ART" BY YASMINA REZA

Suzanne Maynard Miller, New York City College of Technology (CUNY)

IN BRIEF

Hold an in-class auction to question the value assigned to a work of art.

PURPOSE

By engaging in the experiential learning activity of a live auction, students will become sensitive to the feelings of competition and insecurity underpinning the arguments the characters have about art and life.

PREPARATION

Students should read the play in its entirety before class. Then, after doing the exercise, certain scenes—in which the artwork is being discussed and where tensions are running high—should be revisited and read out loud. To do the auction exercise, please see auction letters in the Appendix on Companion Website.

MATERIALS

1. The auction letters. The letters are critical to the exercise; some of the letters say the artwork is very valuable, while others say the value of the work is indeterminate. Also, the letters list the amount of money the students have at their disposal to bid on this artwork. To keep the bidding interesting, the spending amounts are not all the same.
2. A piece of artwork, such as a painting or sculpture, that is not recognizable (i.e., not famous). This can be a simple, quick sketch drawn by you or a student.
3. Optional: Numbered paddles for the auction. Students can also use their hands.
4. Note regarding money: The letters outline the amount of money students have at their disposal; therefore, fake money is not needed.

Nuts and Bolts

Part One: The Auction

1 At the beginning of class, students are told they are participating in an auction. Each student is given a letter. Students must keep the information in the letter to themselves. (See Instructor and Auctioneer Guidelines on Companion Website.)

2 After students have read their letters, the instructor unveils the piece of art. The artwork can be any piece of visual art (a painting, a sculpture, etc.), but—just like in the play—the monetary value of the piece should be uncertain. All the information the students need to start the bidding is in their letters. Note: In order to keep the bidding interesting, the students are *not* all given the same amount of money to spend.

3 The auctioneer (most likely the instructor) briefly describes the painting, but does not indicate its worth in any way. The instructor should make it clear that this is a single-lot auction; in other words, the students will not be bidding on any other pieces today.

4 The instructor leads the students through a mock auction, calling for bids and attempting to raise the price as high as possible

5 SOLD! The instructor declares a winner.

Part Two: The Reflection

This is a critical part of the exercise and must be done after the auction but before any discussion begins. Students should write down answers to the following:

1 Why were you moved to bid the way that you did?

2 If you held back on bidding, why did you do so?

3 If you felt emboldened to bid more, what gave you confidence?

4 What factors influenced your bid amounts?

Part Three: The Discussion

After writing their reflections, students should share their views in an open discussion. Only during this phase of the exercise are students allowed to share the details of their individual letters. The following questions are a guide to help students formulate concrete and specific claims.

1 What is art?

   a What makes a piece of art, art?

   b What makes it valuable in artistic terms?

c When does it become valuable in monetary terms, and how is that value determined?

2 What is value?

a What gives something—anything— value? And when we think of something as valuable, are we only thinking in monetary terms?

b What are some other ways that we assess value aside from a price tag?

3 What makes something popular?

a How do objects, songs, rituals, and customs become prevalent within cultures?

b What role do reviews by experts or endorsements by celebrities play in such popularization?

c What statements are people making or hoping to make about themselves when they adopt the latest fad?

d What are people trying to broadcast about themselves when they actively rebel against something that is culturally popular?

4 How do our peers' actions influence what we do and how we think about ourselves?

a We think of peer pressure as something adolescents face when being pressed to do something that pushes them out of their comfort zone (e.g., drinking, drugs, sex), but how does peer pressure or "keeping up with the Jones's" play out in people's adult lives?

5 How do our peers' decisions about their own lives affect or influence us and why?

a Sometimes the decisions that our close friends make really irritate us, even though those choices do not affect our lives in any concrete way. If others' annoying decisions are not causing you or anyone else harm, why should they matter to you?

6 Are all forms of advertisement "fake news"?

a Just because you are told something is worth a lot of money, do you believe it?

b What are the factors that make you believe it? What makes you question it?

Reflection

In "*Art*," Yasmina Reza asks us to consider the way we determine a thing's value; she also shines light on how we sometimes judge our peers according to what they consider valuable. Often, this judgment leads to self-reflection regarding why we value certain things and/or certain relationships.

After doing the exercise, students should return to the play and read select exchanges out loud, particularly ones in which the argument gets heated, to see if they have any new insights into the characters' frustrations or opinions. In addition, have the students pay attention to the dialogue to see how the playwright's specific word choices—and not just the overall content of what is being said—can accelerate or stagnate a scene depending on what needs to be emphasized at that point in the play regarding plot or theme, or both.

Auction letters are provided. You may use these as is or adapt them. Important: The letters are meant to manipulate the students' thinking as they go into the bidding process.

HOW I LEARNED TO DRIVE
BY PAULA VOGEL

Graley Herren, Xavier University

IN BRIEF

Showing students how non-naturalistic staging decisions can communicate psychological effects distinct from those expressed by the dialogue.

PURPOSE

This exercise shows how Li'l Bit, the protagonist and narrator of *How I Learned to Drive*, uses dramaturgical manipulation to assert control over her legacy of abuse. Through the overt breaking of fourth-wall realism, Li'l Bit is both an actor in her own drama and the orchestrator of the memories she chooses to stage. Though not apparent in reading the text, by illustrating in the classroom the unusual decisions Li'l Bit makes in staging two key scenes, the teacher can show students how Li'l Bit uses performance therapeutically to process her trauma.

PREPARATION

Students should have completed reading the play. The key scenes to concentrate on for this exercise are the opening scene between Li'l Bit and Uncle Peck and the "first driving lesson" scene near the end of the play. If the teacher uses "trigger warnings" to prepare students for potentially disturbing material in class, then that protocol should be followed in teaching *How I Learned to Drive*.

MATERIALS

Two chairs.

Nuts and Bolts

1 Read aloud the first part of the opening scene between 17-year-old Li'l Bit and 40-ish Peck. Remind students that the performer cast as Li'l Bit is supposed to be in her mid-thirties. Ask if this dynamic—viewing two middle-aged people on stage in a "make out" scene—alters their view of the relationship. Why would Vogel do it this way?

2 Set up two chairs facing the students. Read aloud the stage directions dictating that Li'l Bit and Uncle Peck are facing the audience throughout this scene and never touch each other. Perform the second half of the scene according to these stage directions, with the teacher shifting from chair to chair delivering the lines. Why would Vogel position the actors this way? Why would Li'l Bit, who is, after all, the person selecting and staging these memories for the audience, choose to have this memory performed in such an unrealistic, distorted way? What do her dramaturgical interventions say about how she experienced the scene as a 17-year-old and how she looks back on it now in her thirties?

3 Take a similar approach to the "first driving lesson," i.e., the summer of 1962 when Uncle Peck takes Li'l Bit on a road trip. Read aloud the entire scene from start to finish. Acknowledge the many levels on which this scene is deeply disturbing. Consider ways in which this first instance of abuse establishes patterns for Uncle Peck and Li'l Bit's relationship thereafter.

4 Set up two chairs again. Read aloud the stage directions dictating that, unlike in the opening car scene, the adult performers do look at and touch each other in this "first driving lesson." It is impossible for the teacher to literally perform this scene—you can't sit in your own lap, and you certainly wouldn't want to mimic any of the gestures of abuse described in the script. But you can at least turn toward the empty chair and then move from the "passenger seat" to the "driver's seat," demonstrating visually the stark contrast with the prior chair exercise.

5 The key dramaturgical innovation of this "first driving lesson" scene is that all of Li'l Bit's words are spoken not by the adult performer but rather by the Teenage Greek Chorus, who stands off to the side. Rise from your chair and stand in the corner of the room. Read just the lines spoken by the Teenage Greek Chorus from that isolated position away from the "car" and away from the students/audience.

6 Return to your initial place and pose some difficult but important questions. How does this scene differ from the opening encounter? Why stage the "first driving lesson" near the end of the play? What is the impact of having the adult performers physically interact this time? Why split Li'l Bit's part into two, with the adult performer acting out the bodily gestures while the adolescent performer speaks the lines? Again, why would Li'l Bit stage this scene in such an unrealistic, distorted way? What do her dramaturgical interventions say about how she experienced the scene as an 11-year-old and how she looks back on it now in her thirties?

Reflection

How I Learned to Drive is an important play, but it is tough to teach. Vogel displays great courage, compassion, honesty, and creativity in writing the play. One must also acknowledge, however, that the play confronts deeply disturbing subjects and depicts scenes that can be very difficult to discuss. A teacher must approach this material with sensitivity for its potential to upset students. The classroom needs to be a safe place for students to voice their outrage and disgust at certain characters and actions. Some students will resist the play, its subject matter, and its (at times) seemingly sympathetic portrait of Uncle Peck. Even if, like me, you find the play more nuanced and the character of Peck more complex than an avid pedophile, it would be a mistake to insist too early or too forcefully upon counterarguments to this understandable resistance. Students need to know that their initial gut responses are legitimate and will be validated in the classroom before you'll ever have any chance of guiding them into more complicated reactions.

This exercise examines the two most radically experimental scenes in the play. The unexpected performance decisions Li'l Bit makes as de facto director of her own memory play shed light on the damage she has sustained, the lengths to which she will go to avoid, blunt, or censor her past traumas, and the agency with which she wrests control over her past and her future. By staging the scenes in class, even in rough and partial fashion, students come to recognize Vogel's distinctly theatrical approach to addressing trauma. For instance, the split-casting of the final scene provides a perfect dramaturgical translation of the psychological phenomenon of "dissociation," a common consequence of and coping mechanism for sexual abuse. But Li'l Bit ultimately refuses to be defined exclusively in terms of her victimization. Dramaturgical intervention becomes her primary tool for reclaiming control over her life and her story.

Li'l Bit's non-naturalistic staging of these scenes also serves as an excellent example of Brechtian alienation effect. Brecht believed that realist performance tends to breed uncritical identification with the characters and passive acquiescence to the status quo. By contrast, alienated performances draw attention to the artifice of performance, interject critical distance between actor, spectator, and play, and encourage critical interrogation of and active resistance to the dominant ideology. Brechtian alienation provides a useful dramatic lens for viewing Li'l Bit's disruptive dramaturgy. Brechtian theory also helps draw attention to Vogel's broader critical agenda. *How I Learned to Drive* exposes and critiques the values of a society that eroticizes girls from a young age while enabling and protecting the adults who exploit them. The two scenes analyzed in this exercise lay bare the mechanisms of psychological manipulation and sexual abuse. Adult Li'l Bit draws attention to the dramaturgical gears by using them in such unconventional ways. Like a master mechanic, she opens up the hood and shows us how the machinery of abuse works. In the process she remodels her painful past into a vehicle she can finally control. Then she hotwires the play and makes her getaway.

TOPDOG/UNDERDOG BY SUZAN-LORI PARKS

Suzanne Maynard Miller, New York City College of Technology (CUNY)

IN BRIEF

Using card game to help students understand status and power dynamics.

PURPOSE

This exercise seeks to help students understand the power of status as *Topdog/Underdog* shows us that even subtle shifts in status can alter one's fate. The play's three-card monte game provides us with a metaphor through which we can examine the characters' shifting emotional landscape, while the classic improv game "Card Status" (a.k.a. "Status Cards," "Playing Card Status Game," etc.) gives us a chance to empathize with the brothers' feelings of insecurity.

PREPARATION

This exercise can be used at any point during your discussion of *Topdog/ Underdog*, either as a way to introduce the text or as a way to engage discussion once the class has begun reading the play.

MATERIALS

A deck of playing cards. Tape that will stick (comfortably) to skin, writing materials, the *Topdog/Underdog* script (to refer to during the writing exercise).

Nuts and Bolts

1 Playing cards are placed face down on a table; each card has a loop of tape stuck to the back. Each student chooses a playing card at random without looking at it.

2 Once the students have chosen their cards, they stick them to their foreheads. The players see everyone's card value—except their own.

3 Students move around the room, find a partner, and perform the script provided below (or something similar). The attitude a student has toward his or her partner is determined by the value of the card taped to his or her partner's forehead: if a student displays a high card (i.e., ace or face card), the partner should treat him or her with respect or deference; if the student displays a low card (i.e., a number 2 or 3), then the partner should treat him or her rudely or dismissively. Mid-level cards should elicit a somewhat neutral response from partners. The exercise gets interesting when players are—or believe themselves to be—equally matched.

4 When the students finish the script, they should find a new partner and repeat the process. Students continue changing partners until they feel they can approximate their own status—at which point they leave the game to do the writing reflection. Note: Students should not look at their own card values until they have finished the writing reflection.

Script

A(first person to speak): Excuse me.

B(second person to speak): Yes?

A: Do you have the time?

B: The time for what?

A: I mean the time (gestures to wrist).

B: I know what you mean.

A: (Improvise your next line based on your partner's status—indicated by the value of the playing card on his or her forehead.)

B: (Improvise your next line based on your partner's status—indicated by the value of the playing card on his or her forehead.)

Writing Reflection

1 What do you think your card value is?

a What is it about your interactions with others that make you feel you are a certain status?

b What card value would Lincoln assign to himself? What card value would Booth assign to himself?

c What card values would the brothers give each other?

d Would the characters give themselves (or each other) a different status at different points during the play?

e Indicate the scene numbers and lines in the play where shifts in status occur.

Reflection

Lincoln and Booth have had very little familial or economic security at home, in the world, or with each other. The "Card Status" game allows students to experience this feeling of being unmoored. Simultaneously, the game gives students a real sense of what it feels like to be treated and to treat others a certain way simply based on a perceived status or "value." Because students are constantly shifting partners, the game also affords the students the opportunity to experience how one's status can swing wildly at any given moment depending on circumstances—in this case, the card value the student encounters next.

In my experience, it is essential to give students a simple script that can be delivered with different intonations and facial expressions depending on the student's partner's status and on what the student perceives his or her own status to be. I have included a sample script above, but feel free to adapt this in any way. It is important that the script remain simple and basic, allowing room for students to improvise while giving clues about a partner's "value."

This exercise provides a gateway to a rich discussion about power dynamics in general and about those that exist between Lincoln and Booth. The writing exercise following the "Card Status" game is meant to give students time to do some quick textual analysis, which they can then refer to during the group discussion. In other words, the game and writing exercise help the students stay focused on the text while also discussing bigger ideas about shifting power dynamics.

DOUBT: A PARABLE BY JOHN PATRICK SHANLEY

Mauree McDonnell with Alycia Bright-Holland, Eastern Connecticut State University

IN BRIEF

Focusing on the homily and confession as speech acts in order to perceive power imbalance.

PURPOSE

Shanley's play *Doubt: A Parable* features characters with different views on the Catholic Church and the cultural shifts of 1964, stances that affect their faith. This exercise asks students to consider what the performance of Catholic rituals might reveal about character and thematic development, specifically concerning issues of power and gender. The process also invites reflection about the audience members' active involvement and responses within the drama.

PREPARATION

Instructor or students can research one or more of the following topics to supplement their understanding of the religious practice of homily and the sacrament of confession: the Catholic Church's list of mortal sins (in 1964 or now); the function of Catholic homilies; and Catholic teachings regarding gender, particularly the Church's position that priests are the only clergy to offer absolution and that homilies must be restricted to male speakers (see Resources on Companion Website).

MATERIALS

Students may decide to incorporate church bells, music, or other sound cues within the exercise. An enactment of these scenes might include appropriate religious clothing for all cast members, with the color of Father Flynn's vestments reflecting the appropriate season within the liturgical calendar.

Nuts and Bolts

1 Begin by familiarizing students with two features of Catholic practice: the homily, in which a priest interprets the scripture during Mass and extracts its spiritual dimension for the congregation; and the act of confession, in which believers reveal their sins to a priest to become reconciled with God and the Catholic Community. This ritual, one of the Church's sacraments, is alternately known as penance and/or reconciliation.

2 Point out the rhetorical nature of both preaching and the act of confession, that is, they are meant to create a desired effect. When considering rhetorical situations, we focus on the speaker and the speech as well as the listener, drawing attention to how the language influences the speaker, either by persuasion or transformation. Discuss the intended effects for the speakers and listeners when preaching a homily and hearing a confession.

3 Begin with the homily. Ask the students to consider Father Flynn's two homilies in Scenes 1 and 6 not only as monologues but as speeches with a congregation present. Have a student read the homily sitting down or ask students in small groups to read it to one another. Analyze the homily by asking what they believe Father Flynn's message is in the homily, i.e., What does he wish to persuade the congregation to believe?

4 Ask a student comfortable with the homily to stand and speak in front of the class. This reading may involve sound cues of church bells and music, and the liturgical stoles, if available. Tell the student playing Father Flynn to try and persuade his or her classmates about the underlying message. Ask the class to determine what has changed in their experience of having someone sermonize directly to them? If Sister Aloysius and Sister James are present for either homily, how would those actors react?

5 Consider the act of confession. Since there are no scenes that overtly enact confession, the instructor may wish to have students role-play "confessional scenes" simply by having students admit to one another (either pretense or real) something "wrong" they have done. Prepared scripts might read: "I stole a library book" or "I cheated on a test" and responses could range from "Everyone does that" to "You could get in trouble for that." Ask students to analyze the relational nature of confession—what it means to admit to wrongdoing and how it feels to listen and label the action. In classes with more time and performance comfort, an instructor and students might re-create this interaction to demonstrate a confessional relationship with an added authoritative difference.

6 Ask the students to consider the Catholic understandings of confession. We learn in Scene 7 that Sister James has begun going to another priest for confession instead of Father Flynn. How do the students see this change as connected to suspicions around Father Flynn's behavior? In the scenes that follow, what are the ways that these religious characters disclose or abstain from confessing to each other?

7 Turning to the conclusion of the play, revisit the confrontation between Father Flynn and Sister Aloysius. Read the scene when Flynn asks whether she has "never done anything wrong"; how can this scene be considered in light of the ritual of confession?

Reflection

The play is set in the third stage of the Second Vatican Council (1962–5), overseen by a relatively new Pope. During the Council, the Church changed its articulations of Catholic values and practices, including a shift from the Latin Mass in many parishes and a shift from the Baltimore Catechism, the dominant text used in the United States for Catholic instruction from 1885 to the late 1960s. This exercise allows students to explore the ways they see the religious characters acting on their consciences and their religious training during a transitional time for the Church. The possible gaps between the characters' consciences and their doctrinal education can be instructive for actors or for students engaging in literary analysis.

For instance, our production featured devotional organ music as the audience took its seats, engaging the audience as congregants and creating a sense of a larger social community. The actors playing the nuns entered at the beginning of the play and sat in a small pew within the "congregation" of the audience. They repeated the "Amen" at the end of this homily and the subsequent one, as is common in Catholic practice. (Some audience members reflexively echoed the "Amen" as well.) By including those actors within the congregation, playgoers were reminded of the overlap between the different professional and religious roles of these characters. In the sixth scene, we felt the nuns' presence reinforced the pointed overlap between Father Flynn's homily against gossip and his rebuke of Sister Aloysius. Just as the staging offered ways to consider the tensions between public and private conversations, this exercise illustrates the hierarchical relationship embedded in certain religious rituals and the interpersonal dynamic beneath the dialogue. It demonstrates to students the growing tension in the increasingly direct confrontations between characters.

Ask the students to consider how Flynn's monologues are related to his scenes with his fellow religious, Sisters Aloysius and James. The students might unpack what Sister Aloysius claims in Scene 2, that "sermons come from somewhere, don't they?"(19). It is also important to consider whether Scene 8 includes Aloysius "confessing" her bluff that she has called a nun from his previous parish to Father Flynn, as her lie would have been considered a mortal sin in this period. Or is that confession postponed until she is alone with Sister James? How do students understand these characters' decisions to divulge their mistakes outside of the religious institution's ritual for such disclosure?

DEAD MAN'S CELL PHONE
BY SARAH RUHL

Daniella Vinitski Mooney, University of Pennsylvania

IN BRIEF

Emphasizing a silent word in order to develop atmosphere.

PURPOSE

This exercise emphasizes the atmosphere Ruhl can create through character and the manipulation of silence and language. The theme of what is communicated and what is left "unsaid" is paramount to *Dead Man's Cell Phone* as well as many other works by Ruhl. Ruhl appears interested in fundamental human experiences, such as loss and love, and the innately inarticulate quality of these feelings, in both embodiment and performance. The play's use of the cell phone suggests the paradox of people's feelings of loneliness despite being in continual communication. This kind of dramaturgy is typical Ruhl, where she uses mundane objects to explore deeper feelings of loss, unease, or longing. The exercise gets students to understand the frustration and success of trying to communicate feelings to other students, through both image-rich language and physical gestures.

PREPARATION

The instructor may also want to share some Edward Hopper paintings, notable for their melancholic portrayal of mid-twentieth-century city life, and *film noir* excerpts to further students' feeling of atmosphere provided by the play.

MATERIALS

None.

Nuts and Bolts

This simple exercise has three parts, with an advanced modification if applicable.

1 Students will be given the phrase (written on the board or a piece of paper):

  a "When I first experienced real [*thinks this word*], I [*thinks this response*]."

2 The first "blank" to be filled in by the student or randomly given by the instructor can be a simple emotion or experience, from hunger, to love, to anger. The goal is to consider experiences that condition our emotions, attitudes, or moods and to find ways to physicalize that emotion. Triggers like "death" or "loss" should be avoided if assigned by the instructor and not autonomously decided by the student.

3 The student should then create a short response based on this pattern. For example, their sentences might be something like:

  a "When I first experienced real [*thinks the word "love"*], I [*felt my heart expand*]." OR

  b "When I first experienced real [*frustration*], I [*felt my face turn hot*]."

4 Guide the students into producing a physical response by asking or suggesting where an emotion is felt in the body. For a very basic class, an instructor may also create a number of these complete phrases in advance and feed them to a class, although student creativity and autonomy are always best.

5 Students will find a place in the room and a partner to perform this sentence for one another. It is important that students take their time and allow the thought to "land," meaning they complete the thought without rushing or forcing any emotive response. They should practice saying aloud the phrase as well as enacting the gesture.

6 The class will become an audience. One at a time, volunteers will come to the front of the class and perform the "text." No one is forced to perform in front of the class, but aim for 4–6 students to perform. In this second performance, students should choose to withhold the first word in the equation, such as "love" or "frustration" in the above examples. Students should take their time. They should allow whatever emotions or energy surface in the act of being seen and presenting, from laughter to unexpected seriousness.

7 Class discussion: Surprising moments, blocks, emotions, unexpected comical situations, and images can be discussed. Instructor should attempt to tie these discoveries back to the play's theme, i.e., the power/ineptness of communication and language, and from there, specific moments within the play. If time, the instructor may then have some students perform specific moments from the play relating to "the silent word." Examples may be found in Mrs. Gottlieb's eulogy, where the stage directions suggest that she "thinks the word grief," Jean's feeling of love for Gordon, and others.

8 For students with theater training: The instructor may incorporate some breath exercises wherein the students experiment to find the most effective techniques. I suggest that students think about their breath during the silent moments: Are they breathing in, out, or even holding their breath? Students can also employ "the gaze," that is, find a spot in space to focus on when imagining the second "response" phrase. What happens if instead of designing a silent response phrase, students allow themselves to be open to images or an internal improvised response? This additional meditative practice underscores the ethereal quality found in performing Ruhl's work.

Reflection

Ruhl's work evokes an atmosphere that treads the line between the melancholic, mystical, and the profound, but through the vehicle of characters who themselves are quirky, vulnerable, and open.

Much of the way our brains process information is not only through language but through affect, in other words, reading the emotions or attitudes of other people. Ruhl's highly suggestive dramaturgy relies upon scenic elements and atmosphere to create meaning, as well as the physical language the characters share with one another to reveal issues they are sensitive about: Gordon's disgust with the world, Dwight's jealousy over Jean's use of the cell phone, the Other Woman's longing to be acknowledged.

This exercise borrows from some of physical theater Master Jacque LeCoq's methodologies by threading presence, imagery, and intentional silence. In his book *The Moving Body*, for example, LeCoq employs various exercises that explore the actor's physical response to imagery, from environment to emotional circumstance. While the exercise itself has a foundation in physical theater, it loops back to central themes within this play and other Ruhl works, where a paradox lies between the desire to communicate and the ability to do so. The silence evoked in Ruhl's stage direction of "thinking" a concept or word, which is mimicked here, creates a vibration in the performance space reflective of Ruhl's uncanny and atmospheric works.

WATER BY THE SPOONFUL BY QUIARA ALEGRÍA HUDES

Coralyn Foults Nottingham, University of Tennessee, Knoxville

IN BRIEF

Create a multimodal digital text in order to understand how Hudes treats communication and connection.

PURPOSE

At its core, *Water by the Spoonful* is about human connection and communication, like many contemporary plays. However, one aspect of Hudes' play that it is inherently risky, given the form of a dramatic performance, is the visualization and performance of communication taking place in an online space and the deep human connections that form through that medium. Like many plays about family strife, communication succeeds and fails, while connections between family members are shown to be frail and stunted, yet an all-consuming aspect of identity. In this way, Patricia Ybarra sees the play treating Latinx values. Leslie Atkins Durham also observes how Hudes treats technology. In contrast to her contemporaries who treat it with suspicion, Hudes examines how performing within an online space and the real world "enhances each other" and looks for ways that her characters can "reimagine connection and place" (129).

In this activity, students will reimagine selections of Hudes' text by using the content to create a multimodal text through adaptive remediation (see Reflection). To do so, they will need to understand their part of the text and consider which form or genre will communicate the essence of what Hudes intended in her play script or what a theater producing the play would communicate. Further, students will be led to a conversation about how the play script and a performance are different objects of study, and theaters make choices when producing a play for an audience.

PREPARATION

Before the exercise, students should read at least to the end of Scene 6 and bring their laptops to class. The activity would work best if students have read the entire play, but if they read the first half, it will still work. Instructors should also select scenes for students to work with, depending on the class and group sizes. Scenes 2, 5, 6, 7, 8, 9, and 12 are all good choices.

MATERIALS

At least one laptop per group with presentation software like PowerPoint, Keynote, or Google Slides. A projector with audio capability.

Nuts and Bolts

1 Briefly discuss the concept of genre, form, or medium. Genres are a set of socially agreed-upon conventions that help expedite meaning-making. For this activity, genre is not a type of story but a type of writing or text. A Facebook message is inherently different than an email, even though they both inform and use a digital medium, because they use different conventions.

2 Introduce the activity. Let students know that they will take a small part of Hudes' play and adapt her story and words into another genre using images to help them.

    a The product of their labor will use images and incorporate their modifications of Hudes' lines into a new text. Just as Hudes took a risk experimenting with how online communication is visualized, they are experimenting with the play's content and meaning.

3 Brainstorm different potential genres that students can create during the activity.

    a Let students take the lead here. They are familiar with many types of digital genres that are conducive to this activity and can be created during the class session.

b Suggest some genres that work well: a Facebook post, a Twitter thread, a Tumblr post, a Snapchat story, an Instagram post or story, a meme, a storyboard meme, a text message thread with gifs, and a blog post with or without gifs. The activity also works if students choose a more traditional genre like a poem with images or a genre that can be used to communicate narrative.

c Make clear to students that they should choose a genre that they are familiar with and whose conventions they understand.

d Students can also choose images that give more meaning to specific lines and present their text and images together using a program like Google Slides or Adobe Spark.

4 Ask students to split into groups or pairs and ask them to select the part of the text they want to adapt.

a Students should look at a small, yet analytically rich section from one of the scenes, like Odessa tending to her online family in Scene 2. Let them know that they will be adapting the lines to create a new text in a new genre.

b Students sometimes worry that they've picked the wrong option, but reassure them that this, too, is an experimentation with form and content.

5 Using laptops, students work on finding images and modifying the text from their selected scene to create the multimodal text.

a Students should be encouraged to experiment with the images and text in ways that adhere to some basic conventions of the genre. There's no "wrong" answer; instead, they should consider how the images and text work together to display human connection and communication.

6 Presentation or discussion.

a Time permitting, students will present their new texts. Rather than reading through their new text, students should explain to the class how their multimodal text illuminates an aspect of communication and human connection that Hudes worked to do in her play as a whole.

b If time is running short, move directly into a discussion about reimagining/adapting the play and how this activity helps us to understand Hudes' meditation on human communication and connection.

c Optional: Ask students to reflect on the process in writing. Reflection reinforces metacognition and the expanded ways we can examine plays.

Reflection

Theoretical and pedagogical concerns aside, this is a fun activity for students, and the idea of adapting material for another genre is a familiar concept for twenty-first-century students. Still, they usually require reassurance about modifying Hudes' text for the activity or are preoccupied by finding the perfect image. The goal of this exercise is to focus on how technology, images, and digital texts expand our thinking about communication and connection. Every form has boundaries and expectations, but these are opportunities for invention rather than a limitation. By playing with online genres, students are encouraged to understand the difficulties of visualizing connection and communication using a limitless, but risky, medium to understand how the characters struggle to find meaning through online connections.

In our increasingly digital world, literature classrooms can benefit from the concept of adaptive remediation. Kara Poe Alexander et al. define it as "a set of strategies composers can draw on in order to adapt or reshape knowledge across media" (34). According to their article, adaptive remediation is a way for students to take knowledge that they generate (like a research paper) and adapt it for another genre to increase their digital literacy skills. As composition instructors, the authors believe composition classrooms are well-equipped to educate students in digital literacies and multimodal texts. However, the theater, with its roots in rhetoric, can benefit from this thinking. What is the transformation of a play script into a production if not a form of adaptive remediation? The described activity works adaptive remediation explicitly into the literature classroom and takes direction from Hudes' technological experimentation to ask students to adapt the knowledge they gain in a close or analytical reading of the text to another media. Adaptation becomes part of the process and gives students a reason to perform close reading.

From this activity, instructors may choose to discuss the students' multimodal texts as a type of performance. In a literature-based class, students are able to play with different aspects of the concept of performance, as explored by Marvin Carlson in his book on performance. Carlson opens up the definition of performance to include performance as "a recognized and culturally coded pattern or behavior" (4–5); and performance using "a consciousness of doubleness, through which the actual execution of an action is placed in mental comparison with a potential, an ideal, or a remembered original model of that action" (5); and finally, "performance is always performance for someone, some audience that recognizes and validates it as performance even when, as is occasionally the case, that audience is the self" (6). Students have created a "performance" text, as they present the text to the instructor and/or the audience, and they create it with other texts and performances in mind. Thus, the play script becomes the material for another text, and students understand—in another way—that theatrical performances are inherently a collaborative adventure.

Hudes' text makes room for using technology and multimodal literature to understand how human communication continually changes. It is worth exploring on stage and, therefore, in the classroom. Digital communication only complicates human connections, and the activity outlined here asks students to meditate further on this complication.

SWEAT BY LYNN NOTTAGE

Lynn Deboeck, University of Utah

IN BRIEF

Explore how the docudrama style of news headlines shapes the subtext between characters.

PURPOSE

Lynn Nottage's play *Sweat* stages the crisis of the American working class by following a group of steelworkers whose relationships and lives break down as they lose their union-supported jobs in a steel factory. In docudrama style, Nottage bases her play on the interviews she conducted with workers in Reading, Pennsylvania, one of the poorest cities in the country after the stock market crash of 2008.

Through the use of political headlines projected at the beginning of each scene, Nottage portrays the frustrated American dreams of her working-class characters. These news headlines that provide each scene's timely backdrop also reveal the political and economic factors affecting the characters' lives. The breakdown of their relationships results from a sociopolitical situation that the characters do not fully comprehend themselves. Management of the factory, for example, never plays a role in the play; rather, each scene shows the characters' friendships eroding, while the audience perceives the larger political and economic forces such as NAFTA, banking regulations, or the stock market's fluctuations projected above the characters' heads. These projections act as an unspoken text, writ large, for the play—yet, they pay little attention to this larger socioeconomic picture. As an audience, we are granted the privilege of seeing both texts—the political and the personal—side by side in the docudrama format.

The exercise can assist students in developing a greater awareness of how the two texts work in this play, by requiring the students to trace the tension undermining the characters' relationship in each scene by identifying the subtext. Secondly, by putting this subtext within the context of the projected news headlines that underscore each scene, students should understand that the personal frustrations result from larger political and social forces. They will see that Nottage's method of storytelling is contextualized within specific sociopolitical moments and discover a greater subtext for the play, as my students learned: "The human toil or cost of labor, the majority of which goes unseen."

PREPARATION

Have the class read the play. You may wish to do a warm-up exercise or two that helps them identify active-verb choice, since that can be a steeper learning curve, particularly for students who do not have a background in performance. It is also helpful to assign the students to each bring in one current news story on the day you start work on *Sweat*. In this way, you can highlight what news was recognized and what wasn't—making the foundation for how Nottage brilliantly juxtaposes her news headlines projected at the beginning of each scene with the contrary action of the drama to follow.

MATERIALS

A way to project or write words on a board for the class to see. Handouts of "score sheets" (see the Appendix on Companion Website).

Nuts and Bolts

1 Headlines: Have members of the class read aloud a few of the headlines that begin each scene. Ask students to develop a list of word associations based upon the given information. For example, the words associated with the title *Sweat* communicate the major themes/messages in the play: "labor," "toil," "work," "endurance," "perspiration," etc.

One example of a headline is:

> *In the news: The 63rd session of the United Nations General Assembly convenes. The Dow Jones Industrial Average falls 778.68 points, marking the largest single-day decline in stock market history. Reading residents sample fresh apple cider at the Annual Fall Festival on Old Dry Road Farm.* (3; page numbers refer to the Theater Communication Group 2017 edition)

After hearing this read, ask the students to create the word list: e.g., "finance," "worries," "failing," "sweet," and "pleasure." Note the juxtaposition of the Dow Jones falling and the mention of an apple cider sampling and encourage them to keep this type of contradiction in mind when approaching the scenes individually in the next step.

Another use of this tactic from Nottage is:

> *In the news: American think tanks report that the booming stock market is widening the income gap between the poorest and richest U.S. families. Reading passes an aggressive dog ordinance to regulate ownership of certain pet breeds including pit bulls.* (13)

Words here could be "wages," "market," "class," "regulation," and "violence." Conclude your short discussion on these news headlines by pulling again on the juxtapositions used and how they foreshadow or shape the following scene. By revealing for the students these moments of opposition—e.g., the income gap widening and the dog regulations tightening—it will help your students do the same when they realize opposing active forces at work in the scenes as well.

2 Finding subtext: Once the context or "big-picture" words are visible on the board and students have observed the deliberate contradictions in the form, shift to small group work in order to find the specific subtext of each scene. Divide the class into groups, one group for each scene. Have each group discuss what is going on in that particular scene. Ask them to determine what each character wants or needs from that scene or from another character. Instruct the students that a character might have two or three different goals or objectives. Students should also understand that characters might be interacting with one character while thinking of another.

3 Scoring the scene: Once the students have determined what the character needs from another character, ask them to fill out a "score sheet" for the scene, a kind of scene analysis akin to scoring or notating music. See the Appendix on Companion Website for the score sheet.

4 Next, ask them to go back to the beginning of their scene and read the projected/radio headlines to see if they feel the need to adjust the score based not only on what is *occurring* in the scene but on what Nottage is *doing* with that particular scene. In essence, this breaks down the play into character-actions (what is happening) and playwright intention (what the play is conveying to or persuading the audience toward).

5 Returning to headlines: After the small groups have determined the subtext between characters, scored their scenes, and discussed with the class their choices, ask the students to create revised headlines for the scene. The headlines must include some "context words" from step 1 ("Headlines") as well as an abstract noun that refers to the action happening in the scene. Students must incorporate the subtextual motivations and clues they discovered in step 3 ("Scoring the scene"). Finally, the phrase should read like a headline, i.e., abbreviated, to the point.

When the small groups have decided on a headline for their pieces, write up the titles on a board or projected screen in the order that the scenes happen in the play and have members of the class read them out loud in the same manner a news broadcaster might.

6 Analysis: Once all the scene titles are up and have been read out loud, do a retroactive analysis with the whole class, looking back to see what might change in our earlier associations with the title/main messages in the play based upon what we see happening in the scenes collectively. In addition, discuss how making fictional (and yet, very real) small-town altercations into headlines both legitimizes and distances the suffering and toil associated with the period and location.

Reflection

Understanding subtext is one of the more challenging parts of reading a play. In doing so, we not only acknowledge the themes put forth by the playwright, but we also highlight the depth of understanding the audience could experience and recognize the reciprocal communication occurring between audience and spectator. Using transitive, active-verb choices, students can more easily understand what is happening and being done by the characters in a scene and therefore tease out meanings that are below the surface.

Alternating from large class discussion to small group work and back again (with repetition, but not monotony) provides the necessary stimulation to keep the class engaged, and guidance from the professor as facilitator helps hone their observations and empowers them to see what they can bring to the table in the analysis of a script. In the class discussions, as the facilitator, you also might be able to suggest other words in order that the class might see how this changes the subtext. For instance, in the case just mentioned, I might suggest replacing "intimidate" with "threaten." This seemingly small change ends up resulting in changes to the subtext that go deep into character development as well as Nottage's own intentions and messages.

VIETGONE BY QUI NGUYEN

James Jesson, La Salle University

IN BRIEF

This exercise will help students understand how Nguyen's Marvel comics-influenced style, his dialogue, and actors' performances counter stereotypes about Asian-American men.

PURPOSE

To understand *Vietgone*, students should know how past dramatic performances have used facial expression, physical posture, and dialogue to transmit stereotypes about Asian Americans. And students should see how Nguyen and directors of his play have used similar dramatic elements to counter such stereotypes and to humanize *Vietgone*'s characters. The goal of this exercise is to use video clips along with the performing of short scenes from *Vietgone* to familiarize students with long-standing stereotypes of Asian-American men—without reinforcing them—and to convey how Nguyen rebuts this tradition. By mimicking the posture of the actor who originated the play's male lead, students can feel how Nguyen creates a sort of antidote to traditionally dehumanizing stereotypes.

PREPARATION

This exercise works well if students have read the full play and thus have seen the evolution of the character Quang, including his portrayal in the epilogue. However, parts of this exercise could work well after having read the first act only or even before students have read the play.

MATERIALS

Video clips should be screened during class, although, if necessary, students can watch them in preparation before class. It also will be helpful to project color images from productions of the play. See Resources on Companion Website.

Nuts and Bolts

1 Have students watch short clips of films with stereotyped portrayals of Asian or Asian-American men. I recommend the opening scene of *Breakfast at Tiffany's* with Mickey Rooney portraying Mr. Yunioshi. Excerpts of Gedde Watanabe as Long Duk Dong in *Sixteen Candles* can work as well. To help students see how offensive these portrayals are, you can also show the short scene from *Dragon: The Bruce Lee Story* in which Lee, visibly discomfited, watches Rooney's portrayal of Mr. Yunioshi in an American movie theater while on a date.

2 Have the students write a list of characteristics of the performance(s) they watched, focusing on how the actor performs stereotypes through facial expression and makeup, bodily posture and movement, and dialogue and voice. From the class's observations, make a list of these elements on the board.

3 Turning to *Vietgone*, divide the class into groups of three, and give each group three different pictures of Raymond Lee as Quang in either the 2015 South Coast Repertory premiere of the play or the 2016 Manhattan Theater Club production. Select at least one or two pictures in which Lee's posture or actions resemble ultra-masculine actors such as Bruce Lee or Marlon Brando. I also recommend projecting these and other photographs in color so that students can see both the action shots that they won't be able to imitate (such as Quang's jump-kick against ninja assailants) and the colors of the comic-book-style set. Briefly have students discuss and list the differences in body language observed between these photographs and the earlier, stereotyping performances (Rooney and/or Watanabe).

4 Pass out copies of the dialogue between Quang and Thu in Scene 1 (from "Okay. Here we go. Kiss coming atcha" to the end of their exchange, pp. 19–21; all citations refer to the Samuel French acting edition published in 2017). Have the students, in small groups, imitate Raymond Lee's posture from several of the production photographs—each student imitating a different photograph—with their partners giving them feedback. When the students have approximated Lee's posture as well as they can, each group should perform the scene enough times so that everyone has a chance to read as Quang. Each time, as the student portraying Quang reads, he or she should hold the posture of his or her photograph as much as possible.

5 As a full class, discuss which poses seemed to match the scene's dialogue the best and why; also note moments in the scene when the posture did not seem appropriate. And discuss what this experience reveals about the different characterizations of Quang and of Mr. Yoniuchi (or another stereotyped performances of Asians) through language and body.

6 Depending on the time remaining and how far your students have read into the play, have the small groups perform one or two additional scenes in the same way: the dialogue between Quang and Tong in Scene 6 (from the "Cut to Quang working on a motorcycle" through "That sounded less cheesy in my head than it did out loud," pp. 77–78) and Quang's long monologue in the epilogue (the one beginning "You, son, you raised in America and you are American," pp. 97–98). If time remains for only one of these two scenes, I recommend the epilogue. During this step, students might discuss how Quang's quintessentially masculine posture of the first scene needs to be modified in performance given the increasing emotional depth of Quang's words in the play's second act.

Reflection

This exercise begins as one about stereotypes but ideally will lead students into a fuller understanding of how Nguyen's play moves between comic romp and poignant refugee tale. The goal of the initial discussion of Mr. Yunioshi is to establish how stereotypes are not only exaggerated markers of difference but also artificial constructions based on a recipe of gestures and speech patterns. Having observed such stereotyping portrayals, students can then physically feel how the character of Quang combats such stereotypes as he embodies the Vietnamese refugee as superhero.

As a physically powerful and sexy figure, Quang clearly counters the long-standing emasculation of Asian men in popular culture. But a sophisticated class might recognize that making Quang into a superhero is its own form of reductionism, albeit of a more positive type than the vicious stereotypes of the past. As students perform Quang's dialogue with a Bruce Lee- or Brando-type posture, they should notice those places where Quang's words exhibit an emotional depth transcending the superhero model. And the students should have these revelations increasingly in the play's later scenes, especially while reading Quang's final monologue. Students, thus, may be prompted to notice how Nguyen's play becomes more than a comic-book romp by developing its characters into fully human figures, although some students might legitimately feel that Nguyen does not successfully reconcile the comic and serious sides of his play. A productive class discussion can ensue about strategies for combating stereotypes. Is an exaggeratedly heroic character the best corrective to a stereotype? Is the fighter-pilot, ninja-defeating Quang of the play proper compatible with the more realistically drawn father of the epilogue? Are these two portrayals of Quang at odds or somehow complementary?

EXERCISE TEMPLATE

Title of Play: _____ *Playwright:* _____

3. _____
_____
_____

4. _____
_____
_____

5. _____
_____
_____

6. _____
_____
_____

7. _____
_____
_____

Reflection

Reflection that ties the exercise and the specific theme of the play together in a way that highlights the nature of performance.

_____
_____
_____
_____
_____
_____
_____
_____

Resources

Complete MLA bibliographic citations for at least one scholarly article, one review of an important production, one interview with the playwright (if available/relevant), and one media source (a link to a production video, film clip, etc.)

_____
_____
_____
_____